KING HANCOCK

KING
HANCOCK

The RADICAL INFLUENCE *of a*

MODERATE FOUNDING FATHER

BROOKE BARBIER

HARVARD UNIVERSITY PRESS

Cambridge, Massachusetts & London, England   2023

Publication of this book has been supported through the generous provisions of the Maurice and Lula Bradley Smith Memorial Fund.

Library of Congress Cataloging-in-Publication Data

Names: Barbier, Brooke, author.
Title: King Hancock : the radical influence of a moderate
founding father / Brooke Barbier.
Other titles: Radical influence of a moderate founding father
Identifiers: LCCN 2022061150 | ISBN 9780674271777 (cloth)
Subjects: LCSH: Hancock, John, 1737–1793. | Hancock, John, 1737–1793 —
Influence. | Governors — Massachusetts — Biography. | Statesmen — United States —
Biography. | United States — History — Colonial period, ca. 1600–1775. |
United States — History — Revolution, 1775–1783. | United States — History — 1783–1815.
Classification: LCC E302.6.H23 B37 2023 | DDC 973.3092 [B] — dc23/eng/20230301
LC record available at https://lccn.loc.gov/2022061150

To the eighteenth-century Bostonians
whose stories we'll never know

CONTENTS

The Signature

One of the only remarkable things about the morning of Thursday, July 4, 1776, was the weather. It was an unusually temperate day in Philadelphia—topping out in the mid-seventies—and a relief from the typical summer heat and humidity. That morning, as they had for over a year, the Second Continental Congress—the acting colonial government—convened at nine and picked up their business where they left off the night before: debating the document that would declare the colonies' independence. Two days prior, the delegates had voted to break from the British Empire and now they were finalizing the language.[1]

As president of Congress, thirty-nine-year-old John Hancock sat in the front of the room of the Pennsylvania State House—we know it as Independence Hall today—and moderated the discussion. He was one of the richest men in the room, which was saying something, since most of the people there were among the wealthiest in the colonies. He was also a bit unusual, this man from Massachusetts who dressed in fine, embellished clothing and rode in a gold carriage, drawing a sharp contrast to the dour men from his colony who embodied a stern simplicity. He looked out on small wooden tables covered in green cloths that served as desks. Delegates sat with the men from their colony, two or three at a table. They formed a semi-circle facing Hancock, who sat on a raised platform—the ideal stage for someone who enjoyed the spotlight.

Around eleven in the morning, Congress finalized what they called the Unanimous Declaration of the Thirteen United States of America. It went to Hancock's desk so he could authorize it. Americans today have an idea about what happened next: Hancock signed the document and was asked why his name was so large. He replied something about King George III being able to see it without his spectacles.

That did not happen. The reality that day, for both Hancock and the declaration, was more mundane. Hancock signed the document to make it official and Congress resumed other matters. There was no celebration or time wasted praising themselves for finalizing the document that forms the basis of American ideals today. They simply made plans to have the declaration printed and for Hancock to distribute it to the thirteen colonies, foreign powers who might help the war effort, and the general of the Continental Army, George Washington.[2]

Thomas Jefferson, the one man more closely tied to the declaration than Hancock, recalled late in his life that all of the delegates signed on July 4. His memory had failed him, as it often can when looking back after decades. Hancock's was only one of two names—Charles Thomson, Congress's secretary, was the other—on the typeset, printed copies of the declaration. This meant that he, and not Jefferson or the other delegates, had formally announced himself a traitor to the British Empire, an offense punishable by the confiscation of Hancock's considerable property and by death.[3]

The copy Americans call to mind when imagining the Declaration of Independence—the one with Hancock's famous signature—was signed by most of the delegates in August 1776. Congress had ordered that the declaration be engrossed—copied in large script to serve as an official copy—and signed by "every member of Congress." The parchment chosen for the job was nothing special and selected without much thought, likely because it was found in a local store and was inexpensive. But it was a considerable size, measuring twenty-three inches by twenty-nine inches.[4]

When presented with the document to sign first, Hancock held his quill, likely made from a goose feather, between his ink-smudged middle finger and thumb and signed the document in black ink that would later fade to brown. His signature is the largest by far, but not as oversized as is popularly remembered. Its elegance, however, is unmatched. His refined handwriting indicated that he was a gentleman—he knew how to maximize the downstrokes and avoid ink blots. It showed training and practice and required a steady hand; the flourish underneath his name, called a paraph, was a way to further display gentility. When he was a young boy, Hancock received private calligraphy lessons from one of the finest instructors in colonial America.[5]

For that one act of signing the Declaration of Independence, Hancock holds a vaunted place in America's pantheon, but he does not quite fit in with many of the radicals who founded the country. Hancock was not one of the five men chosen to be on the declaration's drafting committee. He had led no movement toward independence. In fact, in 1776, his onetime political ally, Samuel Adams, "had become very bitter" that Hancock was not throwing his influence behind the cause.[6]

This, then, is the story of how a man with middle-of-the-road and often shifting political views came to be one of our country's founders. Hancock was a moderate in a time and place of radicals—in the 1760s and 1770s his adopted hometown of Boston was the epicenter of mobbing, violent protests, and tarring and feathering. Yet Hancock was able to avoid such extremes, remaining popular with the masses and effecting political change in spite of being slow to adopt many resistance efforts.[7]

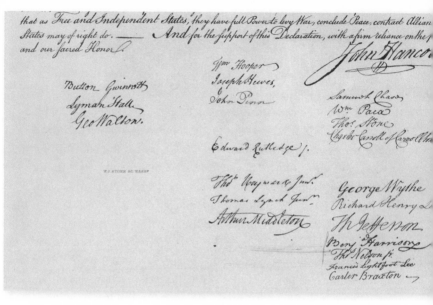

The fifty-six signatures on the only original copy of the Declaration of Independence. National Archives, Washington, DC.

It is easy to ignore or malign moderates, both in the time in which they lived and in the historical record. This is partly because they do not fit in a tidy category demanded during a revolution and when writing about it later. Despite the way the American Revolution is often remembered, the British colonists in North America were not a monolithic body wholly committed to tearing down the political structure they had known for a century and a half. Look even a little bit under the surface, and moderates are visible everywhere. This includes those preserved in US memory as fervent revolutionaries.

Political moderates arise from necessity during times of extreme crisis. As destructive polarization threatens a movement, moderates allay the vitriol on both sides. They are naturally prudent, cautious, and self-protective.[8] During the nearly twenty-five years of resistance,

Commerce, and to do all other Acts and Things which Independent Divine Providence, we mutually pledge to each other our Lives, our Fortunes

rebellion, and revolution, Hancock tempered radicals in Massachusetts and North America from going too far and losing support. He built alliances, appealed to both sides, and identified where many people stood on an issue. And he stepped away from politics altogether when he had other concerns or needed a break. The people trusted Hancock as a result.

Hancock had his detractors, which should not be surprising. Infighting among the founding generation was rampant. As they jockeyed for power and for their worldviews to shape a revolution and then a new country, they often disagreed about the Revolution's tactics and goals. Hancock was less combative than most, but no less shrewd. He wanted people on his side and learned how to win their favor. It was not through violence, fear mongering, or coercion; instead, Hancock assessed the interests of the people, as well as his own, and usually supported those.

As such, contemporaries denounced him for not taking hard enough stances even when pressured to do so. For sometimes taking no side at all. For being frivolous and vain. For putting his own interests ahead of politics. For being wishy-washy on principles. Such detractors were not always wrong. These were the barbs a moderate and someone who often looked out for himself would be used to hearing. And the criticisms have staying power—historians in the twenty-first century frequently echo the judgments of Hancock's rivals and portray him as a one-dimensional and vapid dupe.

He was also denounced as a hypocrite for calling for freedom from tyranny when, for decades, Hancock's family enslaved Black women and men. Then, as he did with other issues—like becoming a leader of the Patriot resistance or declaring independence—Hancock changed his mind about slavery. He emancipated those bound to him and went on to use some of his power and social capital to weaken the institution. It benefits us to see a leader in this complete way—contradictory and unsure of himself—because it is a reminder of how so very human the luminaries of the American Revolution were.

It took more than moderation to build Hancock's popularity with the masses, and in a twist, it was his excess in other areas of life that achieved this. He used his fine clothing and stately appearance to signal his authority. He also had a gift for connecting with people—the ones who were asked to form mobs, sacrifice their well-being for the common good, and enlist in the army. Sumptuous entertaining and plentiful drink were his preferred methods to reach the masses. This separated him from other elites who had little in common with such men and did not feel the need to cater to them. Hancock's generosity, hospitality, and congeniality bridged social and economic divides when others could or would not.

His stature eventually rose so high that he became known by both friends and enemies as King Hancock. For his British critics, the nickname was used sarcastically, as a way to taunt the colonists for being simple bumpkins. But for his many allies, the name showed support and admiration for a man who had sacrificed so much while also acting as a backhanded condemnation of the monarchy. An extravagant moderate had been metaphorically crowned by a people rejecting a king. Such was Hancock's appeal.

A proud man, Hancock would be thrilled that schoolchildren continue to learn his name. If he were being really honest with himself, he would also be surprised. After all, when he was a young boy, he was living in a small town and destined to be mostly anonymous to history, like most people in the colonies. That is, until life as he knew it was rocked off its foundation when he was just seven years old. With his father's death, his world was poised to transform. As it did, so too did the course of American history.

CHAPTER 1

The Emergence of John Hancock

Eight-year-old John Hancock's senses were assaulted as he stood in his new town. The country boy saw a bustling harbor, filled with ships with masts as tall as Boston's ubiquitous church steeples. People—lots of them, many more than he was accustomed to— ambled through the streets, conceding the road to an occasional carriage. The scents of saltwater, tar, brewing beer, burning wood, and animals and their excrement pounded his olfactory system. Church bells clanged their unique peals, fishermen hawked their recent catches, horse hooves clomped through the street, the town crier barked out notices, and vendors rang their tinny handheld bells while pushing rattling carts. It was a crowded, smelly, and boisterous town, and as its energy swirled around him, he likely reflected on how much his circumstances had changed in the last year.

His path in life had seemed pretty assured until recently, for he descended from a line of John Hancocks who served as ministers. Surely, he would do the same. The eldest John Hancock had attended Harvard College—often a feeder school to the pulpit—and became the minister for Lexington, Massachusetts. His son, John, also attended Harvard before landing his own parish in Braintree, a small

farming town ten miles south of Boston. He married Mary Hawke
Thaxter and they had three children. Their first, who would have
been given the family name and path for opportunity had she been
born a boy, was Mary. Two years later, a boy came; the third John
Hancock—the most famous one—was born in Braintree in January
1737. One more boy, named Ebenezer, arrived four years later.[1]

Any sense of a predictable life for the young boy vanished in 1744.
When Hancock was seven years old, his father passed away after
contracting an unspecified illness. He and his family were uprooted
from their residence to make way for the new reverend who would
live in their house, the town's parsonage. Hancock lost his father and
the only home he knew in a short span. These destabilizing shocks
would be stressful enough for a young child, but soon after, his life
shifted again.[2]

His relatives determined that it would be best if Hancock left his
mother and siblings to live in Boston with his wealthy paternal uncle
Thomas and his wife Lydia. More opportunities would be available
to him there than with his immediate family. Hancock was given this
chance because he had hit the eighteenth-century birthing lottery
twice: he was born a boy, and he was the firstborn boy. Although he
likely had little say in the matter, and had recently suffered great loss
and upheaval, he could be considered lucky that such prosperity was
now available to him.

We have no record of what this transition was like for Hancock,
but it undoubtedly came with tremendous insecurity as he tried to
find footing in his new home with his adoptive guardians, all in a busy
town. Braintree had a population of around a thousand people, while
Boston was a town of about 15,000 residents crammed onto a two-
mile-long peninsula that jutted out into the harbor. Its inhabitants
did not make their money from the land, as those in Braintree did,
but from the sea. Boston was the closest large harbor to England,
which had helped the town grow in size, wealth, and prominence
since its colonization by Europeans in 1630.

The town had shed some of its puritanical traditions toward the middle of the eighteenth century, but the legacy of its founding by strict, self-important Calvinists still echoed. John Winthrop, the man who led several hundred people across the Atlantic, had told his followers that Boston would be "a city upon a hill." These immigrants saw themselves as God's chosen people, so their new settlement must set an example. Their leader warned them: "the eyes of the world are upon us."[3] Actually, few people in the 1750s cared about the travels and travails of Winthrop and his people in 1630, but many in Boston still viewed themselves in such presumptuous ways.

In addition to the crowds of blessed people and the myriad smells and noises, young Hancock would find that Boston had many narrow and winding roads compared to the few thoroughfares in his hometown. If the street paths were varied and confusing, their names were quite literal and would help the newcomer navigate: Dock Square was down by the docks, Granary Burying Ground sat next to a large granary, and School Street was home to the Latin School. The same was true of the neighborhoods: the North End was Boston's most crowded and was in the northern part of town, and the South End was, appropriately, at the southern.

Hancock would not live in either of those neighborhoods. There was a large public park called Boston Common that sat between the South End and the Charles River Bay. Rising up from it was Beacon Hill, so named for the beacon that sat atop the hill and acted as a warning device. It was another literal name for a mostly uninhabited part of town. This is where Hancock's uncle decided to build his home in 1735. While Beacon Hill today is the most well-heeled of all of Boston's neighborhoods, it was unusual to settle there when Thomas did.

Most buildings at this time, including private homes, were constructed of wood and brick, but Thomas wanted to stand out, so his house was made of stone. It was completed in 1737 in the Georgian architecture style, a trend named for the kings of England during the eighteenth century. The style valued symmetry and classical details,

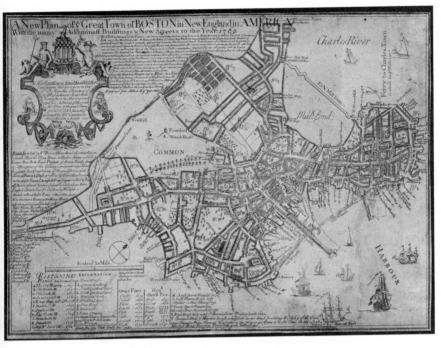

1769 map of Boston. The Hancock mansion is marked by U in the section labeled No 9. Norman B. Leventhal Map & Education Center at the Boston Public Library.

as evidenced by the equal size and number of windows and chimneys on both sides of the building. There was a very large door at the center of the house with pilasters on the side, its placement and decoration also a signal of Georgian design.[4]

"Johnny," as his aunt and uncle called him, would have likely looked with awe at his new home at the top of a steep hill. The house was elevated about fifteen feet above street level with a large front garden. There was a low stone wall topped with a wooden fence to block the way of strangers and cows, which often grazed on Boston Common and sometimes wandered toward the Hancock estate. Twelve stone steps took Hancock to the imposing front door.[5]

Walking through the threshold to the home where he would live for the rest of his life, young Hancock would have been met with unknown luxury. Later in his life he would outdo his uncle in his taste for the extravagant, but for a boy from the country who had previously lived in a modest home, it would have been a shock to see an immense house with such rich interior details.

Uncle Thomas was not of middling means and was certainly not one to have a modest anything. He had spent lavishly on his home. Hancock saw walls adorned with green and red wallpapers picturing birds and bucolic landscapes. Mahogany furniture filled the rooms, oil paintings graced the walls, and silver dishes added sparkle. He may have even been tempted to run his hands along some of the walls—those covered with flockwork, a wallpaper detailed with tufts of wool. Most of the interiors were imported from London, including clocks, marble hearths, and books. He would have peered into the many other spaces: a formal dining room and a more casual one for the family, a drawing room, a family sitting area, and a closet for china. The royal governor and members of the legislature dined annually at the mansion, a sign of Thomas's gentility and deep connections to the crown.[6]

Once adjusted to the interior of the home, Hancock could explore the front and back gardens, in which Thomas took immense pride. He spared no cost to make them beautiful. He imported cherry, pear, walnut, apricot, mulberry, and plum trees, among others. He continued to buy up land in Beacon Hill until his holdings included several acres, which he covered with orchards, a carriage house, stables, and a greenhouse. Though it was just a few hours' carriage ride from Braintree, the estate was a world away.[7]

The Hancock mansion was such a commanding presence that it dominated a teenage girl's needlepoint depiction of Boston Common around 1750. Hannah Otis, sister to the future radical James Otis, portrayed the park with a massive flag of Great Britain overhead while diverse animals roam free and large birds fill the sky. Three of the people she depicted are likely the members of the Hancock

Hannah Otis's needlepoint of Boston Common.
Museum of Fine Arts, Boston.

family, with the finely dressed Lydia and Thomas standing close to
the wall. Nearby seems to be young Johnny, also in elegant clothing,
on horseback. Behind him, a young Black servant in livery tends
to him.

Later, Hancock would be painted by the preeminent male portrait
artists of the era, including John Singleton Copley and Charles
Willson Peale, but it is this portrayal by a girl around eighteen years
of age that best documented how Hancock's contemporaries would
have seen him. Otis did not show a solitary man, as most artists did.
Rather, she depicted a young man with family money and help from
servants, enslaved and free.

Thomas employed white servants and enslaved four Black women
and men. In Braintree, Hancock's father had owned a slave as well, so
living alongside someone in bondage would not have been unusual
for him. What would have been new was the number of people
helping his uncle's house run smoothly. Uncle Thomas had at least
seven people handling the daily needs of three people and their visitors. Hancock relied on them every day when they helped him dress,

cooked and served his meals, drove his carriage, or carried messages for him to others in Boston. Most servants and enslaved men and women in northern colonies lived in their masters' homes—it was an intimate institution.[8]

The homes of eighteenth-century elites, like Hancock's, were often multiracial and multistatus, but everyone lived under the domain of the master. Colonial North America was a hierarchical world with few completely independent people. Aunt Lydia was economically and politically dependent on her husband, as were her servants. Even Hancock was dependent on his uncle until he started a family of his own or until Thomas died. And all of them—the servants, slaves, and privileged Hancocks—were seen as members of one family with Thomas as the patriarch.[9]

This mindset is evident in Hancock's letters when he was abroad. He asked about two of the family's white servants, Betsy and Hannah, and also the enslaved men and women, identifying them as his family. He wanted details about how they were doing and told his brother to tell Hannibal, an enslaved man, "I think of him, as he was the last of the Family I saw on the Wharff."[10] The boy who had lost his father desperately longed to feel close to people—a need that would last a lifetime.

With clear views of the harbor, Thomas Hancock's house on Beacon Hill overlooked the scene that had made his extraordinary wealth. Boston's economy in the eighteenth century depended on the Atlantic Ocean for markets and goods. The North American colonies—and Massachusetts especially—were an integral part of imperial trade networks extending to Africa, the Caribbean, South America, and the mother country of England. As befit a town with a maritime economy, Boston's deep harbor was packed with activity. Longshoremen, laundresses, ropeworkers, prostitutes, and customs officials all worked along the waterfront. Like arms stretching out to receive an oceanic offering, dozens of wharves lined the shoreline. Hancock's uncle eventually grew wealthy enough to purchase one of them, naming it Hancock's Wharf—a meteoric rise for a man of lesser beginnings.

Uncle Thomas was the middle child of three boys. His brothers attended Harvard, but there was not enough money to also send him. Instead, at fourteen, he was apprenticed to a bookseller in Boston. He spent seven years learning the trade, including book binding, printing, and selling. Like most indentured servants, he was to have no fun. His labor contract read "Matrimony he shall not contract, Taverns and Alehouses he shall not frequent, at cards, dice, or any other unlawful games he shall not play."[11]

Thomas served his apprenticeship and then branched out on his own. In 1725, he opened a shop on Ann Street, near Dock Square, a bustling part of town. One could find his store by the sign picturing the Bible and three crowns. He sold a variety of books: religious texts and ones about mathematics, history, and navigation. Scrappy and ambitious, Thomas expanded his store's offerings within several years to include stationery, cutlery, linens and fabrics in several colors, silk shoes, and hosiery for women and men. With his prospects rising, the twenty-seven-year-old Thomas married the only child of one of his business partners, sixteen-year-old Lydia Henchman.[12]

They had no children of their own, so when the opportunity arose, the couple welcomed their nephew into their home.[13] John Hancock's new father figure—an extravagant and shrewd businessman in a competitive urban space—was as far as one could get from an unassuming minister in a country town. The child would have to adapt to his circumstances, which he would grow to be very good at. It was a skill that stayed with him over the years.

John's uncle Thomas was a hulking mass of a man, with a confident air and eyes that didn't seem to miss a trick. Such self-assurance was justified—over three decades Thomas expanded his business, the House of Hancock, to include trading in whale oil, retailing, wholesaling, and land speculation. He would also buy shares in privateering ships, which was risky but could be profitable. The bulk of his wealth, however, came from contracts with the British Empire. Thomas became the lead supplier to the king's army; as such, he made a great deal of money while the empire was at war. And the empire was at war a lot through the 1740s and 1750s, fighting other European powers and Indigenous people for control of the North American continent.[14]

As rich as the British Empire had made him, he was also okay cheating it. Thomas was a frequent smuggler—as many merchants were at this time. Rarely does someone get so far ahead of his competitors without some ruthlessness and cunning; Thomas had plenty of both. British customs duties were high, so instead of buying from London, he procured goods from Amsterdam and the Dutch and French Caribbean islands. His cargo was illegally unloaded elsewhere and then brought to Boston.[15]

Smuggling required a lot of trust and secrecy to ensure the crew or overseas agents did not reveal the ship's contents, its origin port, or its intended destination. Thomas was strict about how to deceive the officials. On one occasion, he told his agent in Holland that no one on board his ships bound for North America was allowed to carry letters for residents of Boston. Doing so would give away where the cargo was intended to go. The goods were to be first transported to Cape Cod, and the crew should "speak with nobody upon your Passage if you c[an] possibly help it." Sometimes asking for discretion was not enough. In 1749, when customs officials were scrutinizing Thomas's business practices, he bribed his entire crew not to speak about the ship's load or route.[16] Learning from his uncle, Hancock would later follow the company's legacy of smuggling, but with far bigger consequences.

This legal and illegal activity led Thomas, son of a minister without a prestigious Harvard education, to accumulate one of the largest fortunes in Massachusetts. The idea of the American dream—working hard to rise above your station and achieve riches and happiness—happened very infrequently in the eighteenth century. Thomas Hancock and Benjamin Franklin were notable exceptions. Most affluent people inherited their money and married similarly wealthy families to solidify and grow their fortunes. A man clawing his way to the very top was remarkable. Fittingly, Thomas epitomized a man with new money: he had expensive taste, dressing finely from the gold tip of his cane down to his silver shoe buckles. He would pass this love of luxury on to his nephew.[17]

In the eighteenth century, an increasingly wealthy man would soon be drawn to politics, not because he was interested in government, necessarily, but because the right connections could boost his fortune. And because men like him—white, wealthy, and genteel—were deemed the only appropriate people to rule. In 1739, Thomas was elected selectman of Boston and would be one of five officials to govern the affairs of the town, much like city councilors today. He held this post for thirteen consecutive years. This job gave him the opportunity to get to know the men with direct access to the crown, helping him secure future government contracts.[18]

Even though Thomas held elected office, he and other colonial merchants rarely muddied themselves with political questions or ideology. Their interest piqued only when specific issues interfered with their business. The reason was simple: Thomas and generations of other merchants had made their fortunes by aligning with a strong and thriving British Empire, its global markets, and its protective army and navy. Such plutocrats did not care to disrupt the symbiotic bond they maintained with their mother country.[19]

Thomas's success had not come from years of schooling, but he wanted to provide a top education for his nephew, who he hoped would take over his prosperous business. Young Hancock was enrolled in South Latin School, a short walk or carriage ride from his home on Beacon Street. On his way to class, he would have passed King's Chapel, the peculiar Anglican church made of stone and lacking a steeple, and its neighboring burying ground, where bodies were interred beginning in 1630. Hancock's school sat just behind the chapel.

It has the distinction of being the first public school in the North American colonies, founded in 1635. Future revolutionary Samuel Adams had gone to school there, as had Benjamin Franklin, although the enterprising inventor dropped out.[20]

The schoolhouse was a small, wooden, two-story building with a sparsely decorated classroom. Students sat on wooden benches with desks in front of them. After the morning bell, Hancock and about one hundred other boys studied classical languages, history, and philosophy. He was a mostly mediocre student except when he studied what he is most famous for: penmanship. His tutor, Abiah Holbrook, was renowned for his handwriting instruction and had a school near Boston Common. Like most students at Latin School and the two John Hancocks before him, Harvard College was the next step, which he entered in 1750.[21]

There are few extant documents relating to Hancock's college experience in Cambridge, but it is clear from one of them that he missed his loved ones while he was away. Harvard was just across the river from Boston, and was close enough that, on a clear day, he would be able to see the rise of Beacon Hill from campus. Still, he felt too far. One surviving letter to his sister is short in length, but young Hancock spent half of it telling her how much he longed to hear from her. He began the letter with a guilt trip: "I believe Time slips away very easie with you, I wish you would spend one Hour in writing to me." He had heard rumors that she was engaged to be married and wanted to make sure he would be invited to the ceremony. He asked twice more for a letter from her.[22] He wanted to be top of mind for those he loved and needed to feel their affection with frequent correspondence.

He balanced his somber moods with typical college diversions. He and some of his friends, along with one of their servants, got drunk at a local tavern. While beer and hard cider were frequently served to students, intoxication was frowned upon by the school, which required students to attend morning prayers at five every morning. After a hearing, the college president determined that Hancock's class rank should be knocked down four places for the infraction, a lesser

Harvard College in 1743. John Hancock lived in Massachusetts Hall, the large building on the right, which still stands today.
New York Public Library.

punishment than what his friends received. They dropped seven spots because they were perceived as the instigators—Hancock was merely a follower. A copy of a drinking song, "A Pot of Good Ale," survives from his college papers, so he continued to imbibe even after being disciplined. He graduated from Harvard in 1754 but, unlike his father and grandfather, he did not enter the ministry. The House of Hancock beckoned.[23]

Hancock had a lot to learn about his uncle's business, which had to include hands-on training. His formal education had prepared him to write weekly sermons and recite classics, but he had not learned how to understand international markets, effectively smuggle, manage employees, invest, and network. After studying the business in Boston for several years, Hancock went to London to further his apprenticeship and help grow his family's connections with overseas suppliers and partners. So connected was the House of Hancock to the British Empire's administration that Hancock would be accompanied by a previous royal governor of Massachusetts, Thomas Pownall.[24]

It was Hancock's first time traveling abroad, and his uncle offered many tips, including staying focused on learning the business, and, more practically, how to avoid pickpockets. Sound advice. Boston was a frighteningly small town compared to London, which had over half a million inhabitants. Luckily for Hancock, London was not nearly as prudish as his hometown. Prostitutes publicly offered their services, and gambling—including on cockfights—was a common form of leisure for men of Hancock's means. He could also pay to spend time in tea gardens, where men and women could drink imported tea, play on bowling greens, or attend masquerade balls. As in his hometown, London residents drank a lot of alcohol, having over seven thousand places to buy inexpensive drinks.[25]

Hancock shopped a lot while abroad—as he would throughout his life—explaining to his uncle that it was a necessary business expense because he must "appear in Character." Clothing was the armor that could hide his lack of experience and help project competence. For centuries, fashion has communicated how we feel about ourselves and our relationships to the world. It can express our status, individualism, and power.[26] As a twenty-three-year-old, Hancock dressed finely as a way to more comfortably step into his role as a prosperous merchant.

He spent considerable sums on clothing and worried that he was getting a reputation for being too exorbitant, especially after Thomas had told him to be frugal. Acknowledging his expensive taste, Hancock justified his spending. Sure, he told his uncle, he shopped and dressed no differently than other gentlemen, but "money some way or other goes very fast."[27]

In fairness to his spending, he was in the hub for shopping sprees and people of means often purchased myriad goods while in the capital. Benjamin Franklin was visiting London at the same time as Hancock, and he too took advantage of the city's offerings, buying clothes and wares for his wife and daughter, including a giant wheel of parmesan cheese. And Hancock was not only spending on himself. Thomas sent a list of items he wanted his nephew to buy for him and Lydia. Hancock also purchased small gifts for others back home, including "a Cap and French Horn" for Cato, one of his family's enslaved men.[28]

Shopping could not beat back his loneliness, however. He was frequently homesick, a grief that afflicted him throughout his life. Like pleading with his sister for a letter while at Harvard, in London he longed to feel close to and loved by the people dearest to him. He wrote frequently to his uncle and brother, but was growing more estranged from his mother, who had since married for a third time. Her husband, Daniel Perkins, was a reverend in Bridgewater, Massachusetts. Hancock wrote to Perkins and complained that despite sending many letters, he had not received a single word from his mother since leaving Boston. "I long to hear of my Mother," Hancock implored. Perkins only wrote once, which Hancock found "unaccountable." He would never again have a close relationship with this mother, but fortunately for a young man yearning for connection, his aunt Lydia would help fill that role.[29]

Hancock did some work while in London, although he was not always helpful. Strong relationships based on respect and trust were paramount to eighteenth-century international business. Very little hard currency circulated, so an ability to get credit from partners overseas was critical. In advance of Hancock's trip, Thomas told his contacts in London that credit should be extended to his nephew for his expenses. With that in mind, Hancock went to a prominent firm his uncle frequently worked with and requested money to pay a debt his uncle owed. The men were justifiably nervous to give over a large sum of money, especially when it was not for Hancock's personal use, as Thomas had directed. They denied his request. Hancock again demanded the money. There was a standoff before the young upstart eventually slunk off.[30]

The partner immediately wrote to Thomas about the episode and noted that care was taken not to embarrass the young man, but Hancock had felt ashamed to be denied credit. He reported to his uncle about the matter and while his letter does not survive, Thomas's reply makes it clear that his protégé had taken the firm's refusal as an insult. Words like "vext" and "distrest" appear throughout Thomas's letter.[31]

Thomas believed that his name should have been enough to extend credit to his nephew for whatever reason. He was sorry the misunderstanding had upset Hancock and proved it by cutting ties with the banker the same day. He gave his nephew the power (and pleasure) to settle out his account with the offending firm, which was obligated to pay Hancock his uncle's balance.[32] Thomas had spent decades cultivating these connections and his young nephew arrived in London feeling entitled to the same treatment.

Hancock's stay in England overlapped with a big moment for the empire: King George II died suddenly in 1760 at the age of seventy-six. The reign of King George III began the day of his grandfather's death, and London celebrated "with great Pomp and Joy" in the midst of a longer mourning period. Hancock observed a new monarch beloved by his subjects, but was upset because the funereal time interrupted his social life: "every thing here now is very dull." The city had lost much of its appeal because all theater stopped and he had few ways to entertain himself.[33]

King George III was just twenty-two—a year younger than Hancock—when he assumed the crown of the mighty British Empire. Hancock wanted to extend his stay in London to witness the coronation. He anticipated it to be "the grandest thing I shall ever meet with." Bad timing prevented it. The king would not be coronated until October and Thomas wanted Hancock to sail home that summer to avoid the dangers of a fall voyage across the Atlantic. Franklin stayed in London for the event, but Hancock traveled back in July, never to venture outside North America again.[34]

The influence of the trip would carry throughout Hancock's life, but had little to do with the family business. London left him with some valuable insights: dress richly to project power and competence; arrogant behavior can be forgiven, especially with money to back you up; pomp and spectacle help people feel connected to their leader. Over the next thirty years, Hancock successfully applied these royal lessons to gain and maintain popularity and power.

———————

George Hewes, a twenty-year-old shoemaker's apprentice, was nervous. In front of him was Beacon Hill and at the top sat the mansion of Thomas and John Hancock. He planned to go up to the door and knock, but his nerves built on the ascent. Shoemaking was one of the lowliest professions and here he was intending to visit Boston's wealthiest family. His master had told him he was lucky for the opportunity, so that morning Hewes washed his face and put on his best jacket. Even though he knew he was fortunate, Hewes's heart was in his throat. Steeling himself, he approached the door, took his hat off, and knocked.[35]

When Hancock returned from London, his hometown was facing a severe financial crisis. Business slowed in much of colonial America beginning in 1760 and came to a grinding halt in 1763. That was the year the French and Indian War—another war waged between Great Britain and France—ended in British victory. The win came at an enormous cost: the crown's national debt nearly doubled. Exacerbating their pecuniary crunch, the British Empire had won vast territory in North America and now needed to secure it. Ten thousand

British troops were to be stationed as far west as the Appalachians. Soldiers required food, shelter, ammunition, and clothing—expenses that the empire could not afford. Since the troops were theoretically there to benefit the North American colonies, Great Britain's legislative body, Parliament, reasoned that the colonists should pay for such protection.[36]

But the colonies, especially Massachusetts, were broke. It was not just the big merchants with fat government contracts like Hancock who were affected when wartime commissions dried up. Men like Hewes were suffering throughout Boston. Credit disappeared; wages dropped—if you could find work at all. Poor relief in Boston increased as more people needed help, especially new widows, whose husbands had fought and died allying with the British. Business across the Atlantic slowed further as an outbreak of smallpox ravaged Boston. Ships coming into the harbor had to be quarantined—necessary to ensure the disease did not spread from port to port.[37]

Hewes's visit to the Hancock house, then, was worth the nerves, as it helped a shoemaker to be connected to men of means because they could hire him or disperse patronage. Hancock was particularly crucial to the local economy because his family business employed several hundred men. "Not less than a thousand Families were every day in the Year, dependent on Mr Hancock for their dayly bread," lawyer John Adams estimated.[38]

Hancock had invited Hewes to his home because the shoemaker had previously repaired a pair of the merchant's shoes. In a world where all garments were bespoke—that is, made by hand and fit specifically to an individual's body—colonists, even very wealthy ones like Hancock, mended shoes and clothes instead of replacing them. Hancock was pleased with the work and asked Hewes to come to his house on New Year's Day to offer him his best wishes for 1763, a tradition of the wealthy. The Hancock mansion was so accustomed to visitors that servants made a tankard of alcoholic punch in the mornings for guests to enjoy.[39]

After knocking, Hewes waited in front of the massive front door until a servant appeared. The apprentice bowed and asked if Hancock was home. Unsure of this visitor's business and seeming to judge by his appearance, the servant brought Hewes to the kitchen—the domain of household help and their visitors—while he went upstairs to alert Hancock. Shortly after, the servant reappeared "with a new varnish of civility" and brought Hewes to the sitting room, a more proper place for an invited guest to wait. Despite the name of the room suggesting that he have a seat, the young man remained standing as the servant left.[40]

Eventually Hancock appeared and Hewes bowed to him. Hancock greeted the apprentice warmly and indicated that he recalled their earlier interaction. Hancock was just five years older than Hewes, but they seemed years apart. They both knew and accepted the eighteenth-century social order that placed a rich, educated gentleman like Hancock on a higher plane than a shoemaker like Hewes. Each of them had roles to play: a common person was to bow and show humility in the presence of a gentleman, while the gentleman was to project superiority, and perhaps charity, to the poor and disenfranchised.[41]

Still standing, Hewes stammered through the reason for his visit with a prepared speech. "Very well, my lad," Hancock replied, offering Hewes a chair. Even in the face of such hospitality, Hewes could not relax, being scared "almost to death." It was not unusual for men of Hewes's stature to feel out of place in a richly decorated mansion that was tended by servants and run by a man wearing lavish clothing and a wig.[42] The differences were so visible and obvious to both of them.

Hancock, too, could have been uncomfortable, not wanting to be in the presence of someone other elite men distrusted or looked down on. Instead, Hancock was a welcoming host, attempting to put his guest at ease. To calm the young man and fulfill his obligation, Hancock reached into his breeches' pocket and pulled out a coin for Hewes, thanking him for coming. Forgoing the punch, Hancock called for wine to be brought out to drink to Hewes's health. The merchant "ticked glasses" with Hewes, a custom the shoemaker was unfamiliar with. Aware of how out of place he was, Hewes bowed again and hastened to leave. Before he did, Hancock made him promise to visit the following year. Hewes agreed before departing.[43]

Hewes had remained anxious during the visit in 1763, but Hancock would improve at connecting with men like him. One observer said of an older Hancock, "he is so frank and condescending to the lowest, that one would think he was talking to his brother or a relative." It was the duty of elite men to show *noblesse oblige* to what people in the eighteenth century referred to as the lower orders or sorts, which included apprentices, artisans, longshoremen, and seamen. Elites should condescend to such men, especially when soliciting votes.[44] But Hancock did not merely condescend. He seemed to genuinely like people and was adept at making them feel seen. And he certainly relished the attention and appreciation they could give him, a man who strove to feel that he belonged. Connecting with the lower orders more authentically than other politicians would help Hancock secure unparalleled popularity.

Amidst the financial crisis impacting Hewes and the town, Thomas named his nephew a full partner in the House of Hancock. It would be a bumpy transition for a couple of reasons. First, Hancock lacked the innate skills to run and grow a business, characteristic of many second-generation business owners. He had shown none of the hunger and tenacity his uncle had demonstrated while building his empire. Second, Hancock was trained during wartime boom years, when money easily flowed in. He was accustomed to abundant credit and open markets, and saw his uncle profit from a financially stable mother country.

Despite the economic downturn and his inexperience, a self-assured Hancock believed he could have a large, immediate financial impact on the company. He thought they should get back into selling whale oil, a business that Thomas had engaged in decades before. One of New England's most important exports, whale oil was primarily used to make candles and had a considerable market in England. Nantucket, an island off the coast of Massachusetts, was home to many of the top suppliers from whom Boston merchants bought before shipping it across the Atlantic. Over half of the House of Hancock's income came from whale oil in the 1730s before Thomas withdrew from the market.[45]

Hancock had an audacious plan to draw the business back in: buy every drop of whale oil available; squeeze out his biggest competitor, Joseph Rotch of Nantucket; and create a high demand and price for the monopolized oil when it landed in London. Hancock went to Nantucket and set up his connections with suppliers—"the best men there"—and felt confident about the enterprise. "I can have what oyl I please . . . which of course takes from the other Channell and is very Chagrining to Mr. R[otc]h," he boasted.[46]

Eagerness and inexperience caused Hancock to forego inspecting the oil. Had he done so, he would have learned that it was of poor quality, and it ultimately sold at a loss. The brash merchant grew angry with his agents in London and accused them of not properly pricing or selling his goods. He took no blame for his role in the fiasco and instead cut ties with some of the partners. He became especially irate after they suggested that he partner with Rotch instead of competing against him. The proud Hancock would not even consider the matter.[47]

Hancock's agents offered another idea that was even more insulting than partnering with Rotch: someone from London would come to Massachusetts and inspect the oil before Hancock purchased it. It was a clear attack on his competence and his ego was wounded. Things got messy.

"I am a judge for myself," Hancock protested, "and if you do not think me a judge for you, I pray you would not employ me." No one from London would know better about the quality of oil than men from New England, he reasoned. But more important to him at this time, and in years to come, was his reputation. He admitted that he could never allow himself to have such an overseer because it would humiliate him in front of other merchants. The House of Hancock's trade in whale oil dwindled after the dispute.[48]

Thomas was a better businessman than his nephew, but he would soon be unable to assuage Hancock's anxiety about bad business deals or smooth over any hurt feelings. As the days got longer and warmer in 1764, Thomas's health was declining, but he continued on with his political duties. He had a seat on the prestigious Council, the upper house in the colonial Massachusetts legislature. After skipping several meetings because of illness, on the first of August, he made his way to the Town House—called the Old State House today—for a Council meeting.

The Town House, a short carriage ride from the Hancock estate, was a three-story brick building where the royal governor and the two-house legislature, called the General Court, convened. Built in 1713, it is the oldest surviving public building in North America. At the top of the edifice sat a lion and a unicorn, symbols of royal authority. The structure still stands today—stoic among the glitzy downtown high-rise buildings that surround it.

In the eighteenth century, the first floor of the Town House was mostly occupied by merchants selling goods. A circular wooden staircase with carved balusters led to the second floor where government business took place. At the top of the stairs was the Assembly Room, which faced west and overlooked Cornhill Street. Because the Council was the upper house, it had the better room. It faced east—to the riches of the Atlantic—and overlooked the harbor and King Street, the busiest street in Boston. For an even better view, one could step out onto the wooden balcony.[49]

Thomas never made it to the Council Room. He got to the top of the staircase before he collapsed. He returned home where he succumbed to "apoplexy" later that afternoon. Thomas had died of a stroke at the age of sixty-one.[50] His beloved nephew was devastated by the news. He was now without a male guardian or mentor and his aunt Lydia was all that remained of a parental figure. He was also about to become supremely rich.

Thomas's will spread his fortune around—including a gift for a chaired professor at Harvard, a school he did not attend, and plenty of charitable donations—but his widow and nephew received the bulk of the estate. Of the two of them, Hancock got much more. Thomas left Lydia money, the Beacon Hill mansion, and all that came with it—the enslaved people who maintained it, its furnishings, land, and carriages. One enslaved man, Cato, received the gift of freedom at age thirty, but only if he "behave to the Satisfaction" of Lydia.[51]

His uncle bestowed to Hancock the entire business: inventory, ships, warehouses, shops, wharfs. Additionally, he received over twenty thousand acres of land in New England. Despite this, he would continue to live in his aunt's home. At the age of twenty-seven, Hancock was now one of the wealthiest men in New England and one of the largest employers in Massachusetts.[52]

Like the death of Hancock's father twenty years earlier, the death of his uncle profoundly altered his life's trajectory. His rise in fortune brought a rapid increase in visibility and responsibilities and drew the attention of the political clubs in Boston—those who helped put men on the ballots and get elected. They were drawn to the young man's wealth, just as they had been to his uncle. Within a year of his uncle's death, Hancock was elected to his first political post, a selectman, an office Thomas once held.

Much later, John Adams claimed that his cousin, Samuel, boasted that the town had done "a wise Thing" by electing Hancock and making "that young Man's fortune their own." John Adams had a special knack for positioning himself at significant moments in history, but it's dubious some of them happened the way he said. This story is surely apocryphal, coming twenty-four years after Hancock's death, but it shows Adams's desire to see the Revolution as inevitable and preordained, despite its path being anything but assured. In the 1760s, even Hancock would not have foretold his own political accomplishments. He was not particularly excited about governing at this time, especially because he was taking office at an inopportune moment.[53]

"Times are very bad & precarious here," Hancock explained to a partner in London. The success of Uncle Thomas may have seemed effortless, but developing a lucrative merchant house was a stressful endeavor—there were tremendous risks and stiff competition. It was particularly challenging during an economic crisis. Hancock was further unnerved when two established colonial merchants went bankrupt. "The great uneasiness & Losses here owing to the failure" of the men "of Note . . . has put us into great anxiety," he said. Hancock was concerned enough about the colony's finances that he ordered fewer goods from London because he did not know "who is & who is not safe."[54]

It was around this troubled time when Parliament passed taxes to pay for the stationed troops in North America. The taxes and subsequent protests by the lower orders would test Hancock. His instincts to avoid radicals and to understand both sides would serve him well, as would the wealth he just inherited. He would be aided by his time spent in London, meeting prominent men there and learning how to project power. His generosity and desire to connect with people would also go a long way, as would wanting to protect his mercantile interests. Hancock had many of the necessary traits and skills to navigate an uprising, and he would acquire more as the resistance turned to rebellion and ultimately to revolution. He was not yet King Hancock in 1764, and neither Adams cousin could have predicted it, but Hancock's rise to power had begun.

CHAPTER 2

Becoming a Man
of the People

Two carts resembling grotesque parade floats were visible on Mill Bridge at the edge of Boston's North End. Even in the darkness, townspeople knew what was on display: figures of the pope and devil with distorted and exaggerated features. Each cart was surrounded by a gang of young men, many wielding clubs and brickbats. Half of the toughs came from the North End and the other half from the South End.[1]

Earlier that day, the rival neighborhood gangs—who had spent the past several days preparing their floats—had marched through town in costumes such as dunce hats, tar and feathers, or monk's robes, and had been surrounded by dancers and musicians.[2] As the sun set, so too did the daytime frivolity. The two gangs now faced each other, tightened the grip on their clubs or picked up stones, eyed the prize of the other side's pope, and squared off.

It was Pope's Day in Boston: November 5, 1764.

The tradition of Pope's Day came from England, where it was known as Guy Fawkes Day. It was named after one of the Catholic conspirators who tried and failed in 1605 to blow up the Parliament building and the members within it. Boston had been celebrating the holiday since the seventeenth century. Over the years, authorities had tried to mitigate the fighting, but the port town's celebration proved immune to regulation and grew in size and violence, all with a clear anti-Catholic sentiment.[3]

While all levels of society could join in, it was primarily a celebration for younger men from the lower orders.[4] An elite man like Hancock would be nowhere near these activities, but shoemaker George Hewes, whom he had entertained in his home the year before, would be a likely participant.

The day began with children going to homes to solicit money. Sometimes they would be sweet and ring bells or recite rhymes to get donations. But they quickly turned sour if purses did not open fast enough. They used profane language, threatened to break windows, and ominously banged on the side of the houses with clubs. The parade followed that afternoon and at night, a massive street brawl among the adults.[5]

Lit only by the moon and some lanterns, the leader of the South End, shoemaker Ebenezer Mackintosh, barked out orders through a speaking trumpet to encourage his gang or have them realign or change strategy. He had been elected their captain earlier that year—a sign of his success in previous years' fights—and he had prepared different tactics to capture the North End's pope. Mackintosh's men were "trained as regular as a military Corps," for both he and many of his followers were veterans of the recent French and Indian War.[6]

Under Mackintosh's direction that night, the South End was gaining ground on the opposition's pope and closing in on victory, but the rival leader was badly hurt. He was lying unconscious on the ground—"near being killed"—and would slip into a coma for a few days before recovering. Bodily harm was expected and accepted on Pope's Day. A few hours previous, the North End's cart had run over the head of a small boy, killing him. The festivities continued despite the injuries, and after a sustained fight with many "hurt & bruised on both sides," the South End nabbed the North End's pope. The participants and onlookers then walked over a mile to the gallows on the neck of Boston, the narrow strip of land that connected the town to the mainland. Bloodied fighters built and stoked a bonfire, and because they won, Mackintosh and his men threw both popes into the pyre. Huzzahs rang out and the men retired to a tavern to take off the late autumn chill.[7]

The Pope's Day festival was tolerated by political leaders because it was a fight among willing participants "and did not directly affect the Government," according to royal governor of Massachusetts Francis Bernard. It did, however, mock and challenge authority, give men experience in working together, and signal their collective power. Bernard's benign assessment of Pope's Day would soon be proved wrong. When King George III's advisors tried to increase colonists' dependency by taxing them, Bostonians would use such experience to protest.[8]

The prime minister of Great Britain, George Grenville, had two taxes in mind to raise the necessary funds to pay for troops stationed in North America. Parliament passed his first measure in 1764 and it had many components, but the most notable—a tax on foreign molasses—gave the bill its nickname, the Sugar Act. It was a course correction from an earlier, ineffective tax. In 1733, the Molasses Act intended to prevent British colonies from importing molasses from French Caribbean islands, but merchants easily bribed greedy customs officials to look the other way.[9]

The Sugar Act aimed to keep profits from the vast colonial market within the empire. It required that colonies import molasses only from British colonies in the West Indies—this both helped the crown and hurt trade with the French West Indies—and it established new ways to enforce the tax. Boston, in particular, would be hit hard by this fee because rum, distilled from molasses, was one of the few commodities the town produced. And they made a lot of it. One visitor to the colonies noted, "The quantity of spirits, which they distil in Boston from the molasses they bring in from all parts of the West-Indies, is as surprising as the cheap rate at which they vend it . . . With this they supply almost all the consumption of our colonies in North America."[10]

Many colonists objected to the Sugar Act for economic and ideological reasons, claiming that it would harm the symbiotic and
lucrative Atlantic trade market and violate colonial sovereignty. Hancock was more concerned with its financial implications than any
infringement on his rights, however. He gathered in taverns with
other merchants to tipple and discuss the state of their trade, worrying
about lost revenue and predicting that "the times will be worse
here."[11]

The times would be worse—Grenville intended to pass another,
more expansive tax the following year. Popularly known as the Stamp
Act, it would levy a fee on printed documents, including newspapers,
deeds, almanacs, liquor licenses, and playing cards. Initially, Hancock
had an acquiescent view of the tax. He believed, as did others, that as
British subjects, they were obligated to obey Parliament's laws. "We
must Submit," he conceded. His uncle had built his wealth by allying
with crown officials, not opposing them, and Hancock was not much
interested in protesting governmental policies. In July of 1765 he can-
didly admitted, "I Seldom meddle with Politicks & indeed have not
Time now." Merchants like him found trading with the British empire necessary and profitable and were willing to accept subordina-
tion to the crown as a tradeoff. Besides, he could simply skirt the tax
with bribery and smuggling.[12]

Despite the new taxes, Hancock was not concerned enough about
his financial prospects to forego a luxury—commissioning his first
portrait. When someone chose to get painted, it not only showed an
excess of wealth—it was out of reach for 99 percent of the population—but of wanting to mark a certain point in their lives. Hancock
had himself painted soon after he inherited his uncle's business.[13]

John Singleton Copley, a year younger than Hancock, was the
chosen artist. He was a Boston native, having grown up in a small
house on Long Wharf. Copley depicts the merchant in his new role
in front of a ledger book, a quill in hand. Hancock was still eleven
years away from the moment that would make him famous for gen-

erations to come—using a quill to sign his name—but there seems a
bit of prescience to pose in such a way.

Hancock's delicate facial figures are contrasted by his full, if shape-
less, eyebrows. He is dressed in a dark jacket with gold trim and
buttons, adornment reserved for the wealthy and a signature look of
his. His slender calves are covered with silk stockings, which his
breeches meet just past his knees. An artisan would not know the
feeling of such a delicate fabric against his legs—its price made it
only available to elites. Hancock was "always genteelly dressed,"
John Adams observed, and the artist shows it in his depiction. The
completed portrait—Copley took longer than most artists to finish—
would hang in Hancock's home, visible to the many visitors who
stopped by for punch or dinner.[14]

Time did not stand still as it did in a Copley painting, though, and
the economic desperation of the town would soon get the attention
of elites, including Hancock. In recent years, the townspeople's stan-
dard of living had steadily declined as the cost of basic goods, including food and firewood, skyrocketed. During the French and
Indian War, taxes for Bostonians increased until the town eventually
had the highest tax rate across the British Empire. Most of Hancock's neighbors were destitute. This was both figuratively and literally true: his mansion was steps from Boston's two-story almshouse,
which had its highest-ever number of occupants in the mid-1760s.[15]

Veterans, especially, felt the taxes were egregious. They had
watched neighbors fall in battle, endured the harsh and uncertain
conditions of war, and returned home to find little work. A committee
formed by the town of Boston summarized the problem perfectly:
"the People of this Province have not only settled this Country, but
enlargd & defended the British Dominion in America, with a vast
Expence of Treasure & Blood . . . And in the late War more especially, by their surprizing Exertions, they have bro't upon themselves, a Debt almost insupportable." The men paid with blood.
Now the crown wanted them to pay with their wages, too. Unlike

John Hancock's first known portrait, by John Singleton Copley.
Museum of Fine Arts, Boston.

Hancock, the impoverished could not afford another financial burden or smuggle their way around a tax, and Parliament did not seem to understand or care. Radical action would be needed to have their protests and interests heard.[16]

───────────

Boston's history of violence hinted that the objections to the Stamp Act would be destructive, for Pope's Day was not the only sanctioned violence in town. Officials and elites understood that mobs would form when the government fell short of promoting public well-being. Over the past several decades, men in Boston had rioted to protest impressment in the British navy, high food prices, and low wages. Crowd action was an effective way to redress wrongs.[17]

Resistance to the Stamp Act would initially be built on both this tradition of street violence and the framework, leadership, and symbolism of Pope's Day. The ideal person to lead the protests was the winner of last year's brawl. Mackintosh, "the Ring Leader of the Mob," recruited men who were indignant that the recent conclusion of the war had not made them any safer or more financially secure. An empire that had already asked so much of them was now asking more. Mackintosh did not limit himself to the South End when recruiting—he asked the rival gang in the North End to participate. The Loyal Nine, a political club of nine tradesmen, also helped Mackintosh plan the attack.[18]

Once the agitators were in place, they identified their first target, an obvious choice: Andrew Oliver, the Stamp Act collector for Massachusetts. Oliver came from a prominent family that had been in Boston nearly as long as the town existed. He had served in politics for almost three decades and was awarded this job because government posts usually went to wealthy men.[19] Hancock knew this all too well. After he inherited his uncle's fortune he was considered for the role of selectman.

On August 14, 1765, the newly unified mob hung an effigy of Oliver from an elm tree—later called the Liberty Tree—on the neck of Boston, which made it the first or last thing one saw on the way in or out of town. Effigies were menacing, but familiar, as ones depicting the pope and devil frequently appeared on Pope's Day. That evening, the mob cut down the effigy, paraded it through the streets, and stopped at the Town House to shout huzzahs "of defiance." The men continued to Oliver's Wharf—like Hancock, he was wealthy enough to have a dock with his name on it—and targeted his warehouse because rumors spread that the stamps from England would be stored there.[20]

"In a few minutes the building was level with the ground," a witness reported. The mob continued to the home of Oliver, who had been warned in advance to leave. The men broke his windows and set fire to his coach. In a macabre twist, the protestors cut off the head of Oliver's effigy and threw it in his yard. The mob demanded that Oliver resign from his post at the Liberty Tree. He did just that the next day.[21]

It had been a frightening crowd, but because it resembled past protests, many in power were not unduly alarmed by it. The crowd had been upset about the Stamp Act and targeted the Stamp Act collector. That made sense to Hancock and other Bostonians. Hancock was so unaffected by the violence that he wished for further action against the Stamp Act: "I hope the same Spirit will prevail throughout the whole Continent."[22]

When other British colonies on the Atlantic seaboard learned of the effective tactics against Oliver, they implemented similarly terrorizing attacks on their officials. A mob in Rhode Island destroyed homes and organized a parade of effigies in Newport, resulting in the closing of their customs house. Seeing which way the winds were blowing, the New York stamp distributor stepped down before any violence came upon him. It took little time before Stamp Act officials from other North American colonies resigned—a remarkable and unprecedented show of intercolonial coordination.[23]

Not every stamp collector under British rule had to resign, however. Our story is confined to the thirteen British North American colonies that became the United States because that was the world John Hancock inhabited and governed, but there was no certainty that those particular colonies would unite or succeed. In the 1760s, the British empire had more than two dozen colonies in the Americas and many were against the Stamp Act in principle, but some subjects, including those in Nova Scotia and Jamaica, paid the tax. Further, there were other inhabitants of North America—Native peoples and Spanish and French colonizers—who were indirectly impacted by British rule and taxes. They allied with or combatted the empire based on their own interests, including money, religion, and revenge.[24]

After Oliver's resignation, the Stamp Act protests in Massachusetts should have ended, but Mackintosh had another target in mind. This time it was the colony's lieutenant governor, Thomas Hutchinson, who descended from a family that helped found New England, including his great-great-grandmother and religious dissident, Anne Hutchinson. He was an easy target because of his vast family wealth and his holding multiple political offices, which many Bostonians saw as corrupt and a conflict of interest.[25]

The lieutenant governor lived in the North End, which was an economically diverse neighborhood, with sailors and prostitutes at the bottom; craftsmen who were higher up on the social rung, including silversmith Paul Revere; and finally at the top, ministers and government officials.[26] The North End today feels like one of the most historic spaces in Boston, even though only a handful of buildings from the colonial period still stand. It is the layout of the streets that harkens back to the time of Hutchinson—crooked and narrow with little pattern.

Hutchinson's family built a large, three-story home that towered over its two-story neighbors. The home's plain exterior did not reflect the interior, which was mostly finished with red cedar and had an estimated fifteen to twenty rooms. There were luxurious furnishings, including clocks, statues and busts, and elaborate bed hangings. Small objects of luxury were scattered throughout: a tortoiseshell box, brushes made of ivory, and mirrors. A cellar was filled with some of the most valuable items in the house: hams, bacon, and over a thousand gallons of fortified wine and sherry.[27]

On the night of August 26, a group of men "well supplied with strong drink" went to Garden Court Street and laid siege to Hutchinson's stocked house. "With intoxicated rage," the rioters used axes to split open the door. For the next several hours, the mob tore wainscoting and hangings, dismantled the roof, knocked down his fence, and chopped his trees to the ground. Feathers rained from above as thugs cut open the beds and threw their contents out the windows. They scattered or destroyed books, papers, and manuscripts — some of them original documents related to the history of Massachusetts, a subject Hutchinson was writing about. They stole his clothing, silver, and cash, and drank the precious contents of his cellar. At the end of the night, there was "scarce any thing left but the Walls."[28]

It was a stunning show of populist power, and this time the destruction of a public official's private property troubled Hancock. A short time after hoping the spirit of violence against Oliver would prevail throughout North America, Hancock condemned the riot against Hutchinson as "quite a different Affair."[29] What was the difference?

The attack of Oliver was an example of grievance-related protests and, therefore, acceptable to Hancock. The assault against Hutchinson was unrelated to the Stamp Act, so it was unacceptable. Hancock continued to believe that opposition to the Stamp Act was "highly commendable," but privately he did not think "every Step that has been Taken is so." People could protest, but not in the way they had against Hutchinson. Of that type of mob, Hancock said, "I abhor & Detest as much as any man breathing." The fiery Samuel Adams, who supported violent protests against the Stamp Act, also condemned the Hutchinson attack, calling it "truly *mobbish*."[30]

The second riot had been about something other than an act of Parliament. The men participating likely relished the idea of destroying something belonging to a wealthy man they hated—being fueled by alcohol only stoked their rage. The raid on Hutchinson's house had not been orchestrated by the Loyal Nine, as the mob against Oliver had been, and it showed that when the lower orders were angry, they could target any man of privilege. This was worrisome to Hancock and other wealthy men.[31]

Detestable as Hancock may have found the Hutchinson mob, one had to be careful in openly condemning any protests against the Stamp Act. Throughout the North American colonies, men calling themselves the Sons of Liberty organized to oppose the tax. In Boston, the group grew out of the Loyal Nine and they could be quite intimidating. Merchants in Massachusetts—but also New York, Pennsylvania, and Virginia—were now caught between enraged, mobilized men and a desire to make money by continuing their trade with the British Empire.[32]

The Sons, however, were intolerant of nuance or sitting the conflict out. As happens during times of extreme conflict, the Sons became more convinced of their own superiority and grew more baffled and annoyed with those who did not agree with them or their tactics. They declared that the men in power who supported the Stamp Act are "either Traitors to their Country, or so little acquainted with the British Constitution as to render them unfit to be trusted to represent you again."[33]

Notice the Sons' commitment to and faith in British principles. They considered someone a traitor because he was not adhering to the *British* constitution. Many Britons opposed the tax precisely because of their confidence in the empire. The new tax violated a right they thought subjects were entitled to—the government could not take their property without their consent. The Sons of Liberty believed that a few bad actors had misled the king and his ministers; consequently, they had faith the tax would be repealed.[34]

Before that happened, Hancock changed his mind about the Stamp Act. "This letter I propose to remain in my Letter Book as a

Standing monument to posterity & my Children in particular, that I by no means Consented to a Submission to this Cruel Act," Hancock wrote.[35] He had no children yet, but wanted to condemn the tax in case any questions arose about his loyalty now or in the future. For him, opposing the Stamp Act was not about heady political ideas, but rather preservation for himself and his property. This should not be surprising. The town's violence against the Stamp Act had been terrifying.

In July 1765, Hancock had said he had no time to meddle in politics, but just a few months later, after two destructive riots against wealthy officials, he found the time. He would not oppose the Stamp Act by taking to the streets armed with a club, but in a more influential and respectable way. It began with a letter-writing campaign to London.

Hancock was in a unique position as a prominent merchant. People in London cared what he had to say because he was a reliable client and a connection to the vast colonial market. He threatened his overseas partners with the "Stagnation of Trade" if the Stamp Act went into effect and demanded that they "rise up & Exert themselves" in defense of the colonies because "we are worth a saving." Enlisting the help of overseas merchants was a strong strategy because they could directly and more persuasively appeal to those in Parliament, many of whom thought of Americans as lesser subjects with little clout.[36]

Hancock's pleas to his London associates also reminded them of the debts he and other colonists owed. If the Stamp Act remained, he threatened his London partners that "you may bid Adieu to Remittances for the past Goods . . . yor Debts cannot be Recover'd here." This was no idle threat. Hancock was not the only man beholden to the British—other colonial debts had been steadily increasing over the past two decades. If Parliament would only lift the Stamp Act and return to free trade, Hancock promised that they would be able to pay their bills.[37]

Over time, Hancock began using ideological arguments to shroud his pecuniary interests. "We look upon it as unconstitutional," Hancock said of the Stamp Act, invoking his rights as a British subject to justify opposition to the tax. This was an evolution from his pragmatic arguments about the destruction of trade and unpaid debts. As he heard more from those around him, his thoughts shifted. He also came to embrace what would become key language of the American Revolution: the fear of being enslaved by the British Empire. "The people of this Country will never Suffer themselves to be made slaves . . . to that D[amne]d act," Hancock wrote.[38] Hancock needed to go no further than his bedroom to see true slavery, but that did not stop him from using this common phrase.

Hancock was one man, but if more like him worked together in other towns, they could form a powerful coalition. That fall, merchants in New York and Philadelphia, along with Boston and other coastal Massachusetts towns, agreed to stop importing British goods until the Stamp Act was repealed. Hancock promised that he and other merchants "will by no means carry on Business under a Stamp." Colonists were the primary purchasers of British goods, and their boycott would devastate the mother country's economy. Using their financial might to get Parliament to notice them was a new power the colonists, especially those in urban centers, were testing out.[39]

Before the boycott began, however, Hancock wanted to maximize potential profits. If one of his ships arrived before November 1—the day the tax was to go into effect—he would quickly unload the ship, reload it, and send it back to London. He also submitted "a small order for Goods to be sent by the first Spring Ship" if the Stamp Act was repealed. Hancock knew there was money to be made if his vessel landed first filled with items colonists had not recently been able to buy. He was very clear, though, that if the Stamp Act was not repealed, they should send no goods "in consequence of the united Resolution of the Merchants here & the other Trading Towns."[40]

Hancock's desire to beat the Stamp Act deadline showed the blurred edges of resistance. He was not going to operate with stamps, but the merchant still wanted to trade with Britain. When Parliament passed the Sugar and Stamp Acts, colonists did not drop their own interests and become full-fledged revolutionaries ready for independence and war. A couple of taxes did not change Hancock's desire to do business the way his family had for decades.

As the implementation of the Stamp Act approached, some Bostonians grew anxious. Heightening nerves was Pope's Day, falling just four days later. Fearing violence, Governor Bernard called out two companies of militia to guard the town from October 31 to November 6, but they told him "they could not execute" his orders. To ensure his own safety, Bernard fled to Castle William, a fort on an island in Boston Harbor.[41]

Hancock had a better idea than hiding or using military force: bring the lower orders together and convince them to act respectably. Such conciliation was characteristic for a political moderate. Hancock hoped to prevent violence by lowering the temperature in town — efforts no doubt inspired, in part, by self-preservation. In November 1765, he and another leading merchant hosted a party at a local tavern for men from the North and South End gangs.[42]

Colonial taverns were spaces where men debated politics, gathered for camaraderie, and built connections. There was no shortage of watering holes in colonial Boston; the town had a strong culture of drinking, but men from different social classes rarely found themselves in the same space. The grog shops at the waterfront catered to seamen and the poor, with maybe a prostitute or two lingering, while the taverns on King Street, with higher rents, catered to a more elite crowd, as evidenced by the variety of alcohol served, the silver from which to drink, and the plentiful candles illuminating the space. Hancock was comfortable drinking with men outside of his class, mostly because his status in society was so assured. He chose to entertain at a tavern familiar to him and popular with artisans.[43]

The Green Dragon Tavern had been around for a century and was a large, brick structure between Dock Square and the North End. A connected stable was used by travelers who arrived on horseback, and for those who needed a place to stay, beds were available in the attic. It got its name from the decades-old copper dragon—with a curled tail and a "frightful looking tongue"—that hung out front, oxi-dized green by the salt air. It was "the wonder of all the boys" who played on the large parcel of land in front of the building.[44]

Over time the tavern had served diverse functions. Samuel Sewall, of the Salem witch trials ignominious fame, attended a court session there—it was already heated and lit, which saved the courts money—and a short-lived dancing school also popped up at the Green Dragon. In the 1760s, the upstairs became home to the Ma-sonic chapter of St. Andrew's. Hancock belonged to this fraternal organization, as did silversmith Paul Revere and doctor Joseph Warren.[45] The colonial-era tavern no longer exists in Boston, but an establishment of the same name is near the original location.

Green Dragon Tavern. Its distinctive sign is visible over the door.
Boston Public Library.

That night at the Green Dragon, Hancock was a generous host, as he would be throughout his life. He paid a large sum of money for supper and drinks and gave a speech, encouraging both sides "to lay aside their animosity" and to realize "the necessity of their united efforts." To protect the town's reputation, he asked for peaceful demonstrations going forward. Hancock "possessed a most happy talent of adapting his conversation to the taste of all," which helped him influence men with interests very different than his own. No doubt also aided by the warmth of alcohol, they all shook hands as they parted.[46]

Governor Bernard, however, saw Hancock's party in a more dangerous light. He thought the reconciliation would lead to more powerful riots, not a ceasefire. Hancock united them "for other Purposes, I fear, than burning a Pope."[47] The merchant definitely had ulterior motives, but it was to prevent violence, not stoke it. Not only was he keeping the peace in his town, but he ensured the mob would not turn on a wealthy man like him, as they had with Hutchinson.

Hancock's plan worked. Instead of violent protests, there was a safer and more festive atmosphere on November 1. The day began with a tolling of the bells and effigies on the Liberty Tree. This time, the hanged represented officials in England, not those of their neighbors. Around two o'clock that afternoon, the effigies were cut down and became part of a procession with over two thousand observers from Boston and the countryside. The parade wrapped its way around the Town House and shouted huzzahs. They proceeded to the gallows where the dummies were "tore to pieces" before being hanged.[48]

Four days later, Pope's Day also had a new and orderly feel: Mackintosh donned special clothes, including a blue and red hat laced in gold. He led his followers and officers—who also wore distinctive hats and carried "wands"—through the streets. In the afternoon carts and stages were brought to King Street. They were topped with the customary popes and devils, but this year, they also carried "hanging Stampmen," merging Pope's Day with politics. "In a very ceremonial manner," the North End and South End publicly confirmed that they were now allies. The carts and men stopped at the Town House and asked the legislators inside to contribute to their evening's fund. Bernard, back from his asylum, directed that "my People should give money to the Pageants."[49]

Thanks to the governor and others, the year had been an especially prodigious one for donations. "Many contributed from affection, much more from fear," Bernard resentfully noted. As usual, the gangs put the money toward an afterparty at a tavern. Hancock and as many as two hundred others attended. Mackintosh and the North End leader sat at each head of the table, with Hancock occupying a distinguished position alongside one of them.[50] In just a few months, Hancock had changed his mind about taxation, raised his profile among the lower orders, found ideological reasons to justify his financial interests, and used his important voice to lobby his contacts in London. He was stepping into the role of town leader.

Meanwhile, his protests to London and the merchants' boycott were successful. Suffering greatly, British merchants and manufacturers petitioned Parliament to repeal the Stamp Act. Some legislators were sympathetic to colonial protests and their cause was aided when Grenville was replaced by Lord Rockingham, who felt no need to retain his predecessor's failed taxes. Rockingham had a tough job, though. He needed to do two conflicting things: assuage British merchants' concerns by eliminating the tax and establish Parliament's ultimate authority. Bernard summed up the predicament: "Thinking Men know not which will bring most danger, a Repeal or a Confirmation: the Latter they say will make the People mad with desperation; the former insolent with Success."[51]

As a way to assert their power while conceding to the colonies, members of Parliament repealed the Stamp Act but also passed the Declaratory Act, giving themselves the power to tax the colonies "in all cases whatsoever." While this was menacing language, colonists throughout the British Empire—from Kingston to Glasgow to

New York City—rejoiced in the tax's repeal. Britons toasted to being loyal subjects and part of a free empire, all while praising the king.[52]

Today, this successful colonial rebellion against unfair taxation conjures the familiar beginning of the American Revolution, but that is not how people in the eighteenth century viewed it. The Stamp Act was a mistake by Parliament and after effective pressure, the legislators repealed it. Hancock had been awakened politically, but only temporarily. He and many others throughout North America were happy the threat was gone and felt no need to become permanent activists against the empire. Radical colonists, however, would not forget the threat the Stamp Act had posed. Even as they were grateful for its repeal, the tax became a festering wound that would reopen in the coming years.[53]

Given the time it took for news to cross the Atlantic—about eight weeks—it was not until May 16, 1766, that Bostonians heard of Parliament's decision. Luckily for Hancock, word came aboard one of his ships. "It is worthy Remark that the Vessel which bro't us the glorious News of the total Repeal of the Stamp Act is owned by that worthy Patriot, John Hancock," a newspaper reported.[54] This tied his reputation to the revocation of the Stamp Act, a connection he would further cement with a party that complemented the town-wide celebration.

Boston's church bells tolled, guns fired, drums beat, and cannons boomed. "All Sorts of Musick" accompanied the martial sounds and merchants' ships were festooned with "a Display of Colours." The Liberty Tree had also been decorated, and the afternoon "was Spent in Mirth and Jollity." Throughout the revelry, commitment to the king and Parliament was affirmed.[55]

The festivities centered around Boston Common. Lawyer James Otis hosted an open house, as did other families who lived near the park. The party covered several blocks—"the Sashes of the Houses round were covered with Illustrated Figures as large as Life." Even Bernard stopped by and was happy to see "Demonstrations of Loyalty and Joy."[56]

Since the Common was directly in front of Hancock's house, he had a chance to show off. All of his house's windows were illuminated, drawing townspeople's eyes to him. He "gave a grand and elegant Entertainment to the genteel part of the Town."[57] He did not host anyone and everyone in his home that evening, but he still knew how to charm the masses.

To the townspeople, he gifted a pipe — which amounted to over 120 gallons — of Madeira wine, setting up the oversized barrel in front of his house. By offering alcohol to the lower orders, as he had at the Green Dragon, he helped gain loyalty. Political authority in the eighteenth century often came from wealthy men giving work, extending credit, or supplying men with food and drink.[58]

Hancock would have recognized some of the people enjoying his gift, including the shoemaker, George Hewes, who partook in Hancock's hospitality for a second time. As people drank together outside, Hancock blurred the usual social stratification and made himself a man of the people, even as he entertained the elite separately. He mingled with the crowd and "treated every Person with Cheerfulness."[59] Unlike other politicians who interacted with common people merely to gain recognition or secure votes, Hancock enjoyed their company.

Late that afternoon, an obelisk engraved by Paul Revere was set up on the Common. It was covered with "various Hieroglyphics, and Poetical Lines" and at dusk, it was lit from within by "lamps." Fireworks followed, including "rockets, bee-hives and serpents." Again, Hancock would not be outdone. He erected a stage in front of his house for his own pyrotechnics show, "which was to answer those of the Sons of Liberty."[60]

Afterward, "the Populace retired to their respective Dwellings, the Lights were put out, and the Town was hushed in unusual Silence." Accounts claimed that everyone made their way home by midnight. As townspeople went to bed in a festive and grateful mood, Revere's obelisk accidentally caught fire at one o'clock that morning and burned down.[61] Boston's peaceful celebration literally went up in flames.

CHAPTER 3

The Bold and Brash
Idol of the Mob

On April 8, 1768, two nosy tidesmen wanted to pry into Hancock's maritime activities. The customs officials' jobs were to ensure there was no "clandestine running" of goods onshore without merchants or captains paying proper duties. Yet, Hancock had allegedly boasted that "he would not suffer [the] Officers to go even on board . . . any of his London Ships." Owen Richards and Robert Jackson wanted to prove him wrong by snooping around one of his vessels.[1]

A customs board had recently been established in Boston to help enforce a new tax. In 1767, Parliament passed the Townshend Duties, which imposed a fee on imported British goods, including tea, glass, paper, paint, and clothing. To both radicals and moderates in the colonies, this measure demonstrated that the Stamp Act and subsequent protests had taught Parliament nothing. Many in England did not appear to value the mutually beneficial commercial relationships they had with the North American colonies because the duties would decimate the House of Hancock's profits and those of other merchants. The new customs men were also loathsome, earnestly patrolling the harbors, eager to stop and search nearly any vessel.[2]

Bostonians were unhappy with these intruders, but the customs officials were equally unimpressed with the townspeople. The bureaucrats despised many of them because they thumbed their noses—the literal act of which was a sign of disrespect in colonial America—at the crown with their rampant smuggling. One bureaucrat said of the residents, "the common cry being, Pay no Duties!, Save your Money and you save your Country so that running of Goods and Smuggling is become public Virtue and Patriotism."[3] Smuggling was not new—the Molasses Act of 1733 had been revamped into the Sugar Act of 1764 because captains had perfected bringing in cheaper sugar from the French West Indies. Recall, too, that Hancock's uncle Thomas bribed his crew not to disclose his illegal running of goods. When people could skirt the law to save money, they did.

Pervasive smuggling and Hancock's public threat to undermine their work helped explain Richards and Jackson's enthusiasm to closely investigate his ship. At Hancock's Wharf, they embarked on *Lydia* around one that afternoon. Three hours later, they were still on board when Hancock arrived with several men. The merchant asked Richards what business he had on his vessel. Richards answered that he was simply performing his duty as a customs officer. Hancock ordered James Scott, his ship's captain, not to permit Richards or Jackson "or any Custom House Officers to go under deck, on any Acc[ount] Whatsoever." Anyone who disobeyed would be fired.[4]

The tidesmen left, but they planned to return the following evening, hoping to nose around undetected. It is difficult today to fathom the darkness that could blanket an eighteenth-century town at night. Boston did not install streetlamps until 1774, so the light after sunset came only from the moon and handheld lanterns.[5] One could easily think he would get away with clandestine activity.

About seven o'clock, Richards and Jackson returned to Hancock's pier. They illegally boarded *Lydia* and went into steerage, which

Hancock had forbidden. Ten minutes passed before they were spotted. An employee of Hancock's grabbed them by the shoulders and pushed them above deck, telling Richards "he should lose his Bread" if they stayed below.[6] But the tidesman did not leave or even take the threat seriously; instead, Richards snuck below deck again.

At this point, someone had likely gone to the mansion on Beacon Hill to warn Hancock. When a man of his stature had urgent business, so, too, did the people who worked for him—paid or enslaved. Hancock arrived accompanied by eight men, including a Black man who carried a lantern and likely "belonged to Mr Hancock."[7] As a British official noticed here, and the teenaged Hannah Otis showed in her needlepoint of Boston Common, it was not unusual to see Hancock with a Black enslaved man nearby.

With the confidence of a man used to wielding authority, Hancock ordered Richards to immediately come above deck. The brash tidesman refused. Hancock sent four of his men to fetch him. Only two of them were necessary because Richards saw any "resistance would have been in Vain." One man got on each side of him, put an arm under each of his, and grabbed one of his legs. "Damn him hand him up, if it was my Vessel I would knock him down," a spectator threatened as Richards was hauled up. Taverns lined the waterfront, and people in and around them heard the commotion and gathered around.

Once Richards was on deck, Hancock requested to see his orders. Richards turned them and his commission over. "I deny it, it has no date," Hancock asserted.

Richards did not answer before the merchant pressed on: "Do you have a writ of assistance?" Such a writ acted like a search warrant and would have allowed broader access to Hancock's ship, including below deck.

Richards replied that he did not, but that he must remain on board until the goods were unloaded and the vessel was discharged. Hancock reiterated that the tidesman had the right to search the deck of the ship, but he "shall not tarry below."[8]

With that, Hancock readied to leave. He had made his point, and *Lydia* had kept her secrets.

Excited by someone standing up to the hated customs officials, spectators wanted to escort Hancock home and cheer for him along the way. He had become a hero by defending his own financial interests, which, fortunately for him, aligned with many of the radical townspeople's political interests. He downplayed the moment, however, and asked the crowd "not to huzza him through the town" as he made his way home.[9]

Hancock's public, swaggering display may have made him popular with the masses, but it drew the ire of powerful people. Customs officers felt he was "an infatuated man" who was too cocky and smug for his own good. After this confrontation, they claimed to have heard Hancock threaten that if the customs officials were not recalled, "he will get rid of us before Christmas." They feared Hancock's outsize influence and worried men would seek to imitate him. To humble him, the customs board wanted to bring charges against the merchant.[10]

Richards, too, became a target. Over the next two years, he would continue to annoy Bostonians until they hit a breaking point. In the spring of 1770, he was tarred and feathered while two thousand people looked on. In a rare twist, the mob set Richards's feathers on fire so that the skin underneath would burn.[11] He would survive.

Officials turned the matter with Hancock over to the attorney general of Massachusetts, Jonathan Sewall. He had been enriched by being loyal to the crown, so they hoped to find a sympathetic ear. Sewall examined the case against Hancock and decided that he could not prosecute him for two reasons. First, to be convicted of resisting a customs official, a person must be "armed with Clubs or any Manner of Weapon." Hancock's men had carried no such items. Second, the law gave customs officers the right "freely to go and remain on Board until the Vessel is discharged of her Lading," but Sewall thought "on board" did not include going below deck. Richards had acted outside the acceptable bounds of customs officers. "Tho Mr. Hancock may not have conducted so prudently or courteously as might be wished . . . it is probable his Intention was to keep within the boundaries of the Law," Sewall wrote.[12]

The customs board was furious about the decision because they thought it would embolden Bostonians, who were "ripe for any mischief." Hancock had shown with this episode that the only consequence for mistreating customs officers was an increase in popularity. "We have every reason to expect that we shall find it totally impracticable to inforce the execution of the Revenue Laws, until the hand of Government is properly strengthened," they fumed.[13]

The board tried other ways to gain control. They asked Bernard to station soldiers in town to help enforce their authority. While he favored having troops, the governor needed his Council's approval for such a move and he knew they would not give it. The board also sent Sewall's ruling to England directing them to reverse the ruling about Hancock. This, too, was denied. Until the crown stepped in to aid the customs commissioners, they were in a position of weakness, and they knew it.[14]

Hancock, meanwhile, made no effort to keep a low profile with the customs officials and even antagonized them further. He and other selectmen voted to block such bureaucrats from attending Election Day, an annual event when the colony's representatives from the lower house nominated the men to serve in the upper house. Hancock and the selectmen told Governor Bernard that if he invited the customs officers, he could not host the party in Faneuil Hall, a large, centrally located building frequently used for town meetings. Hancock also threatened that the Corps of Cadets, a prestigious and mostly ceremonial militia that protected the governor and of which he was a member, would not attend if he welcomed the commissioners to the banquet.[15]

Bernard refused to be told what to do by Hancock and ordered the Corps commander, Joseph Scott, to command the entire company to report on Election Day. If anyone did not attend, they should be dismissed from service.

Defiantly, Hancock "tore the Seal off his Commission." All but nine men followed his lead, also quitting their duties. Hancock even met with some members of the Corps and discussed forming their own military company.[16]

His recent successes against customs officials may have caused him to overplay his hand, however. Bernard called Hancock's dramatic resignation a "high Indignity" to the king's authority. The governor supposed that Hancock was not "aware what a high Offence it is" to discuss forming a separate military command without a warrant or order. If Hancock continued to meet with these men in this manner, it "will incur the highest Penalties of the Law."[17]

This warning sufficiently scared Hancock, whose agent wrote to Bernard claiming that the cadet's conduct had been misrepresented and he hoped to meet with the governor to demonstrate his respect. Bernard agreed because he hoped to "see Mr Hancock reconciled to Government," but the governor wanted witnesses friendly to both sides present at the conversation. Hancock dutifully assented, promising to be "open and Explicit with Respect to his Conduct."[18]

It was quite a turn for the merchant to seek reconciliation after ripping the seal from his jacket, but he was a man inclined to moderation. Hancock may have (rightfully) worried about the reputation he was getting among the highest ranks of colonial government. Perhaps, also, Hancock had his eye on the upcoming Election Day and hoped that Bernard would approve him to the Council. We have no details about the meeting, but it did not help Hancock in his bid for the upper house. In 1768, for the first time, he had been nominated to the Council, demonstrating his rising political prospects. The governor and his sweeping powers could veto any person, though, and when given the shot to knock Hancock off his pedestal, he did not miss. Bernard denied him the post.[19]

———————

Despite the new tax and snooping tidesmen, the House of Hancock continued its trade, especially in wine. Madeira was a favorite of Hancock—the fortified wine came from an island off the coast of Africa under Portuguese control. It was typically only available to the elite—unless they gifted gallons of it for a celebration—because it was subject to significantly higher duties than wine from England, thanks to the Sugar Act. Unfazed by the steep price, Hancock ordered the wine to stock in his stores and sell to local taverns. He also wanted some for his own table, which should be superior to the others: "I pray they may be the very best." He was exacting, mentioning the desired quality of the wine five times in one letter and requesting that his be marked with a special symbol so he could identify them. "I don't stand at any price, let it be good, I like a Rich Wine," he ordered.[20]

On the night of Monday, May 9, one of his ships returning from Madeira, *Liberty*, docked at Hancock's Wharf. Hancock reported to the customs officials that he had twenty-five casks of madeira on board. Tidesman Thomas Kirk and another official accepted that number and the merchant paid the duties on it. Except, *Liberty* likely held more than twenty-five casks of wine. Such a small amount would fill less than half his ship's capacity and it made little business sense to sail across the Atlantic without a full vessel. Hancock was too experienced to do that.

Suspicious, customs commissioners questioned the two tidesmen the next day, and they confirmed that everything had been on the level. Even though one official reported that he overheard Hancock claiming that "he wo[ul]d run her Cargo of Wines on Shore," Kirk and his partner maintained that no goods had been illegally unloaded.[21]

Despite that, customs officers were convinced that Hancock was smuggling goods. "It was commonly reported that he had a much larger quantity on Board," claimed customs official Benjamin Hallowell. Primed for a fight after Hancock had embarrassed Richards and Jackson two months earlier when he kicked them off *Lydia*, customs officials wanted to make an example of him.[22]

They had a stroke of good luck in early June when the tidesman, Thomas Kirk, changed his story. The reason for his altered testimony, Kirk claimed, was because he had previously feared Hancock's captain, John Marshall. Since the captain had recently died, Kirk now felt comfortable telling the true account of the *Liberty*. It was not only to set the record straight: there was a big incentive for him to implicate Hancock. The value of any seized goods would be split three ways between the informant (Kirk), the governor (Bernard), and the crown.[23]

Kirk spun quite a tale. He now claimed that the evening he went to check on *Liberty*, Captain Marshall asked him to "consent to the hoisting out several Casks of Wine" before duties were declared. Kirk refused. With the help of five or six men, Marshall then grabbed Kirk and forced him below deck, shoved him into a cabin, and nailed the top down. The tidesman managed to break through a door, was discovered again, and was locked back in the cabin.[24]

Above his wooden hovel, Kirk allegedly heard the voices of several men and the unmistakable sound of "hoisting out goods" and "the Noise of the Tackles." For three hours this continued. Once it was silent, the door opened and Captain Marshall filled the doorway. He threatened that if Kirk breathed a word about how he was treated or what he heard, he and his property would be harmed.[25]

This story was the work of an imaginative mind. The tall tale's details were no doubt influenced by the testimony of Owen Richards about his treatment on board *Lydia*, as they bore similarities. But it did what was needed: it incriminated Hancock. With Kirk's revised deposition in hand, two customs commissioners, Benjamin Hallowell and Joseph Harrison, walked toward Hancock's Wharf, resolute in purpose. They intended to seize his vessel and had a convenient charge to pin on the merchant: the failure to load goods without a permit, a violation of law.

Typically, this rule went unenforced in Boston because nearly every ship would have otherwise been seized. Merchants usually loaded their goods first, then sought the necessary clearance. *Liberty* had laid idle at Hancock's Wharf through May while it was packed with new cargo for London, including tar and whale oil.[26] The customs officers were ready to get Hancock on a rarely used technicality. And they had Kirk's story as further proof of the House of Hancock's wrongdoing.

Rumors that Hancock's ship was going to be seized "provoked the People who had collected at the Shore." Little else but a hint of wrongdoing by a customs officer was needed for a crowd to gather in Boston at this time, especially in defense of Hancock. One crown official claimed that the merchant "had always a Mob at Command." While this was an exaggeration, Hancock had worked the past couple years to ensure that the lower orders did not turn against him. On this day, there would be violence, but Hancock had nothing to fear.[27]

Rough characters gathered at the waterfront—"a mix'd Multitude" of longshoremen, ropemakers, and sailors who shouted at the officials that they should not take the sloop unless they wanted to be thrown overboard. Joseph Warren, Hancock's fellow Mason, warned Hallowell that towing Hancock's ship would cause a "great uproar." Despite the threats, the two men continued their work, with Harrison branding the main mast with the king's mark. *Liberty* was hauled to the British warship *Romney*, while the townspeople "swore revenge," grabbing stones and pelting the seamen and officers.[28]

Romney was being targeted for more than its connection to Hancock's ship. A few days earlier, on June 5, *Romney*'s captain sent press gangs into Boston to force men to serve in the British navy. For decades the royal navy had a dearth of men—desertion, death, and illness contributed to the shortage — and they forcibly entered men into service. In 1747, Bostonians rioted for two days to protest impressment, a practice sailors thought was a flagrant example of excessive and arbitrary power. Despite such violence, the navy had recently grown more desperate for manpower because of losses in the French and Indian War and returned to impressing men.[29]

Romney had become a symbol of the abuses of the British Empire, and with Hancock's ship now tethered to it, townspeople were ready to erupt. The sun had not yet set when Harrison and Hallowell saw the danger they were in. Men grabbed "Clubs, Stones and Brickbats" and surrounded Harrison, who was repeatedly struck with rocks and sticks. One thug landed such a blow that the customs official staggered back. A sympathetic stranger pointed Harrison to an alley where he could flee. He made it into the house of a friend; had Harrison headed home, he would have seen his residence's windows broken.[30]

The mob's behavior was "grow[ing] more outrageous as they increased in numbers." Men pummeled Hallowell, throwing objects at him until he was "knocked down and left on the Ground covered with Blood." He suffered several whacks to the head, including one "of a dangerous nature" that later confined him to bed. When he did make it home, it was hardly a restorative convalescence. The mob resorted to familiar behavior by shattering some of his windows and trying to forcibly enter the house.[31]

Harrison's son, who was not a customs officer but had helped in the seizure of Hancock's ship, was also overrun. Grabbing him by his hair, the mob dragged him through the streets, all the while hitting him with sticks and throwing dirt on him. "Some friendly People" helped him find refuge in a nearby house where he tended to the wounds on his arms and one of his legs.[32]

The crowd's numbers continued to grow, as they were joined by "a number of Sailors, and vagrant Persons who were suspicious of an Intention to put them on board the ship." The men's reasons for joining the riot may have been different — defending Hancock, fighting against impressment, or simply wanting to break windows—but they had one goal: terrorize the hated customs officials.[33]

Notably present, too, were strangers who wanted to help the bureaucrats. Some townspeople took pity on the men being savagely treated and directed them to safe houses or offered ways to escape.[34] Not everyone wanted crown officials to be publicly assaulted or to have such chaos in the streets. Some colonists thought the new taxes were odious, but they opposed the violent and terrifying actions to protest them. Any townsperson who had been in Boston three years earlier could flash back to the fear and uncertainty of the Stamp Act riots and just want peace.

People's political beliefs rarely fit in tidy categories, especially during a time of insecurity. Despite the challenges of labeling people within a static group, historians have attempted to quantify colonists' loyalties. They estimate that about 20 percent of the population were loyal to the crown—or at least supported British control of the colonies—but they were not a unified group with the same ideological reasons for siding with the empire. In the 1770s, they began to be referred to as Loyalists. Opposing them were about forty percent of the population who became rebel Patriots. The rest were apathetic or uncommitted to a political side and were referred to as the "disaffected." Such wavering men and women were not flaky or indecisive—they were not happy with either side and mostly wanted to be left alone. Being on the wrong political side at this time was minimally punished with threats from your neighbors and more severely punished with harm to one's personal property or body. As a result, they sometimes switched loyalties to ensure personal safety or, at risk to themselves— like on this day in June—they helped those they felt were being unfairly treated.[35]

The bullies continued to the home of John Williams, the inspector general—who had nothing to do with *Liberty*'s seizure—and broke "100 panes" and "did other damage to the House." Williams's wife bravely came out to tell the crowd her husband was not at home and they left. Bernard was grateful the mob did not access Williams's alcohol-stocked cellar because "the Mischiefs would have been greater and more extensive."[36]

The records show that the men found alcohol anyway, which fueled a new level of destruction. They grabbed a large sailboat Harrison had built in an "elegant manner." The mob, now numbering between five hundred and one thousand men, hauled his boat out of the harbor, carried it through the streets—"with loud huzzaing all the way"—and dropped it on Boston Common. There, they set the boat on fire. As the boat burned, the mob "got some rum & attempted to get more."[37]

Terrified customs officers and their families fled to Castle William and planned to remain sequestered "till we can receive such Protection as will enable us to act in safety in Boston." The security they desired would arrive in a few months and it would devastate the town. Before it came, though, Boston's denizens could revel in their collective power. They had caused crown officials and some residents to think twice about crossing Hancock, impressing men into the royal navy, and enforcing unfair taxes.[38]

———————

Despite the violent mob in defense of Hancock, he was not nearly as troubled by the politics of it all. His top concern was making profits, not opposing taxes. As long as British officials held on to his ship, he could make no money. The day after the riot, he "was very earnest and desirous" to cut a deal with the crown.[39] His politics were not radical enough to stop trading with London forever—he was a businessman who employed hundreds of men and he wanted to get back to his work.

Joseph Warren, a man respected by both radicals and crown sympathizers, acted as Hancock's go-between. He offered a deal to Hallowell: customs officials would return Hancock's ship and, in exchange, the merchant would stand trial if the crown chose to charge him with smuggling. On the morning of June 12, Warren reported to Hallowell that "all matters were settled." The deal was to go in effect the next day and Hancock agreed to give "his own Bond as a Security."[40]

Hallowell and Harrison were disposed to make a deal. They had heard rumblings about a "general Insurrection" that would break out if Hancock's ship was not returned. Groups of men were standing by throughout Boston ready to attack any customs officers, friends of theirs, or their abettors. Hallowell and Harrison had just experienced — in very visceral ways — the menace that mobs could bring, and they took such a threat seriously.[41]

Radicals, including Samuel Adams and James Otis, were furious, however, when they heard about Hancock's agreement. Late Sunday night they went to his mansion and told him he made a bad deal. With no commercial interests, they lacked empathy for someone with more to lose. Other Sons of Liberty came too: "his House was full." The visitors explained that Hancock could not legitimize British taxes and policies by agreeing to stand trial. With mounting pressure, Hancock reneged on the arranged deal.[42]

Warren broke the news to Hallowell and apologized that the matter could not be settled. Hancock took the advice of his friends, Warren explained, and was going to let things run their course. Harrison was disappointed, calling Hancock "unluckily subject to the influence of Otis and other Incendiaries." He found Hancock to be a timid and "pliable" man who disagreed with Adams and Otis but was "bullied into Compliance."[43]

Notably, Hancock's first instinct had been to bargain with the British, not attack them or stonewall them. Just as he reconciled with Bernard after his resignation from the Cadets, he sought practicality when living under British rule. But when faced with strong opinions from the Sons of Liberty — and likely the memory of terrifying mobs

The Hancock house. New York Public Library.

in the past few years—Hancock backtracked. He would have to protest the tax the way Otis and Adams wanted. It was safer that way.

This acquiescence showed the power of radicals and the fear they inspired. Over the past three years, Hancock's renown had grown, with news of the *Liberty* riot spreading across the empire from Halifax to London.[44] His popularity among the lower orders had further increased; yet, Hancock still felt pressured to go along with the most imperious rebels.

The day after Hancock backed out of the deal, he attended a town meeting with hundreds of people who composed a petition for Governor Bernard. They requested that *Romney*'s captain stop impressing men and they reiterated their opposition to the Townshend Duties. After the town meeting, twenty-one gentlemen, including Otis and Samuel Adams, gathered at Hancock's house. Piling into eleven carriages, the men traveled to Bernard's country house in Roxbury, outside of Boston, wanting to personally hand him their petition.[45]

Bernard found the procession "very respectable" and received them "with all possible Civility." He offered them wine and heard their concerns. Hancock and the other town leaders were satisfied with the governor's responses, but Bernard knew better than to think they had reconciled. He explained, "Just at this time I am popular: whenever my Duty obliges me to do any thing which they don't like, theres an End to my popularity, and therefore I don't expect to enjoy it a Week."[46] Being liked for even a week was optimistic because many in Boston still felt aggrieved.

Hancock, Otis, and Adams helped draft another letter; this one was addressed to the king and stated their opposition to the Townshend Duties. They and other representatives in the Massachusetts House, also called the Assembly, claimed that colonists could no longer be considered free if Parliament continued to take their property—in this case, money—without representing them in the government. They circulated their letter to other North American colonies, asking them to petition crown officials and boycott British goods until the duties were repealed.[47]

Bernard and secretary of state to the American colonies, Lord Hillsborough, demanded that this circular letter, as it became known, be retracted. They understood the risk of the colonies uniting. The Massachusetts legislators voted on whether to recall the letter, and in an overwhelming majority of 92 to 17, they unsurprisingly decided against it. Hancock became one of the "Glorious 92," the lofty name given to the men who did not rescind. Silversmith Paul Revere created a punch bowl honoring the men and moment. Hancock was there at its unveiling, no doubt sipping rum punch—a popular cocktail that included Boston's ubiquitous spirit, citrus juices, and sugar— from its silver rim.[48] You can view the bowl alongside other pieces of Revere silver at the Museum of Fine Arts in Boston.

Bernard dissolved the legislature in exasperation, and Massachusetts functioned without its lawmakers for the rest of the year. As a member of the House of Representatives, Hancock cited the "great Grief" people felt because "they are Depriv'd of the Benefits of a General Assembly." Even without a functioning legislature, the town seemed to be running the governor, rather than the other way around.[49]

To get Boston under control and prevent a "total Revolt of the Colony," the crown took drastic steps. Before he had even heard about the *Liberty* riot, Hillsborough directed General Gage to station soldiers in Boston to enforce the new duties. When the witness statements about the *Liberty* affair arrived in London, Hillsborough saw "the Necessity of strengthening the Hands of Government," and ordered two additional regiments to the Massachusetts capital.[50]

Officials also wanted to put Hancock on trial for smuggling. On October 29, 1768, Sewall, the attorney general who had chosen not to prosecute Hancock in the *Lydia* case, filed a suit. The charge was for 9,000 pounds sterling, triple the damages of the estimated wine the merchant illegally unloaded in May. Court officials went to Hancock's mansion and arrested him. We do not know if that involved anything more than Hancock turning himself over, but he was given a staggeringly high bail: £3,000, which he "prudently" paid, not wanting any more violence to erupt.[51]

The case against Hancock came down to whether he knew about or helped to illegally unload the cargo. Hancock hired the smart and feisty attorney John Adams, whom he had known since they were young boys in Braintree. Adams claimed that a ship's owner "may be asleep in his Bed, and not so much as know or dream that any Body is unshipping and landing his Wines." Hancock surely knew about his employees' actions—and may have directed them many times before—but the crown's lawyers could not prove it, despite countless witnesses, including one attestor who was later convicted of perjury. The trial dragged on for months and bored Adams—who was

"thoroughly weary and disgusted with the court"—before the case
was dropped in March 1769.[52]

Even though Hancock was not convicted of any wrongdoing related
to the riot, his *Liberty* suffered. The vessel would endure an ironic
and, in the end, just fate after being repurposed by the British navy,
which had outfitted her with arms. The ship patrolled the New
England coast, hoping to find smugglers. The captain of *Liberty* had
"exasperated" the people of Newport, Rhode Island, with his unnecessary searches and seizures. Newport was a tough town in the same
vein as Boston, and they decided to end his "imprudent behavior." A
mob set fire to the ship.[53]

The entire *Liberty* affair, including the riot and trial, was frequently
reported in newspapers, and increased Hancock's fame throughout
the colonies and across the Atlantic, which would typically pay little
mind to a colonial smuggler. Most of the attention in London was
negative, but one prisoner in England was glad to learn of Hancock's
defiance. John Wilkes was a hero to the radical colonists because he
championed the rights of Britons and warned about encroachments
on liberty, having recently been jailed for libel. He offered sympathy
to Hancock and claimed that the merchant's persecution was because
of "his known zeal to the cause of his country, which our common
enemies desire to punish, when they cannot suppress it." In later
months, Wilkes again singled out Hancock and sent his respects. Customs official Harrison told the former prime minister of Great
Britain that Hancock is "the Idol of the Mob, just as Mr. Wilkes is in
England."[54]

Trying to prosecute one of the town's leading citizens on trumped-
up charges did nothing to endear the crown to the colonists. Instead,
for those paying attention, over the past year, the crown seemed to
be acting more tyrannical. It had imposed a new tax, ignored pleas
to repeal it, dissolved the legislature, and brought in aggressive new
customs officers. All that paled, though, to British soldiers disem-
barking at Long Wharf in October 1768.

Paul Revere's depiction of British ships, deliberately oversized, arriving to Long Wharf. Library of Congress.

While some in Boston found the soldiers a welcome sight, including Bernard, customs officials, and single women looking for marriageable men, many people throughout North America feared a standing, or permanent, army. The colonists relied on local civilian militias to fight when necessary. Standing armies were considered dangerous because they had their own rules and authority. Hancock claimed that they were often comprised of men "unfit to live in civil society . . . who have given up their own liberties, and envy those who enjoy liberty." Colonists feared these mercenaries would subject them to military rule.[55]

Until the occupying redcoats' housing was settled—the Quartering Act of 1765 prohibited soldiers from staying in private homes—Bernard told one regiment that some of them could camp on Boston Common. Looking out from his mansion, Hancock would now see pedestrians strolling or cows grazing in the park, but also dirty tents and flashes of red uniforms. He would smell their waste and stink, and hear their martial music, drills, and savage whippings of offending soldiers. And if he heard the "dead beat" of their drums around eight in the morning on October 31 and looked out his front-facing windows, he would have seen a soldier shot by a firing squad for desertion.[56]

Despite the unsettling military occupation, Hancock professed Bostonians to be "as Loyall a people as any in the King's Dominion."[57] His fealty to the empire shows that resistance happened in fits and starts. Hancock considered himself a loyal subject, but he stared down and intimidated customs officials, voted against repealing the circular letter, and made demands to the governor. He also sought to reconcile with Bernard for his impudent behavior as a member of the Cadets and struck a deal with customs officials. He pushed the law's boundaries and then retreated using peaceful, petitioning means. He sought to both protect his own interests by keeping his business profitable and prevent the ire of radicals from turning on him. He was in on resistance and then he was out.

The next year would test him in new ways, though. John Mein, an unpredictable and vindictive man with sympathies to the crown, began to systematically attack Hancock in the press. As suspicions grew about the merchant's loyalty, "the idol of the mob" would soon have a hard time defending himself.

CHAPTER 4

Bad Press

With a barn as their backdrop, hundreds of Sons of Liberty gathered around two large tables in an open field. It had rained earlier that day, and a tavern keeper suspended a sail cloth above their heads to keep them dry. Music played and colors flew and cannon fired—hallmarks of Sons' celebrations. The guests, numbering around 350, were key members of resistance efforts: Joseph Warren was present, as was Paul Revere. The *Boston Gazette* printers, Benjamin Edes and John Gill, also showed up.[1]

Some were there more willingly than others. John Adams, whose cousin Samuel had helped to organize the event with James Otis, felt he had to be there. It had been an inconvenience for him to come, but he wanted to show that he was "hearty in the Cause." If he was absent, he feared people may have wondered who and what he was loyal to. Hancock may have felt similarly—that it was his "Duty to be there"—because he also attended. A year earlier, Otis and Samuel Adams had persuaded him to abandon his deal with customs officials despite at least one person involved believing that Hancock "disapproves of [Adams's and Otis's] Proceedings."[2] Hancock was conciliatory to those with radical views because it was more prudent to pacify them, especially now.

The soldiers' occupation after the *Liberty* riot had made the atmosphere in Boston especially tense. Redcoats aggressively guarded the neck of town, which made coming and going more difficult; they brutally and publicly punished infractions; and they were drunk and loud, especially on the Sabbath.[3] It was an easy time to promote an us-versus-them mentality, which left little room for moderation. As John Adams observed, suspicions were easily cast if someone veered from the crowd or skipped a certain event.

When there was levity in the town, as there was on this drizzly summer afternoon in 1769, the party's organizers had motives. Every year since 1765, the Sons of Liberty celebrated the destruction of Andrew Oliver's home on August 14 to honor their collective and successful action against the British Empire. According to John Adams, Otis and Samuel Adams created this holiday and other "Festivals" to foster resistance. Events like these filled men with "the sentiments of Liberty" and "render the People fond of their Leaders in the Cause, and averse and bitter against all opposers."[4]

By turning people against their enemies—anyone who disagreed with them—and elevating their leaders, the resistance movement gained loyalty and power. Activating shared identities is an effective way to unite a group of people, even as it polarizes another. Samuel Adams knew the power of such tribalism and saw the world in binary terms. His political motto was uncompromising: "Put your enemy in the wrong, and keep him so." He was especially adept at using the power of the press to rally people against an adversary and organizing anniversaries to reinforce a common group identity.[5]

The celebration began at the Liberty Tree around eleven that morning. There, the men made various toasts before taking carriages to the Liberty Tree Tavern in Dorchester. Once settled at their outdoor tables, the Sons of Liberty enjoyed food and drink. In the

A 1768 depiction of Boston Common. The Hancock mansion dominates
Beacon Hill and the occupying soldiers and their tents are visible below.
New York Public Library.

eighteenth century, the big meal of the day was dinner and was
served in the afternoon. Food offerings could be more diverse and
local than what Americans eat today. There were usually multiple
courses, consisting of roasted meats—which might include turkey,
pork, duck, chicken, beef, or goose—and chicken or beefsteak pies.
A meal typically ended with sweet pies, plum puddings, or tarts. All
would be accompanied by various alcoholic drinks.[6]

Entertainment followed the food and included singing songs
together, including two versions of the "Liberty Song." One was
written by the doctor Benjamin Church and all attendees joined in
for the chorus, which "cultivat[ed] Sensations of Freedom." A hatmaker,

Nathaniel Balch, known for his sense of humor and later a good friend of Hancock's, did impressions.[7]

But the real joy came from the toasts, with each accompanied by a tipple. Numerous and vigorous huzzahs were a common occurrence in colonial taverns, as men heartily drank to each other's health and people and events they wanted to honor. That afternoon, the men raised their glasses forty-five times. That number had special meaning: John Wilkes, the British revolutionary who praised Hancock after the *Liberty* affair, had been imprisoned for his pamphlet entitled *No. 45* in which he criticized the king. The Sons' toasts reveal what was on the minds of the attendees in the summer of 1769. Some matched the suspicious mood—sounding more like threats than cheers.[8]

"May Sir Francis Bernard . . . soon meet with condign Punishment!"[9]

Following this popular toast, three cheers rang out from the participants. Just a few weeks earlier, Governor Bernard had been recalled to London and Bostonians were ecstatic. Massachusetts was soon going to be run by Thomas Hutchinson, the hated man whose house had been destroyed during the Stamp Act riots. He and the town would frequently clash, but now was not the time to worry about him.[10] Bernard was gone and there were other things to praise.

"Success to the noble Efforts of the public spirited Merchants on this Continent, who are generously sacrificing private Interest to the Welfare of their Country!"

Three cheers accompanied this mouthful. The Sons were praising a new nonimportation agreement—a clunky term, but Charles Boycott, the Irish landlord who gave us the term boycott, was not yet born in 1769. Hancock had more reason than others to raise his glass—he had helped organize the movement the year before. Its goal was to render moot the Townshend Duties, the recent tax on any goods imported from Great Britain. Hancock explained the simple terms of the arrangement: "upon a Meeting of our Merchts it was thought prudent to Stop the Importation of Goods, at least for one year." With the exception of a few articles, no British goods would be imported beginning January 1, 1769.[11]

The crucial part of the toast, though, was the recognition that it was a colonies-wide effort, not one isolated to Massachusetts or its neighbors. General Thomas Gage, who was in charge of British forces and stationed in New York, had been skeptical because the colonies in North America rarely thought of themselves as being part of a larger whole. He believed the Boston merchants' agreement "will not be followed by other provinces."[12]

And yet, when Boston sent the details of their deal to the two largest colonial towns—New York and Philadelphia—both agreed to join after initially hesitating. The southern colonies took longer, but most of them also adopted some resolution by that summer. Colonists throughout British North America had been particularly influenced by a series of pamphlets out of Philadelphia. In *Letters from a Farmer in Pennsylvania*, John Dickinson—actually a wealthy lawyer—argued that colonists should resist the Townshend Duties by petitioning the king and limiting their purchases of British goods.

The colonies had to cooperate for the boycott to be effective, though, because if Boston boycotted, but Philadelphia did not, British merchants would happily send their goods there. The agreement required a lot of intercolonial trust, which did not exist much at this time.[13] Colonists would now also have to make goods that they had previously imported, so that too was honored.

"Success to the Manufactures of America!"

Relying on American-made goods would be harder for colonists than you might think. Elites were not the only ones who imported items from London. Myriad effects, including textiles, furniture, gunpowder, copper, sail cloth, and cheese, poured into the continent. In New England, there was a particular appetite for overseas goods—British imports doubled between 1740 and 1760.[14]

It would be a sacrifice for both Hancock and his aunt Lydia to forgo such wares. For decades they had furnished their home, enriched their gardens, transported themselves in style, and dressed to showcase their wealth, all thanks to items from overseas. "People here are Determined to be more frugal," Hancock reported. This was a trait he lacked, but would have to temporarily cultivate. Colonists were now touting the fashionability and patriotism of wearing American-made clothing, called homespun, a movement that also brought women into the political arena.[15] The attendees did not forget them.

"The fair Daughters of Liberty!"

White women became crucial to the boycott and the men who rarely acknowledged women in toasts or other political matters recognized this. The fairer sex may not have been allowed to vote or hold office, but that did not mean women had no thoughts on the events happening around them. Women in Boston signed agreements pledging not to import or buy British goods, mirroring those of elite male merchants. Being involved, even with something as seemingly simple as choosing clothing, awakened a political consciousness for some women and girls. It happened as early as twelve years old for Anna Green Winslow of Boston, who referred to herself as a "daughter of liberty" because "I chuse to wear as much of our own manufactory as pocible."[16] And for those who were not on board with the boycott as Winslow was, there was a clear message.

"May the detested Names of the very few Importers everywhere, be transmitted to Posterity with Infamy!"

Cannon boomed after this important toast. Not everyone had agreed to sacrifice their livelihoods for the Sons' goals and they continued to import British goods subject to the Townshend Duties. Such violators were named as enemies on the first page of every issue of Edes and Gill's *Boston Gazette*, a mouthpiece for the Sons of Liberty. Governor Bernard had believed that most merchants went along with the boycott—which would harm their businesses more than paying the new import duties—because they feared the repercussions if they did not comply. "I make no Doubt but above half of those who signed against the Importation of British Goods were brought to it by Intimidation," he noted. And if they had not felt pressured into joining, seeing their business suffer might do the trick. Newspapers and pamphlets encouraged Bostonians not to patronize the stores of the importers. Such publicity was vital for the movement, so the Sons also recognized the freedom allowed printers.[17]

"The Liberty of the PRESS!"

In the 1760s, there were usually about five local newspapers operating in Boston, all of which were notably partisan. The press allowed ordinary people to attack and hold those above them accountable, which made them feel more powerful and politically involved. The colonial resistance movement had stronger control of the press than those sympathetic to the crown. For the entirety of 1769, for example, one Boston newspaper included daily updates on the offenses of the soldiers occupying the town, keeping people aware of a common threat. Newspapers' influence increased when tavern owners had the rags read aloud, giving the news to the illiterate and unsubscribing.[18]

After several hours of merriment, the toasts and entertainment wound down. Satiated guests clambered into their carriages or those of friends. Once the 139 coaches were loaded, they formed a procession back to Boston. The vehicles extended for a mile and a half with Hancock out front and Otis as the caboose. They took an impromptu detour through town, including around the Town House—an unnecessary parade but one to flex their power and size.[19]

As Hancock retired at home that night, he may have felt satisfied from the alcohol and camaraderie, but uneasy about some of the toasts. The ones about liberty of press and the merchants committing to the boycott would soon come back to haunt him.

One man who had been outed as an importer in the newspapers, John Mein, would prove to be a tough opponent for the Sons of Liberty. A Scotsman and "stout fellow," the fiery Mein immigrated to the colonies in 1764 and set up a bookstore with a fellow countryman. In December 1767, he and his partner started a newspaper, the *Boston Chronicle*. Shortly after, Mein assaulted John Gill of the *Boston Gazette* for publicly criticizing his political views. This was merely the opening gambit for Mein, who seemed to relish confrontation.[20]

In a *Boston Chronicle* article published on June 1, 1769, Mein alleged that 190 people had been importing British goods since the start of the year, many of whom had agreed to comply with the boycott. He declined to print the names of the violators, feigning concern that it might "excite great uneasiness in the province." Because the non-importation agreement was tenuous and existed in a climate of watch-dogs and snitches, people grew defensive. A notice appeared in the *Boston Evening Post*, calling on the public, merchants, and traders to "suspend their Judgment" about Mein's claims because "the Matter will shortly be set in a *true* Light." Another newspaper pointed to the flaws in Mein's facts: some of the ships he identified as violators had sailed from England before the boycott began and many of the goods he listed were allowed under the agreement. Those that were not "are trifling, and of little Value." According to these defenses, none of the ships or goods identified had genuinely qualified as violating the agreement.[21]

If Hancock was inclined to superstition, he had reason to grow nervous. Shortly after Mein's first public attack, a severe thunderstorm ripped through Boston. Lightning struck two ships at his wharf, damaging masts and striking down an employee who had been in steerage. An unnamed worker had "one side of his head burned" and another "had both his shoes struck off, and one of his feet burned."[22]

Like that summer storm, Mein was ready to inflict damage. He was going to name names and Hancock would be "singled out by Mr. Mein as an object of his particular resentment." On August 21, 1769, the front page of the *Boston Chronicle* detailed the manifests—lists of cargo— from two of John Hancock's ships. Mein provided the shipping dates and the specific goods that arrived on the vessels and showed that they had left London after the nonimportation agreement began. The inventories also revealed that Hancock's ships carried items for several people in Boston. That was not unusual. Eighteenth-century merchants earned money on Atlantic voyages by freighting merchandise for others. While it was common practice, it became problematic when customers ordered goods barred by the nonimportation agreement because such contraband implicated the ship's owner.[23]

The leaked manifests also showed that Hancock had imported "100 pieces British Linen" for himself. British linen was definitely not homespun and Hancock's employee, William Palfrey, rushed to defend his boss in the newspapers. The clerk claimed that Mein "in such an artful and evasive Manner . . . intended to mislead People" because the 100 pieces of British linen were actually "One hundred Pieces of RUSSIA DUCK, an Article particularly excepted in the Agreement." Duck is a heavy, tightly woven cotton fabric and was a permissible import. Palfrey claimed it was all a misunderstanding, swearing that "Mr. Hancock has not directly or indirectly imported from Great-Britain any one Article contrary to the Agreement of the Merchants."[24]

Hancock had, in fact, ordered duck from George Hayley, not linen. He was still importing goods from London during the boycott, but only those that were allowed in the agreement. Other merchants were doing the same. Palfrey said that his employer's "Reputation as a PATRIOT and a Merchant . . . is too well established to suffer any Injury from the Aspersions of Mr. Mein."[25] Palfrey's sanguinity was misplaced because Mein hit back with specifics that cast further doubt on Hancock.

Mein provided details from Hayley, Hancock's contact in London. The printer showed that Hayley had entered British linen, not Russian duck in his notes, which was also how it was recorded by the comptroller of the London port. It could have been a clerical error or an intentional attempt to evade export duties, but either way, it looked bad for Hancock.[26]

If this seems like a petty issue with Mein and Palfrey nitpicking over a small detail, it was not. Hancock was a town leader and prominent merchant who had helped to organize the colonies-wide boycott. The difference between Russia duck and British linen was critical to Hancock's reputation and the legitimacy of the nonimportation deal across the colonies. He had to appear compliant and there were now reasons to doubt him.

Rhode Island's *Newport Mercury* ran a piece by "American Spy" openly questioning Hancock's commitment to the cause. It claimed the merchant was considered "one of the foremost of the Patriots in Boston, and the strictest observer of the agreement for nonimportation," yet his deeds reflected otherwise. He would "be less suspected in this character if he did not keep a number of vessels running to London and back, full freighted, getting rich, by receiving freight on goods made contraband by the Colonies." Hancock, they argued, was enriching himself as others sacrificed. The newspaper called on Palfrey to put forward evidence to prove his boss's innocence.[27]

Once again, Palfrey defended his employer and implied that "American Spy" was either Mein or one of his allies. Mein had it out for Hancock, Palfrey claimed, and may have been manipulated into "a mode of Conduct dictated to him by his Abettors." Palfrey was implying that Mein was on the royal payroll. What he only speculated about is known today: in April 1768, Mein was named the stationery supplier of the customs commissioners and likely had officials tipping him off about potential boycott violators.[28] Since Hancock was a frequent target of Mein, the vitriol may have been fueled by vengeful officials. It was only a year ago, after all, when Hancock had embarrassed and undermined the board of customs during the *Lydia* and *Liberty* confrontations.

On September 6, 1769, the day after a comet appeared in the early morning hours of Boston's sky with "its Tail very long," Hancock began to clean up his affairs. To avoid potential problems with freighted cargo on board, merchants in Boston decided that their vessels could no longer transport prohibited wares for anyone. Hancock updated Hayley: "I beg you would . . . prevent any fre't except Coals, Hemp, Duck & Grindstones being put on board any of my Vessels." He also requested that one of his ships be sold in London, "as there is no prospect of a Freight back."[29] Mein's attacks changed the boycott by eliminating freighting and putting Hancock on the defensive.

Mein may have ignored the subtle differences between permissible goods and those carried for someone else, but his accusations successfully sowed distrust, as persistent, unfounded claims often can. His newspaper was read from Florida to Nova Scotia and some of those reading lost faith in the nonimportation enterprise. New York merchants were angry with those in Boston, and Philadelphia, too, began to doubt the town's devotion. Mein bragged that it was his exposure of importers that waned enthusiasm for the boycott.[30]

Because of the misgivings surrounding him and his hometown, Hancock tried to improve his standing in other colonies. He went to Philadelphia and met with John Dickinson, who had initially suggested the boycott in his *Letters*. He received Hancock "with the greatest politeness" and the merchant enjoyed "the company and conversation" of the "farmer." Hancock returned home in October and a report from Philadelphia claimed that his "engaging Behaviour, added to their Firmness in the Cause of Liberty."[31]

It is not clear that Hancock's trip did anything for Boston's nonimportation movement or his reputation because he still needed to defend himself against claims of impropriety. Hancock had been sufficiently maligned in a New York newspaper that a rejoinder from his clerk would no longer do. Hancock gave an unequivocal denial. "This is ONCE FOR ALL to certify whom it may concern, That I have not in one single Instance, directly or indirectly, deviated from said Agreement; and I now publickly defy all Mankind to prove the CONTRARY."[32] The suspicion had clearly exhausted him.

And still, Mein was not done. He resorted to printing insults about many Sons of Liberty. He called Otis "Counsellor Muddlehead," an especially cruel name, given that Otis had recently been severely injured in a tavern fight and would never again be completely clear of mind. Hancock was "Johnny Dupe," who was the "Milch-Cow of the 'Well Disposed.'" He had a "silly, conceited grin . . . a fool's cap on his head—a bandage tied over his eyes." All of these traits prevented the merchant from seeing the people who used him for his money. They professed to be his friends, even as they were "riffling his pockets."[33]

This was a familiar criticism of Hancock: he was a gullible dupe. It's easy to see why he could be characterized this way, but like Mein's charges of boycott violators, it neglects the full picture. Hancock made choices to preserve himself and his business. When the radicals' interests no longer suited him, he no longer allied with them. Exploitable was one way to see Hancock, shrewd was another—they both led to the same result: Hancock sometimes went along with people with whom he disagreed.

Mein's attacks may have felt good to publish in the moment, but after, the printer worried he could be in danger. Just a day after the newspaper circulated, a man who looked like Mein was jumped in an alley and beat with clubs. Thugs thought they were assaulting the printer. Unnerved, Mein armed himself with pistols.[34]

The following afternoon, he and his partner, John Fleeming, were walking on King Street. A crowd "began to collect together pretty fast" and circled around Mein. William Molineux was among them—a frequent leader of Boston's violent protests and someone who had also been mocked in the Chronicle. Mein pulled out his gun and threatened to shoot the first man to touch him. Shouts of "kill him" rang through the crowd. Mein ran toward a guardhouse and made it to the steps before a man hit him with a shovel on the back, leaving him with a two-inch gash on his shoulder.[35]

Mein got inside, disguised himself in a soldier's uniform, and fled to one of the royal ships in Boston Harbor. The crowd turned their ire on a sailor, George Gailer, accusing him of providing Mein with shipping manifests. Gailer had the dubious distinction of becoming the first person to be tarred and feathered in the colonies. He was "script naked & painted . . . all over with Tar & then covered . . . with Feathers," before being dumped into a cart. He was made to hold a lantern so "People might see the doleful Condition he was in, and to deter others."[36]

Men pulled Gailer through the streets and out to the Liberty Tree, huzzahing the whole time. The procession stopped in front of Mein and Fleeming's print shop and some participants threw rocks at the windows. When someone fired a gun from the office, members of the mob stormed inside. The assailant had fled, but his loaded guns were still there, which the intruders took. This "did not interrupt the Carting the feather'd Informer thro' the principal Streets in Town for about three Hours." After they were finished, they made Gailer promise not to inform again and returned his clothes, and the participants went home.[37]

Not everyone cheered about this assault, including those who often sympathized with the rebel Patriots. John Rowe, a merchant who helped organize the boycott, said Gailer's torture "occasioned much terror."[38] Politics during the American Revolution were not black or white, despite popular memory portraying colonists as unified and decisive. Rather, there was a lot of gray, as people brought their own experiences, risk tolerance, temperaments, and interests to political resistance.

Mein may have gotten away the night Gailer was tarred and feathered, but a fortuitous opportunity soon came to Hancock to retaliate against the printer he held "in such thorough Contempt." Thomas Longman was a bookseller in London and an ocean away from Mein, who owed him a considerable sum of money. Longman was looking to collect and needed someone in the colonies to help. He recalled Hancock offering assistance a few years back, so in the summer of

1769, Longman requested that Hancock recover the money Mein owed him. Recently, the printer's newspaper subscription list had plummeted by half, his bookshop was no longer profitable, and he could not pay his debts.[39]

We can only imagine the glee Hancock felt in receiving Longman's letter. It would have arrived in the midst of Mein's antagonizing. Hancock's reply has not survived, but we do know that he answered that he would be able to assist. He began by seeking power of attorney for Longman. English stationers Wright & Gill were another creditor of Mein's and Longman arranged for Han-

John Adams circa 1766.
He was Hancock's
lawyer for the *Liberty*
case and the suit against
John Mein.
New York Public Library.

cock to also settle their debts. The powers of attorney for both firms arrived on March 1, 1770.[40]

Hancock enlisted his lawyer from the *Liberty* case, John Adams, to litigate the matter. Adams had Mein's property seized, including two printing presses and his stock of books. "The Effects are in the Hands of the Sheriff, and as soon as it has gone thro' the Law, & the Effects turn'd into money, the neat proceeds shall be remitted you," Hancock informed Longman. He worried, however, that the sale of Mein's property would not come close to recouping the debts and suggested that "You get further Security of Mr. Mein in London."[41]

After seeing his effigy hung on Pope's Day in 1769, Mein had fled to the English capital, leaving the newspaper in his partner Fleeming's hands. When Mein arrived overseas, Longman had him arrested and put in debtors' prison. Ever provocative, Mein unsuccessfully tried to lead several prisoners to escape.[42]

Hancock heard that Mein and his associates were spreading nasty rumors about him in London, "but I Despise them, being confident that their case and false representations can do me no Injury." Hancock could feel such certainty because he was close to financially ruining Mein and silencing his public criticisms. After opening the case, it took just three months for Fleeming to shutter *Boston Chronicle*, the newspaper that had given Hancock so much grief.[43]

Mein believed that it was too coincidental for the man he had mercilessly attacked to become his creditor. He claimed that Hancock had sought revenge by seeking out Longman.[44] There is no evidence that this is true. Longman's letter to Hancock was crossing the Atlantic before any major trouble with Mein and Hancock began. It was Hancock's great luck that he was asked to settle Mein's affairs.

Hancock's feud with Mein illustrates the power of the press; the deep, and sometimes terrifying, suspicion fostered by the nonimportation agreement; and the importance of Hancock appearing dutiful. It also exposed the hypocrisy of many Patriots. When Hancock and the Sons of Liberty had toasted to freedom of the press, it seems they meant it only for the people on their side. Such a narrow definition of liberty did not go unnoticed by those who disagreed with the revolutionaries.

———————

By the turn of 1770, Boston was beleaguered by several factors: the hatred between townspeople and two thousand occupying soldiers, the press inflaming tensions about the boycott, and the Sons of Liberty's increasingly aggressive tactics. There was also disagreement about if the nonimportation agreement should continue. It was originally scheduled to end on the last day of 1769, but since the Townshend Duties had not yet been repealed, some hoped to extend it. Others wanted to return to business without being told what they could buy and sell. Hancock, for one, was eager to resume business. He placed orders with London for goods to ship immediately if and when the Townshend Duties were repealed.[45]

At a town meeting to discuss the boycott, street tough William Molineux proposed visiting the homes of importers. After a year, the nonimportation movement had shifted from a nonviolent solution in the hands of the merchants to one influenced by radicals relying on intimidation. The town, in turn, grew more polarized.

Molineux asked people to accompany him on his house calls and Hancock refused. Other leaders agreed to confront the importers, despite it being cold enough outside for the harbor to freeze. Molineux, Samuel Adams, James Otis, and a few others braced against the January chill and went to the house of Thomas Hutchinson, whose sons were violating the nonimportation agreement. A thousand people followed them. The governor bravely met them out front. He defended his sons and condemned Molineux and the others for going to individual homes because it "must strike the People with Terror from your great Numbers."[46]

The Sons' tactics scared many, especially as the violence against importers increased over the next few weeks. "I own I was intimidated," admitted Theophilus Lillie, a shopkeeper in the North End who had also been named an enemy. He publicly called out the Sons in a newspaper article, claiming that he had done nothing wrong by importing—there was no law against it—but still men harassed him by frequently defacing his store's sign and threatening to break his neck. He denounced the extralegal committees of inspection who came to his home and shop searching for imported goods.[47]

Lillie articulated the feelings of many colonists who were willing to accept Parliament's taxes as a justifiable cost of being a part of the British Empire. To them, the radicals who encouraged or comprised the mobs seemed more tyrannical than a distant monarchy. Several Boston shopkeepers suffered indignities simply because they were trying to make a living, including sisters Ame and Elizabeth Cuming, who had their shop windows broken. Lillie used the Sons' language against them, arguing that "he would not submit to such slavery any longer." Besides, the mob was too unpredictable and inconsistent: "I had rather be a slave under one master; for if I know who he is, I may perhaps, be able to please him, than a slave to an hundred or more, who I don't know where to find, nor what they will expect from me."[48]

Just as the Puritans who settled Boston in 1630 sought religious freedom but executed Quakers and excluded Anglicans, Lillie exposed the hypocrisy of town leaders who cried for liberty in 1770 but only had one idea of freedom: theirs. "It always seemed strange to me that People who contend so much for civil and religious Liberty should be so ready to deprive others of their natural Liberty," Lillie posited.[49]

No matter how clearly or rationally he spoke on behalf of importers, Lillie remained in the radicals' crosshairs. On February 22, 1770, a group of schoolchildren and teenaged apprentices protested outside his store. They had a cart with a massive painted likeness of Lillie's head on top. This spectacle drew the attention of customs informant

Ebenezer Richardson, who was a neighbor of Lillie's and widely disliked, as informants often were. Richardson yelled at everyone to disperse and tried to grab the children's signs. He even asked passersby to ram their wagons into the crowd.[50]

Instead of diffusing the situation, Richardson made it worse. The crowd followed him home, all the while taunting him for being an informer. Once Richardson was inside his house, he and his wife shouted at the crowd. The throng responded by throwing trash, rocks, and stones. Richardson then grabbed his gun and fired birdshot into the crowd. A boy about eleven years of age, Christopher Seider, was mortally wounded.[51]

For as violent as Boston had been over the past few years—burning ships, tavern brawls, tarring and feathering, assaulting newspaper printers, destroying homes, breaking windows—not a single person had been killed in these conflicts. Not one. But here was a young boy slain.

The funeral for the "little Hero and first Martyr to the noble Cause" became a town-wide affair. Several hundred boys marched two by two through the streets, with over two thousand adults trailing behind them. Hutchinson imagined it to be the "largest funeral perhaps ever known in America," although it would take just two weeks for him to see a bigger one. Like the Stamp Act riot against Oliver, the Sons of Liberty used this tragedy to rally people.[52]

Seider's death made a difficult situation for the soldiers stationed in Boston even worse. Captain Thomas Preston complained that "the utter hatred of the Inhabitants to the Troops increased daily." The townspeople were "constantly provoking & abusing the Soldiery." The tension broke ten nights later.[53]

On March 5, a lone redcoat, private Hugh White, was guarding the customs house on King Street when a young man insulted him. White struck him in the face and about thirty people gathered around. John Adams famously referred to this crowd as "a motley rabble of saucy boys, negroes, and mullatoes, Irish teagues and outlandish jack tarrs."[54]

Seven soldiers and one officer, Captain Preston, arrived to assist White. The mob, now numbering as many as two hundred, threw snowballs, oyster shells, and trash at the soldiers and taunted them to fire. When an object—likely a "large stick" or a "piece of ice"—hit one of the redcoats' shoulders, his gun discharged. "One after the other" the other soldiers fired into the crowd. Three men were struck and killed, and two others died later of their wounds.[55]

This event was immediately politicized and became known by colonists as the "bloody Massacre." It was depicted in a now-iconic engraving by Paul Revere that portrayed the townspeople as innocent, defenseless victims against trigger-happy soldiers. His print helped shape the town's perception of the event we know as the Boston Massacre.[56]

The next morning, three thousand residents met in Faneuil Hall to discuss the shooting. Hancock, who felt "extremes of grief, astonishment, and rage," was named the meeting's chairman. The assembly decided that the governor must send the troops out of town. A committee went to Hutchinson's home and threatened that ten thousand armed men would march into Boston if he refused to send the troops away. The governor complied and the only soldiers who remained in town were those standing trial. At a British officer's request, Hancock agreed to help the redcoats safely board their ships.[57]

Hancock shared the news about the soldiers' imminent departure at a town meeting. His speech was "Received with a shoute & clap of hands, which made the Meetinghouse Ring."[58] Hancock had a knack for finding these moments, or rather, for them finding him. He presented good news to the town as if it was he who created it. The same thing had happened in 1766 when news of the Stamp Act repeal came on one of his ships.

While there would be no murder convictions—only two of the nine soldiers were found guilty of manslaughter—the radicals used the tragedy to garner attention and sympathy. More than ten thousand people attended the victims' funeral. Most of the town's shops shut tered and all church bells, including those in nearby Charlestown and Roxbury, tolled "a solemn Peal." There was a procession through town that was followed by "Carriages belonging to the principal Gentry of the Town."[59] Hancock's gilded chaise was no doubt a part of the ceremony.

The deaths of five people at the hands of soldiers could have spurned the town to more violence and extremes, but ultimately, it did not. Hancock, for one, needed a break. Over the past two years, he had been burdened with the *Liberty* trial, the newspaper feud with Mein, the atmosphere of suspicion cast by the Sons of Liberty, and coexisting with soldiers. In that span, he'd even had a man armed with pistols stalk him, intent on killing him. For the next couple of years, he and many others—including John Adams, who was also worn out—stepped away from the radical politics of Samuel Adams and James Otis.[60] Hancock instead wanted to focus on his personal life and his business.

It is only with hindsight that we can look back on the American Revolution and feel assured of its progress and its outcome. Those who were living through it, however, had no such perspective or certainty of when or how it would end. In 1770, the soldiers had left town and Mein was bankrupt and back in London. Hancock could have easily thought that any political trouble was behind him.

CHAPTER 5

Life Outside of Politics

The widow Dorcas Griffiths kept a retail space on Hancock's Wharf for over twenty years. She lived upstairs from the shop where she and her daughter sold groceries, tea, and linens. Like most stores in Boston, hers may have had a wooden sign hanging out front, hinting to her illiterate customers what they could buy inside. At some point, Griffiths applied for and received a license to also sell alcohol. She then had a dramshop: a place that retailed rum, cider, and beer, but it was not a tavern, where one could drink, eat, and lodge. Town officials rarely let women run taverns for fear they could not limit customers' consumption the way men could.[1]

Looking out from Hancock's Wharf and seeing the harbor filled with ships and motion, you'd think selling alcohol would be a lucrative business—customers were all around. But there was no shortage of places in town to buy booze. Even with a customer base known for its drinking, selling alcohol—whether retail or in a tavern—was a very competitive business in Boston. Being located on the docks also meant Griffiths catered to the poor and transient drinkers because the more elite customers drank further from the hectic waterfront.[2]

To turn her store into a dramshop was an act of desperation, rather than of independence. The eighteenth-century poor and widowed were often associated with the drink trade because officials granted them liquor licenses as an act of charity, hoping to prevent them from becoming public charges. In such needy circumstances, Griffiths may have turned to make money in other, unseemly, ways. There was an allegation that she was "a Common prostitute" and had a prominent client: John Hancock.[3]

That she was seventeen years older than Hancock may not have been a hindrance for him, if he had been a patron. Benjamin Franklin believed that if a man was not ready or willing to be married, he should take up with an older mistress, for mature women were more discreet, knowledgeable, useful, and grateful than younger ones. Franklin noted one crass additional benefit: "it is impossible of two Women to know an old from a young one" when considering "what is below the Girdle."[4] It is not out of the realm of possibility that Hancock had a liaison with an older woman as he sorted out who he might make his wife.

It was certainly unusual that Hancock was in his mid-thirties and unwed. Especially because "There can be no doubt, that . . . he had his Choice of a Companion," according to John Adams. His family wealth made him a desirable match, yet he waited much longer than most. New England men typically married in their mid-twenties and women around the age of twenty-three. Many men were eager to wed because it changed their role in society: they became the head of a household and often moved into a new home with their wife.[5] Hancock had no need for a change in status, but for a man who craved connection, he probably wanted the companionship.

It was not that Hancock had no interest in marriage, necessarily. While in his twenties, he courted Sally Jackson, who came from a wealthy family and whose father served as a selectman with Hancock. Their relationship lasted for a decade before he broke things off, but we have no records about why. As with most of his romantic life, there are few extant details, and they often come from people other than Hancock. John Boyle was an apprentice of the *Boston News Letter* and kept a diary of Boston's many social happenings. Sometimes his entries were printed in his newspaper, much like a gossip column. His entry on February 22, 1770 (aside from referencing eleven-year-old Christopher Seider's death at the hands of customs official Ebenezer Richardson) noted the marriage of Sally Jackson to Henderson Inches. Boyle added, "Mr. John Hancock hath paid his addresses to Miss Jackson for about ten years past, but has lately sent her a Letter of dismission."[6]

After breaking things off with Jackson, Hancock put renewed effort into finding a suitable match and had the time to do so. Over the past five years, he had been at the center of many acts of resistance—intentionally or not—but when troops left town after the Boston Massacre, Hancock turned his attention to his love life and revitalizing his business. A big concession from Parliament helped distance him from politics. Legislators repealed all of the Townshend Duties except for the one on tea. Bostonians learned of the happy news, once again, from one of Hancock's ships.[7]

The remaining tax on tea muddied the nonimportation agreement because some colonists, including merchants in New York and Philadelphia, wanted it to continue until the last tax was repealed. Many in Boston, however, felt the continued measures "too severe." This included Hancock, whose imports had plummeted over 75 percent during the boycott. He was eager to get back to trading, especially because he heard that the tax on tea was unlikely to be lifted any time soon. One of his employees wrote from London in 1771, "The affairs of America are scarcely mention'd here, and there is not at present the least prospect of the Duty on Tea being taken off."[8]

Knowing this, Hancock abandoned the boycott and resumed importing tea, as did other merchants in Boston. He advertised in the local newspapers an assortment of goods for sale in his store in Faneuil Hall Market. "After the most strict Compliance with the

Non-Importation Agreement," the House of Hancock was back in business.[9]

His employees, including the loyal and competent William Palfrey, also helped reignite his romantic life. After being Hancock's mouthpiece during the newspaper feud with John Mein, Palfrey became his matchmaker. There was a potential love interest in London that would have connected Hancock to the revolutionary hero John Wilkes. One of the House of Hancock's overseas business partners was George Hayley, who had married Wilkes's sister, Mary. They had one daughter, Dinah, born in 1759—twenty-two years Hancock's junior—and the favorite niece of Wilkes. Hancock had an eye on her and sent Palfrey to scope out the possibility.[10]

Palfrey arrived in London in February 1771 and visited the Hayleys. He was not subtle about his boss's intentions. Palfrey told Dinah that Hancock sent her his respects. He then turned to Dinah's mother and, while "looking steadfastly at Miss while I spoke," said that she might expect Hancock to visit London in two or three years. The vivacious and eccentric Mrs. Hayley did not want to wait for Hancock to court her daughter. "In two or three Years, why don't you think Miss will do as she is. She's a strapping Girl of her Age." Expectedly, Dinah was mortified by her mother's banter and "blush'd to the Eyes." Palfrey felt embarrassed for her and dropped the subject.[11]

While Mary may have been content to marry off her eleven- or twelve-year-old daughter, or at least heartily joke at her expense, Hancock felt the need to wait until she was slightly older. His uncle Thomas married his aunt Lydia when she was sixteen years old—there was family precedent for a teenaged bride, but not a tween one. Lydia, too, had been the only child of one of Thomas's business associates, so just as his adopted parents' union strengthened their businesses, marrying Dinah would provide a strong alliance with a prominent London merchant. In the eighteenth century, men and women wed with an eye to economic, social, and family connections as much as love.[12]

Ultimately though, as they had with Jackson, things fizzled with Dinah, and we have no details about that relationship either. Hancock was hedging his bets at this time, anyway. While Palfrey was still overseas, Hancock took an interest in someone much closer to home.

In March 1771, he began pursuing a woman with a strong family name. "'Tis said that John Hancock courts Dolly Quincy. 'Tis certain he visits her and has her company in private every evening," reported a Boston merchant. Dorothy Quincy, called Dolly, was the youngest daughter of Edmund Quincy IV, a descendent of Edmund Quincy, who settled in Massachusetts in 1633 and eventually landed in Braintree, Massachusetts, where Hancock was born. The "Choice was very

Dorothy Quincy.
New York Public Library.

natural" for she was the "Daughter of the great Patron and most re-
vered Friend of his Father."[13]

When Dolly was young, her family had been quite prosperous, but
by 1757, Quincy IV had declared bankruptcy. The family had to sell
many of its possessions and downsize to a smaller place in Boston.
Despite the family's unsettled financial circumstances, Dolly's family
circulated in the same circles as Hancock and the two would have
known of each other for years.[14]

They both contributed something important to the union. She
brought her lineage and he brought much-needed wealth. The match
was a boon for the Quincy family, as Dolly was reminded, likely more
than once. Her father told her that she had "the honor of Col° Handcock" inviting her places. The merchant may have been busy,
Quincy IV wrote, but "He appears to rise the higher the greater y^e
burdens." Later, her father would solicit Hancock for appointment
to political office, so he understood the power of having an influential family connection.[15]

We know little about Quincy, as she left few letters behind. It was
not unusual for women to write less during courtship because
eighteenth-century men were expected to show more affection. Even
after marriage, though, she wrote to Hancock infrequently, even when
he begged her for letters. Both Hancock and her father complained
that she did not correspond with them enough. Women of Quincy's
status received lessons in both reading and writing and had high
literacy rates, so it may have been that she did not enjoy or feel confident writing. It also could be that she never cared much for Hancock, something she later hinted about.[16]

Years after Hancock's death, Quincy recalled their courtship and
claimed: "I should have been very glad to have got rid of him." It was
only because Aunt Lydia "would not let her go" that Quincy stayed
with Hancock.[17] This was a cruel admission, but Hancock also took
his time with their courtship and may have, for a period, felt lukewarm about her. Their relationship began in 1771 and they did not

marry until 1775, so he could have still been deciding whether to pursue Dinah or may have been looking for someone else entirely.

And what of the shopkeeper on Hancock's Wharf? There is only one piece of evidence linking Hancock to Griffiths and it is problematic. When war broke out, Griffiths and her daughter fled to England and petitioned the government for a pension, something many Loyalist refugees did. For two years, she received a steady income from the crown until her claim was more closely investigated. Despite leading officers vouching for her character and business operations — including General Thomas Gage who claimed that Griffiths and her daughter "humanely assisted the Sick and wounded Officers of the King's Army" — her pension was now denied.[18]

Thomas Flucker, a prominent Loyalist who served as secretary of Massachusetts before he fled to England, claimed there was more to it than her helping wounded soldiers. He alleged that Griffiths was a prostitute and "bred up her Daughter in the same way."[19] There could have been some truth to this accusation, or sexism may have made it easy for Flucker to leap from unwed woman and daughter shop-keepers to them being prostitutes.

Flucker then dragged Hancock into it: "She was kep^d by the famous Handcock, & when he turned her off, she lived with Capt Johnson." Based on Flucker's testimony, the commissioners determined that Griffiths was unsuitable to receive a pension. His account may have been credible enough to deny her payments, but it's questionable. Flucker surely hated Hancock and had a motive to malign him, having witnessed the merchant's previous conflicts with Francis Bernard. Flucker was so virulent against the rebellion and its leaders that he forever severed connection to his daughter, Lucy, for her chosen spouse: bookseller and future secretary of war, Henry Knox.[20]

Flucker's timing is also off. Griffiths began taking care of Captain Johnson after June 1775, so if Flucker was correct—that after Han-cock "turned her off" she began her relationship with Johnson— Hancock would have been seeing Griffiths while courting Quincy and spending months on end away from Boston. It's possible that Hancock visited prostitutes in his life, but the connection to Griffiths at that particular point in his life is unlikely.[21]

Beginning in 1770, with the House of Hancock back in business and a renewed focus on romance, Hancock wanted to step away from the inflammatory, demanding politics of the past few years. After all, the troops were out of Boston and most of the taxes were lifted. This was good enough for him. Hancock's liberation coincided with other men who had been involved in the previous acts of resistance, but now wanted to distance themselves from radicals. This was especially true for merchants who had sacrificed so much during the boycott.[22]

Yet, Hancock continued to serve in public office. This was not surprising given that he had all of the necessary qualities to lead, if not the enthusiasm. In the eighteenth century, white, educated, privileged men were expected to hold office because they were deemed the only fit leaders. They could also afford to neglect their business from time to time by attending frequent meetings. Town and province leaders also needed to be genteel in manners and form, reinforcing the hierarchical social order pervasive in colonial life.[23] Hancock exceeded those qualifications.

In May 1770, for the fourth year in a row, Hancock was voted into the Massachusetts House of Representatives, receiving 511 of 513 ballots cast, the most votes of any candidate. Thomas Hutchinson estimated that there were about 1500 eligible voters in Boston that year, which meant that only about a third of qualified men actually cast ballots. Colonial voting was notoriously spotty, owing to bad roads, inconvenient polling places, or no issue on the ballot men cared about.[24]

Massachusetts, like other colonies, took their suffrage cues from Great Britain, requiring that men be at least twenty-one years of age and own enough property to support themselves and their dependents. John Adams explained that it was natural to exclude so many people from voting. Women should not have suffrage, for example, because "their attention is So much engaged with the necessary Nurture of their Children, that Nature has made them fittest for domestic Cares." And men without property were incapable of thinking for themselves, he argued, because they would simply side with their landlord or other men of property to stay in their favor. Such people "are also too little acquainted with public Affairs to form a Right Judgment."[25]

Adams also believed that because many folks were too simpleminded, they would cast ballots for candidates who provided them with alcohol. George Washington successfully used this tactic in 1758, rolling out over a hundred gallons of alcohol—including rum punch, wine, brandy, cider, and beer—to secure the votes he needed.[26] Hancock, too, had this down, as attested by his party at the Green Dragon and the madeira giveaway after the Stamp Act repeal.

While alcohol was a safe bet to help a man be competitive in an election, it did not always secure every vote. When two people did not cast ballots for him in 1770, Hancock resigned from the House, complaining that he had been "spoken ill" of. Samuel Adams told Hancock that if he stepped down, he would be rejecting the wishes of the 511 men who did vote for him "merely because one contemptible person" had "blessd you with this reviling." Adams mentioned only one dissenting vote and not two because custom dictated that Hancock should not vote for himself. Adams even hinted that the detractor may have been "hired for the purpose" of not allowing Hancock to secure unanimous votes.[27]

A man who took politics as seriously as Samuel Adams could not have respected Hancock's tantrum, which was likely motivated by vanity. Hancock wanted to be elected to office and feel people's affection at this time, even if he did not want to spend considerable time on political matters. He liked the attention and prestige that came with the office. Adams was persuasive enough and they both served on the House that year.

It was around this time that Hancock wanted to have a second portrait done. He turned again to John Singleton Copley and also hired him to paint Samuel Adams, who would have been unable to afford such a luxury on his own. The portrait was likely not out of affection, which Hancock rarely seemed to have for the firebrand, and Copley was no fan of Adams either. Rather, the portrait was a way to curry favor with or express gratitude to the man who just convinced him to serve in the House. Adams's likeness would be displayed in the Hancock mansion to spark conversation and show off Hancock's taste and political connections.[28]

The two portraits, like the two politicians, are a study of physical contrasts. Adams's hair is slightly messy, the lapels on his coat are rumpled, his jacket is missing two buttons (whether because he forgot to button them or because they had fallen off), and there is no ornamentation on his clothing. Poor sartorial choices plagued Adams so much that in 1774, friends chipped in to buy him new garments before he embarrassed them at the First Continental Congress.[29]

Hancock, however, was thin, sleek, and polished. Unlike the portrait he commissioned in 1765 where he was pictured at a work setting and not looking at the painter, this waist-length portrayal of Hancock has him gazing directly at the viewer. There are clues throughout that point to his wealth and status. His smug expression hints that he has more than you. His clothes prove it. His black jacket blends into the background, but its gilded embroidery—and that on the waistcoat—shines brightly. Such accents were not functional; they were there to show that Hancock could squander money, that he was a success.[30]

His snugly fit clothing, especially the waistcoat, further identified him as a gentleman because it would only allow for an erect posture. A tradesman, for example, would wear looser clothing, including an unbuttoned vest—as Paul Revere did in his Copley portrait—which

Samuel Adams by John Singleton Copley.
Museum of Fine Arts, Boston.

A self-assured John Hancock by John Singleton Copley.
Collection of the Massachusetts Historical Society.

gave a freedom of movement that someone like Hancock did not need. Hancock's face is well lighted and his accompanying tight cravat at the neck was a requirement of the genteel. His short wig with clean lines further reflects a confident and privileged man because it, like the jacket's golden details, was not necessary. Wigs were impractical and ornamental—not to mention costly—so they, too, signified a man of status.[31]

Make no mistake: these sartorial choices matter to both men. Adams was not able to or could not be bothered to dress well. Hancock, however, deliberately chose to spend time on his appearance and his clothing communicated his taste and membership in the elite. He was above others in very visible ways—an asset in colonial leadership.

And yet, Hancock was not to the manner born. He was the son of a humble minister in a country town. His self-made uncle accumulated extravagant wealth that Hancock was lucky to inherit. Because Hancock was *nouveau riche*, he could better associate with the middling and lower orders than if he had the generational wealth, power, and prestige—and the accompanying envy and hatred it inspired—of men like Oliver and Hutchinson.[32] He was more at ease among the lower sorts, even as he was distinctly not one of them. Improbably, despite his elite status, he was relatable.

Buying a portrait of Adams guaranteed no allyship between the two men. Shortly after, Hancock distanced himself from the ideologue and focused on personal concerns. His health needed special attention: "For some months past I have been unable to attend to Business & being now Confin'd to my house." Likely suffering from gout, he skipped many selectman meetings over the span of several months and delegated more of his business affairs to Palfrey.[33]

This was the beginning of Hancock's lifelong battle for a sound body, a fight that he would often find himself losing. Colonial women and men were used to frequent ailments and health concerns, but Hancock's could overwhelm him, especially when he felt political pressure or had a heavy workload. In the twenty-first century, we take for granted knowing there is a connection between body and mind, but even without such proof, Hancock sensed a direct link between stress and poor health. He wished an associate "some Relaxation from Business wch is absolutely necessary for the preservation of Health that best of Blessings." Later in his life, Hancock's health would fail him at times of intense conflict. Many would accuse him of using illness to bow out of messy political fights, but it's clear that his body was sensitive to stressors. Hancock needed downtime to recover from the toll of recent years.[34]

Hancock stepping away from politics was noticed by others. "There was a breach among the patriots in Massachusetts Bay," Governor Hutchinson reported. Hancock "had been firmly attached to Mr. Adams," but then, to Hutchinson's delight, in 1771, "All friendship between them was suddenly at an end, and Mr. Hancock expressed his dissatisfaction with the party." Word reached London, too. Secretary of state Lord Hillsborough wrote to Hutchinson informing him that Hancock "had deserted the Cause of Liberty." He urged the governor to capitalize on the rupture "telling him that he had it in Command from the *highest Authority* to enjoyn to promote Mr H."[35]

The governor had previously tried to sway other rebels to the crown's side, with mixed success. He had solicited John Adams, who turned him down. Undeterred, he appealed to several different men, including Benjamin Church. Hutchinson was able to convince Church, who anonymously published newspapers articles critical of the Sons of Liberty. He would later completely sell himself out and spy for British military forces.[36]

Hutchinson relied on the generations-old tactic of patronage to court his desired conquests. The governor understood the value in giving money or political offices—including judgeships, militia officers, or local appointments—in exchange for loyalty. For example, printer John Mein had been on the royal payroll and repaid that by publishing scathing attacks about political opponents. Offices could also be denied, as Bernard and Hutchinson had done with Hancock for the Governor's Council.[37]

Hutchinson promised Hancock that he would not block him from the upper house in the future if he had "a change of sentiments." The governor assured him, "Every thing past would be entirely forgotten, and it would be a pleasure to the governor to consent to his election to the council." That was not an appealing enough offer for someone who wanted to be less involved in politics altogether. Hancock replied that he "intended to quit all active concern in publick affairs, and to attend to his private business." He even swore that he will "never again connect himself with Adams."[38]

For his part, Samuel Adams was not ignoring political matters as Hancock was, but was growing more determined to broadcast any imperial overreaches. Tenaciously advocating for colonists' rights, he was adept at finding lesser-known instances where he believed liberty was threatened. For example, in 1772, Adams was outraged about Parliament's new policy of paying judges' salaries, which had been previously funded by the colonies and would now likely bias the jurists toward favoring royal policies. He set up a committee of correspondence to communicate with other colonies about the crown's "Infringements and Violations."[39]

The Boston committee was comprised of many prominent members, including merchants, lawyers, and doctors. One third of the men had Harvard degrees and many were Masons. Hancock checked these boxes but declined to sit on the committee. Thomas Cushing, a merchant and friend of Hancock who also had moderate political leanings, passed as well. Without Hancock's star power, the committee lacked prestige, which some Loyalists viewed as a further sign of division.[40]

Adams blamed Hancock and Cushing for not joining, not the committee or its ideas. Privately, however, Samuel and John Adams were concerned both merchants had not signed on. The cousins met at Samuel's house and "had much conversation about the state of affairs, Cushing . . . Hancock." Samuel loathed their tepid politics, fuming, "For the sake of their own Ease or their own Safety, they preach the People into paltry Ideas of Moderation." Hancock had also moved away from John Adams as his lawyer, who was offended: "For about three or four years I have done all Mr. Hancock's business, and have waded through wearisome, anxious days and nights, in his defence; but farewell!" Samuel Adams claimed that Cushing and Hancock did not realize "the evil Tendency of their Conduct" by declining to be a part of the committee.[41]

Avoid being ensnared in the trap set by Adams: that of a false binary. He believed Hancock either joined the committee of correspondence or his conduct was evil. Rarely is life—much less revolution—that clean. Hancock and Cushing did not want their businesses to suffer because of taxation, but they also were not as agitated as others about crown policies, especially after most of the Townshend Duties were lifted. People are complex and make political choices for myriad reasons. What may be good for them one year will not be good for them another.

Recall that in 1769, John Adams was obligated to attend the party in Dorchester for fear that if he missed it, the Sons of Liberty would question his loyalties. He attended and toasted and huzzahed, but he had felt pressure to be there. Three years later, he was suspicious about people who did not think like him. Rebellion shape-shifted, and as it did, so did many of its leaders.

We also know things the revolutionaries did not. Hancock had no idea that Parliament would pass another ill-conceived tax in a couple years and that he would join in to resist it. For he was not living in pre-war society—with violent resistance, deadly battles, and colonial independence just a few years in the future—but a post-war one, in which Massachusetts had allied with British forces less than a decade before. Because he did not feel threatened by the crown's policies in the early 1770s and had reason to hope any turmoil was over, he literally went about his other business.

Despite Hancock's indifference, Samuel Adams was able to get his tacit support for the committee of correspondence's "Boston Pamphlet," which was to be distributed throughout the colony. The document enumerated grievances with Parliament, railed against the change to judges' salaries, and restated their colonial rights. Hancock was selected moderator of the meeting that would discuss the pamphlet, so even though he had no part in drafting it, when it was approved, his name graced the first page of text. The people in the Massachusetts hinterlands responded very favorably to the ideals outlined in the tract, which further raised Hancock's profile outside of Boston, even as he pulled away from politics.[42]

With his mind on almost anything but the crown, Hancock sought out fun. While most had to toil for a living—if they were lucky enough to find work during a time of contracted credit and employment—Hancock was financially comfortable enough to temporarily ignore such concerns. Hancock took a summer vacation, going on a sailing trip with seven friends and two servants. They sailed "to visit the Eastern Parts of this Province and also on a Party of Pleasure" and were gone for seventeen days.[43]

We know that Hancock was a fine host and loved entertaining richly, so surely there was no shortage of food, madeira, and conviviality. A professor at Harvard attended because of "asthma and the prospect of pleasant companionship." The fresh air likely helped Hancock, too, as did having guests who avoided harping on political issues. Samuel Cooper, the minister of Brattle Street Church where Hancock and his aunt were members, also joined. Hancock had recently pledged to help Cooper build a new church because Hancock "suffers no body to outdoe him in acts of public utility." He also paid for a new mahogany pulpit, pews, and a bell, the largest one of any church in Boston—one of many acts of charity he committed during his lifetime.[44]

Hancock may have felt more generous than usual after winning the "the Highest Prise" in the 1772 lottery: $1500. It was the second time that he had taken home the largest cash award. Boston frequently offered raffles to raise funds for Faneuil Hall, which had been damaged by a fire the decade before. That Hancock would be an "Adventurer"—the term for those who bought tickets—seemed appropriate. The lottery supported the town-wide goal to restore the marketplace and meeting space and he was one of Boston's leading men.[45]

Hancock also gambled on himself when he accepted a new role, believing he could make a difference. He had recently been elected colonel of the Corps of Cadets—Boston's militia and governor's guard. He'd served in the group for six years and acted as their de facto leader in 1768 when he resigned and tried to form his own company, which Governor Bernard shut down. By accepting the new rank, Samuel Adams worried that some would believe Hancock had fallen for Hutchinson's patronage because the governor had to formally approve his nomination. Adams wrote to friends in Virginia, desperate to let them know that any rumors that Hancock had defected were untrue. He called it "an imaginary conquest." Adams was mostly right because Hancock was unanimously elected by nearly one hundred fellow cadets and Hutchinson had no legitimate right to deny the post. Adams's concern, however, showed that some continued to believe Hancock could be wooed by Hutchinson.[46]

Hancock threw himself into the position and eagerly used his new military title. He posted a newspaper ad for two fifers. "WANTED Immediately! . . . Those that are Masters of Music . . . are desired to apply to Col. JOHN HANCOCK." Understanding better than anyone that clothes can make the man, Hancock outfitted his men in new uniforms "trim'd in ye most elegant manner." The Cadets wore crimson coats—the color borrowed from the British army—and white waistcoats. Thigh-high gaiters—thick stockings worn over boots with buttons running down the sides—were worn to protect the legs. Black tricorn hats completed the look.[47]

Hancock drilled them on Boston Common and "you'd scarcely believe your eyes, they are so strangely metamorphos'd." He turned around a ragtag group, instilling them (and the town) with pride because they now "vie with [the] best troops in his majesties service." Militia training days were often public occasions in New England where men got to show off their uniforms and skills. The days usually ended with sharing food and drinks. Serving as colonel was the perfect role for Hancock because it gave him a chance to socialize and be generous. He footed the bill for one Cadets party, which included paying for over one hundred bottles of punch, sherry, and madeira. As fit a raucous party, glasses and bowls were broken and Hancock was charged for those, too.[48]

The Cadets recognized that it was Hancock who had transformed them: "It is principally owing to you, Sir, that the Company acquired such reputation." Under Hancock's influence and leadership, the Cadets became orderly and impressive. "Colo. Hancock turned out this forenoon with the Cadet Company—they made a Good Figure & behaved . . . much Better than usual," a fellow merchant observed.[49]

Hancock's activities at this time show that for a few years, he wanted to be in a calmer and less contentious place. We often imagine the American Revolution as an inevitable and unified march toward war and independence, with one crown offense building on another. But it was not. A man like Hancock had a wife to find, friends to spend time with, and hobbies to pursue—all while not wanting to be stirred up by minor political issues. That is, until the crown began again to interfere with his business.

In May 1773, Parliament brought Hancock's political respite to an abrupt end. The British East India Company (EIC), which controlled Great Britain's tea trade, was on the verge of economic collapse. In an effort to get rid of a surplus of tea, Parliament passed the Tea Act, requiring colonists in North America to buy tea exclusively from the

EIC and pay a tax on it. In an effort to crush smugglers—who had caused legal imports of tea to fall by 75 percent in recent years— Parliament slashed the price of EIC tea, so that even with the tax, theirs remained cheaper than their Dutch competitors.[50]

This new law was going to drastically affect Hancock's business because after the repeal of most of the Townshend Duties, he had enthusiastically resumed trade, especially in tea. He ordered or carried on his ships nearly a third of the total tea imported into Boston, some of which was duties. John Adams was a guest in Hancock's home at this time, and said that they "drank Green Tea, from Holland I hope, but dont know." Possible, but not likely. During these years, Hancock was filling his ships "as full as an Egg," and still had to turn cargo away.[51]

Under the new Tea Act, however, Hancock would be unable to import and profit from the commodity. It could only be sold by consignees designated by the crown, and he, unsurprisingly, was not one of them. Instead, elite families who had ignored the nonimportation agreement a few years back were chosen. This included Hutchinson's sons and Richard Clarke, a prominent merchant who also ran his business with his sons.[52]

It was this interference with his business, rather than ideology, that temporarily ended Hancock's political indifference. Tea became an especially touchy commodity in Boston and Hancock was prescient enough to see which side would best protect him and his interests. He was savvy about knowing when to come off the sidelines and after a three-year break, it was time. Hancock's transformation would include teaming up with Samuel Adams, the man he had distanced himself from, and going from an ardent importer and server of tea to someone who called for its destruction.

A Coronation

Hancock was growing impatient, as were the hundreds of other people standing with him. They were at a familiar spot: the Liberty Tree. Given the time of year—late fall—the elm's canopy was likely sparser, with just a few yellow leaves hanging on. This had been a site for both toasts and effigies, a place where the Sons of Liberty gathered for camaraderie or for bullying. On this day, their purpose was intimidation.

Their anger stemmed from tea: who could sell it, who could not, and who was going to drink it. The tea consignees—those chosen by the crown to sell the taxed tea—were the primary targets, including Richard Clarke and Governor Hutchinson's sons. Early one November morning in 1773, they stepped outside their homes to find notes demanding they appear at the Liberty Tree to relinquish their posts. The Sons wanted them to resign at the same site that stamp collector Andrew Oliver had eight years before.[1]

An hour passed before Hancock, Joseph Warren, Samuel Adams, and five hundred others realized that, unlike Oliver, the consignees were not going to show. Furious at being stood up, eight or nine men, including street tough William Molineux, marched to Clarke's warehouse and asked the merchant to send back any East India Company (EIC) tea that arrived in Boston. In a "haughty manner," Clarke refused. The thugs ripped the Clarkes' door from its hinges before storming off.[2]

Confrontations like this had Hutchinson nervous. He knew how violent many in Boston could be, so he called on the colonel of the Cadets for help. Hutchinson ordered Hancock to "summon each person belonging to the company to be ready & to appear in arms." Boston's militia, Hutchinson reminded him, was to show up "whensoever there may be a tumultuous assembly of the people." The Cadets, however, were not going to comply with Hutchinson, whom Hancock considered a "Tool of Power and Enemy of his Country."[3]

This was quite a distance from a year earlier when the governor thought he could woo Hancock to his side. The colonel now seemed firmly allied with the Patriots. When he had ignored politics for the three years after the Boston Massacre, there had been no real threat to Hancock. That changed with the tax on tea. Hancock had imported loads of the commodity in the last two years and this law would cut directly into that business. He got involved by sitting on a committee to agitate the consignees into resigning and moderating several town committees aimed at preventing the tax from going into effect.[4]

On November 17, news came from one of Hancock's ships that EIC tea was crossing the Atlantic. This was a rare bit of bad news from his fleet, but it served as a call to mobilize because once the tea arrived, a countdown began. British law required that cargo be unloaded within twenty days and any taxes paid. If that did not happen, customs officials could seize the goods, at which point they and the ship would be sold at auction. With tea imminent in Boston Harbor, the situation grew more urgent. Patriots stepped up efforts to force the consignees to resign—including making house calls.[5]

That night, men went to Thomas Hutchinson's house but no one was home, so the crowd continued to the Clarke residence. Horns blew and shouts rang out from as many two hundred angry men. The

Clarke women sought safety upstairs and the men blocked the entrances. As the mob tried to force open the house's locked door, one of Clarke's sons hung out of the window and shot into the crowd. No one was injured but the crowd spent an hour throwing objects at the house. The crowd eventually dispersed with the promise of another meeting to impel resignations.[6]

On November 28, 1773, "the Tea that bainfull weed is arrived," reported Abigail Adams, wife of John. It was stored on a ship called *Dartmouth*, and according to Hancock, the townspeople were "much Agitated" that it had docked. Worried that the ship might be unloaded under the cover of night—as Hancock knew from experience was a possibility—the Patriots set up a watch. Every thirty minutes, volunteers patrolled the wharf and shouted, "all is well!" Leading the watch one night was none other than Hancock and his well-dressed cadets. They had refused to turn out for Hutchinson but were willing to guard the tea.[7]

Simply monitoring the cargo was not going to be enough, though. The twenty-day deadline ticked and Boston felt increasing pressure to reject the tea in some way. A letter from Philadelphia was printed in a Boston newspaper and taunted its residents: "You have fail'd us in the Importation of Tea from London since the Non-importation Agreement, and we fear you will suffer this to be landed." Philadelphia and New York reminded Bostonians that their town's merchants, including Hancock, resumed importing tea back in 1770, despite other colonies wanting to continue the boycott. Both towns had already intimidated their consignees to resign, so they promised: "you need not fear; the Tea will not be landed here or at New-York. All that we fear is, that you will shrink at Boston."[8] The town's reputation was at stake and drastic action was needed.

On December 16, the day before the deadline to unload the tea, a crowd gathered at Old South Meeting House, a large church in Boston. It was a cold and rainy day, but that did not stop nearly five thousand people, by Samuel Adams's estimation, from cramming into the building. They were waiting for the arrival of Francis Rotch, the owner of *Dartmouth*, who needed a pass from the governor to send the tea back. He'd gone earlier that day to Hutchinson's country house seeking permission for his ship to leave the harbor.[9]

It had been a tough year for Hutchinson. Private letters he wrote in the 1760s were exposed and reprinted throughout the colonies, subjecting him to fierce and unrelenting criticism. His sons had been continually harassed for being tea consignees. He could have made things easier on himself by letting the ships return to London. It would have instantly calmed the mood in town. Instead, he chose to take a hard line. His answer was no.[10]

Rotch brought word back around 6:00 PM and the crowd swung into action. They shouted for the harbor to become a teapot while "a number of people huzza'd in the Street." One of the attendees—George Hewes, the shoemaker's apprentice who Hancock hosted at his mansion ten years earlier—recalled that as the people flooded out of the church, Hancock cried out, "let every man do what is right in his own eyes!"[11]

Thousands of people walked to Griffin's Wharf where three ships with EIC tea were now docked. Hancock, along with other rebel leaders, including Adams and Warren, stayed behind—it was too risky for them to be seen or caught at such an event. About 150 young, working-class men who were not well known or easily recognized participated, including Hewes. One man, Thompson Maxwell, recalled years after the event that Hancock had recruited him. He and a few other men had loaded goods at Hancock's warehouse earlier that afternoon. The merchant invited Maxwell back to his house where he "informed me what was to be done." That night, Maxwell and the others destroyed well over a million dollars' worth of tea, in today's value.[12]

"In a very few Hours, the whole of the Tea on board . . . was thrown into the Salt Water," Hancock told a contact in London. He admitted knowing only in broad terms what happened that night and had few details, "as indeed I am not Acquainted with them myself." He wisely distanced himself from the destruction of the tea, as the Boston Tea Party was referred to at the time. Even as he claimed to not know much about it, Hancock justified the action and opined about the Tea Act: "No one Circumstance could possibly have Taken place more effectually to Unite the Colonies than this Manavere of the Tea, it is universally Resented here."[13] One cannot fault him for such thinking, but we have the benefit of hindsight and access to other viewpoints, both of which show that Hancock was mistaken in three ways.

First, the Tea Act was not "universally resented." Some people, like the consignees, stood to profit from it and many townspeople wanted the intimidating behavior to stop. Second, not everyone approved of destroying the tea, including some towns in Massachusetts. Calling the tea party a "Disastrous Affair," merchant John Rowe favored paying restitution for the tea losses and lamented, "I am sincerely sorry for the Event." Leaders in other colonies also felt it went too far and feared mob rule. George Washington expressed his dissatisfaction with the event and Benjamin Franklin wrote from London pleading with Boston to make amends. "Making voluntarily such Reparation can be no Dishonour to us or Prejudice to our Claim of Rights," he believed. He predicted that Parliament would react explosively when they heard about the destruction of the tea. Franklin correctly thought that "Society at large" will be blamed for "the Mischief" of a handful of men.[14]

Finally, Hancock's claim that the Tea Act would "Unite the Colonies" did not prove to be true. It was neither the tax nor the tea party that united the colonists. Rather, it was Parliament's reaction to the destruction of the tea that banded together more men up and down the Atlantic seaboard than Hancock or crown officials could have imagined. It would take some time for the colonies to find out what it would be—a round trip to England took a minimum of ten weeks—but when it came, it escalated the imperial conflict like nothing before.

———————

On the morning of March 5, 1774, townspeople awoke knowing that a big day was ahead. John Hancock was giving a speech. Those who were planners would have correctly anticipated a large crowd and arrived early to secure their spot. After assessing the number of people who wanted to get in, the organizers moved the event to Old South Meeting House, which had more than double the capacity of the original location of Faneuil Hall, and was where thousands of people gathered a few months earlier on the night of the Boston Tea Party.[15]

As attendees walked the short distance to the church—keeping its steeple with the recently installed clock in sight—some may have rushed or pushed to ensure they made it to the doors first. Built in 1729, the wooden church was the largest building in colonial Boston, but it was still not massive enough to hold everyone interested. Money and influence did not help with admission, as merchant John Rowe discovered when he "tryd to get in but could not."[16]

"A prodigious Crowd of People attended," eager to see the local icon speak. Every year on the anniversary of the Boston Massacre, townspeople honored the occasion with a speech. Just like annual celebrations of the Stamp Act riots against Oliver, this event was intended to keep people angry about the crown's authority and overreach. This was especially helpful when little was happening of political consequence, as in the years immediately after the Massacre. Some thought that Hancock was chosen to give that year's oration because of his wavering politics the previous years.[17]

People flooded into the church and would have filled the wooden benches on the ground floor, which were separated by hip-high dividers with small doors to enclose the box. Others could go to the upper galleries. At the front of the room, daylight streamed though arched windows. As bodies crammed into the church any late winter chill likely abated.

Hancock had to climb a short, enclosed staircase to get to the pulpit. Used to the admiring gaze of townspeople, Hancock began his speech with some false modesty and claimed his "unworthiness" to speak to the audience. He was surely pleased to have their attention, though, and he planned to impact them.

After the opening, he elucidated the purpose of government: "Security to the persons and properties of the governed." A righteous government, he contended, would not proclaim the right to tax the colonies "in all cases whatever"—a reference to the Declaratory Act of 1766—especially after their subjects had protested the taxes. The crown further trampled on colonial rights when it stationed soldiers in Boston in 1768 to enforce their laws. Hancock reminded his neighbors that the redcoats had harassed and insulted them, were loud and debaucherous—especially on the Sabbath—seduced the town's young women, and by their vile examples even taught "our infants . . . to lisp out curses."[18] And then, on the night of March 5, 1770, they had shot five men dead.

Hancock's tone darkened at this part in his speech. "Satan with his chosen band opened the sluices of New England's blood, and sacrilegiously polluted our lands with the dead bodies of her guiltless sons." He continued for some time about the "treacherous knaves" and "bloody butchers." Hancock hoped that the ghosts of the five murdered men—he named each of them, the first Boston Massacre orator to do so—terrorized the soldiers when they were sleeping and haunted them when awake.[19]

The vitality he displayed while speaking would have been surprising to those who knew of Hancock's recent health problems. After the destruction of the tea, he had felt unwell with unspecified symptoms. He had attended only two selectmen meetings between December and March and declined to serve any longer as fire ward, which was a small job, "on account of his Health." He may have wanted to keep a lower profile after the Boston Tea Party since he had been an instigator, or stress had taken its toll and he needed to rest. His employee claimed that he "is prevented by indisposition, & is at present confin'd to his Bed." But here he was a couple months later emotionally stirring a "vast Concourse of People."[20]

Hancock then drew attention to a young man who was wounded in the shooting. This was another anniversary first. Hancock was an expert at connecting with people, and publicly identifying the men killed or wounded was an effective way to do that. Christopher "Kit" Monk had been about seventeen years old and working as a ship-building apprentice when he joined the crowd in March 1770 to confront the soldiers. When the firing started, Monk was shot in the back near the spine and the ball came out through his chest. It should have been a mortal wound, but Monk was still hanging on in 1774 and "Doomed to drag on a pitiful existence."[21]

"Observe his tottering knees, which scarce sustain his wasted body; look on his haggard eyes," Hancock cried, his call amplified by the wooden sounding board suspended above his head. "For us he bled, and now languishes" and will surely die as a result of his wounds that "were aimed at our country!"[22] The crowd was so moved by the tribute that they took up a collection to support Monk.

Further motivating the crowd, Hancock asked for solidarity between the colonies and praised the committee of correspondence—the one he had declined joining—for uniting Massachusetts and those of their "sister colonies." Hancock also suggested a "general congress" comprised of other North American colonies because it would be "the most effectual method of establishing such a union."[23]

Professing confidence that the "struggle for liberty would end well for America," Hancock's speech was nearly done. The son and grandson of ministers ended on a religious note, calling on Bostonians to leave their concerns to God, for surely he would guide their righteous path. In forty-five minutes, he had angered, saddened, empowered, and then galvanized the crowd.[24] It was quite a show.

"Universal Applause" rang throughout the church. Townspeople clapped and clapped for one of their favorites. John Adams called it "an elegant, pathetic, a Spirited Performance." (Pathetic in the eighteenth century meant full of pathos, or passion.) The "Composition, the Pronunciation, the Action all exceeded the Expectations of every Body," the usually tough critic proclaimed.[25]

As moving as the speech was, it was likely not written by Hancock alone. The language and ideas stand out as more inflammatory and radical than his actions over the past decade. Religious language and imagery were not usually a part of his writings and ideas either. But they were for minister and friend, Samuel Cooper, and the devout Calvinist, Samuel Adams, both of whom may have contributed to the speech. The idea about a congress did not originate with him either—the year before, Benjamin Franklin thought such a body would be beneficial.[26]

Word spread about Hancock's performance when the owners of the *Boston Gazette*, Benjamin Edes and John Gill, distributed the speech. It became one of the twelve most frequently printed political pamphlets in the ten years of resistance, going through five American editions and appearing in four different cities and towns.[27] This undoubtedly raised Hancock's colonywide profile, which could use a boost after suspicions about his commitment to the boycott.

Just when Samuel Adams and his allies would have thought Hancock had committed to their cause, the orator exhibited his independence a few days later. The lieutenant governor and former Stamp Act collector, Andrew Oliver, had recently died and Hancock wanted his Corps of Cadets to fulfill their duty by attending his funeral. Samuel Adams, however, thought that Oliver deserved no such respect. The colonel stood his ground, believing that it was the office he was recognizing, not the person who filled it.[28]

As Oliver's body was laid in the Granary Burying Ground, the Cadets fired three shots. "Great numbers of People were collected to see the Cadet Company perform their Exercises," a newspaper reported. Oliver's coffin was not even in the ground when Samuel Adams and his associates "huzzaed at the intombing of the body." It was tacky, to say the least. One account called it "Rude Behaviour," and others accused these men of forgetting "the Command, '*Rejoice not when thine Enemy falleth.*'"[29]

In a matter of three months, Hancock helped agitate against the Tea Act, spoke to the crowd before the destruction of the tea, and gave the Boston Massacre anniversary address. He also felt it was necessary to honor those he disagreed with, like Oliver. He made decisions based on circumstances, not a rigid ideology, and he avoided holding tightly to an extreme. Hancock's moderation would soon become more difficult to sustain, however. London's punishment for the destruction of the tea was imminent.

———————

In May 1774, Hancock's Cadets had another assignment that Samuel Adams would have disdained: welcoming a replacement governor. General Thomas Gage, commander in chief of British North American forces, arrived in Boston to great pomp, which suited his new position as governor of Massachusetts. Gage succeeded Hutchinson because the crown wanted someone more authoritative running Massachusetts. After the destruction of the tea, they were done coddling the colonists who continued to reject their authority. As cannon boomed from Castle William, Hancock and his snappy Cadets greeted the general at Long Wharf and escorted him up King Street.[30] Despite the show of decorum, Gage probably eyed the colonel suspiciously—he'd been familiar with Hancock since the *Liberty* trial six years earlier.

Gage was not the only imperial response to the Tea Party. Given the relative quiet in the first months of 1774, it would have been easy for townspeople to forget that punishment would be coming. But come it did, in a series of laws known as the Coercive Acts. Gage personally assured the king that he could enforce them, confidently arriving in Boston with thousands of soldiers to do just that.[31] The town was once again occupied by soldiers and under military rule.

The Coercive Acts were harsh and far-reaching. The Port Bill shut down Boston's harbor until townspeople paid for the value of the tea destroyed. As intended, this crippled the maritime economy almost immediately. Such a measure would devastate the House of Hancock. Other laws aimed to weaken colonial power. The Massachusetts Government Act prohibited town meetings and allowed the governor to appoint Council members instead of the House of Representatives. Another law permitted any civil or military official on trial for a capital offense in Massachusetts to instead be tried in England, where they would be more likely to be acquitted.[32]

Gage acknowledged he was on an "unwelcome errand" to enforce the laws, and it only took the summer for him to become exasperated with the job. He dissolved the General Court in June, and then in August, put men loyal to the crown on the Governor's Council.[33] He also took his frustration out on Hancock—a poor choice, as he would learn.

Gage stripped Hancock of his title as colonel of the Corps of Cadets, claiming he had "done me ill and not treated me with the respect that it is due to the Governor." It's unclear what happened between the two, but when Hancock informed the company of Gage's decision, they stood with their leader. The militia had always cherished the right to choose their officers, so "[t]hey look upon this dismission as disbanding the Corps." They all voted to step down, even returning their uniforms and musical instruments.[34] Gage was being shortsighted here. Hancock was too popular and influential to anger and just a few weeks later, the general would need his help.

Four regiments of soldiers were camping on the Common and by late September, it was getting cold at night. Gage was having barracks built, but construction had abruptly stopped when workers walked off the job after pressure from Boston's committee of correspondence. Townspeople also withheld "labour, straw, timber, flitwork, boards" and anything else the troops might need to subsist, short of what "meer humanity requires."[35]

Gage could not find laborers to finish the job, even when offering generous wages, so he asked Hancock to convince local carpenters—who the merchant had likely employed before—to build the barracks. When Gage thought Hancock had been rude to him earlier with the Cadets, it may have been a miscommunication. This time, there was no doubt that Hancock was not obliging to Gage. The soldiers "had taken every possible measure to distress us," Hancock explained, and he refused to help make them comfortable. Desperate, Gage offered to temporarily lift the Port Bill and let ships come into the shuttered harbor, but still Hancock would not help.[36]

The governor's trouble was not limited to Hancock and Boston, however. "Nobody here or at home could have conceived, that the Acts made for the Massachusett's Bay, could have created such a Ferment throughout the Continent, and united the whole in one Common Cause," Gage lamented. This was not an exaggeration. Nothing did more to motivate the colonists across North America than the Coercive Acts. Not the Stamp Act or the Townshend Duties or the Boston Massacre.[37]

Colonists were surprised by the severity of the laws because they punished all of Massachusetts for the actions of 150 men. John Adams overheard a conversation among farmers in Shrewsbury (a town forty miles west of Boston) who were concerned that "if parliament can take away Mr. Hancock's wharf and Mr. Rowe's wharf, they can take away your barn and my house." The laws were even difficult for those loyal to the crown to justify, as Britons throughout the empire grew more concerned about tyranny and arbitrary power.[38]

Banding together as never before, colonies chipped in and sent food and resources to help afflicted Bostonians. Virginia forwarded goods but also proposed a meeting for all the colonies to discuss the increasingly tense relationship with Great Britain. Hancock had suggested this in his March 5 speech, calling for a "general congress." The First Continental Congress met in Philadelphia beginning in September 1774.[39]

While the intercolonial congress met, the men of Massachusetts were holding their own assemblies. The Government Act banned any town gatherings, but Patriots cleverly got around that by making them county-wide. The meetings had no formal authority—yet—but they were influential. Counties in the countryside convened, forced their courts to close, and impelled Gage's hand-selected councilors to resign. The meetings of Suffolk County, home to Boston, became especially significant because their ideas about resistance spread far outside the colony.[40]

Curiously, Hancock did not attend the Suffolk delegation or the Continental Congress. He was bothered by Gage, the soldiers, and the Coercive Acts, but he avoided political matters in the summer of 1774. He may have found the measures on both sides too extreme, or he may have been unwell. It was an uncertain time for many moderates in North America as they realized an imperial crisis seemed to be drawing nearer.[41] Hancock was likely waiting to see how the situation would play out before deciding where to align himself.

Joseph Warren, a thirty-three-year-old doctor whose profile was steadily rising among the Patriots, had no such concerns about seeming too radical. He led the Suffolk convention and wrote the Suffolk Resolves, an incendiary document that called for the creation of an alternative government—a Provincial Congress—to operate outside the bounds of royal authority. He also proposed that Massachusetts boycott British goods, raise their militia, and start preparing militarily for a potential confrontation.[42]

In Philadelphia, the Continental Congress approved the Suffolk Resolves and, in doing so, transformed themselves into a governing body that made decisions for the colonies separate from the crown. It is impossible to overstate how significant this was. Over the past decade, protests and riots had not legally separated colonists from the crown. Not even a little bit. What did was the Continental Congress sanctioning the Provincial Congress. Massachusetts residents now claimed to have the political authority in their colony—not Gage, Parliament, or King George III.[43]

In October 1774, the extralegal Provincial Congress held its first meeting and Hancock decided to attend. Perhaps his ego had nagged him for missing such pivotal gatherings, or he was feeling healthier, or he felt safer allying with the new government. No matter the reason, he was rewarded by being selected the body's president. With that new position, Hancock became, for many, the most powerful and authoritative man in Massachusetts.[44]

The delegates created a committee of safety to prepare for war and Hancock, Warren, and Benjamin Church—who was selling details about the colonists' preparations to Gage—were chosen to serve on this delegation and manage an army of 15,000 men. The committee recommended Massachusetts residents "use their utmost diligence to perfect themselves in military skill" and gather adequate arms and ammunition. None of these men had experience in such an enormous task—Hancock's military participation was limited to his service with the Cadets—but the former colonel worked with a new urgency.[45]

The Provincial Congress did not have universal approval in Massachusetts, for good reason: it was a rival government that was collecting money from residents and preparing for war. It was a stunning escalation in the imperial conflict. One man hoped the Congress would dissolve because he thought it had few prudent members. "They were about establishing a standing army to be compos'd of fifteen thousand men: a scheme not only ridiculous, but fraught with a degree of madness at this juncture," he complained. Such efforts by the Provincial Congress were thought to be just as dangerous to liberty as Gage and his troops. A Boston resident preferred the noises of the army in Boston "to the infernal Whistle and shout of a lawless and outragious rabble."[46]

By the fall of 1774, Boston had an unmistakable military cast. The committee of safety was readying the colony for battle while Gage was stockpiling ammunition and artillery, including fortifying the neck of Boston with cannons. Hancock only had to walk to his front door to feel the changes to his town. "The Common wears an Entire new face. Instead of the peacefull Verdure with which it was cloathd when you left it, it now glows with the warlike Red," a Beacon Hill resident wrote. During the day, the soldiers' noise interrupted the previously tranquil and quiet feeling the park offered. Cannons fired, drums rattled, and fifes shrilled.[47]

Not long ago in the same place, Hancock—who could no longer call himself a colonel—had drilled his cadets and townspeople had taken pride in the militia's discipline. But it was different now. These young soldiers were not comprised of or led by one of their own; instead, they were a hostile occupying force. As the leader of the rogue government with a house overlooking this scene, Hancock soon "apprehended his person was in danger."[48]

So reviled was he that redcoats invented an epithet that captured Hancock's popularity and poked fun at colonists for their lack of an aristocratic ruling class. In the summer of 1774, a Bostonian named Samuel Dyer was held captive by British soldiers. They asked him who ordered the destruction of the tea. When Dyer answered "nobody," the officer told him, "he was a damned liar, it was KING HANCOCK and the damn'd sons of liberty."[49] A nickname used derisively by British soldiers, it suited the regal Hancock who, remarkably, even King George III had heard of by now.

British officers also modified the folk song "Yankee Doodle" to poke fun at Hancock. The ditty had been around for at least three decades and was easily customizable and appropriated. The redcoats sang, "Yankee Doodle came to town / For to buy a firelock: / We will tar and feather him, / And so we will John Hancock." These verbal attacks could be written off as silly jests, but it was worth taking them seriously. As 1774 turned to 1775, the threats to Hancock's safety became more real.[50]

Such danger was obvious at the Boston Massacre anniversary speech in 1775. It was attended by thousands, including forty British officers and many soldiers, who crowded toward the front of Old South Meeting House. Dressed in a toga, Warren—that year's orator— spoke melodramatically about the men who died in the Massacre. He lamented the orphans left behind because their fathers had been killed, despite none of the Massacre victims having children. Another collection was taken for Christopher Monk.[51]

After Warren stepped down, Hancock stood up and made a short speech. The officers cried out "fie, fie!" Except the spectators did not hear "fie"—the eighteenth-century equivalent of booing—they heard "fire." The attendees panicked, pushing toward the doors and jumping out of the windows.[52]

Just as people believed they were escaping a conflagration, a regiment of soldiers marched by and the already-startled Bostonians thought they were about to be attacked. It was an uneasy few moments before townspeople realized that there was no fire and the redcoats were only drilling.

An officer spoke of the very real dangers that day: "It was imagined that there wou'd have been a riot, which . . . wou'd in all probability have proved fatal to Hancock, Adams, Warren, and the rest of those Villains." Hancock would have been an easy mark because he and the other leaders were huddled up at the pulpit together, "and the meeting was crowded with Officers and Seamen in such a manner that they cou'd not have escaped."[53]

The officer was glad it had not come to that for Hancock in the church. Not because he did not want to see him dead. But because it would "indeed have been a pity for them to have made their exit in that way, as I hope we shall have the pleasure before long of seeing them do it by the hands of the Hangman."[54]

Two weeks after this close call, redcoats came to Hancock's mansion and harassed him. They "with their swords, cut and hacked the fence before his house in a most scandalous manner." A day or two later, four officers and four soldiers "were sent to insult John Hancock, under pretense of seeing if his stables would do for barracks." Such behavior would be unnerving, especially coming from officers, but an intrepid Hancock confronted them. He instructed them to leave his grounds, and they refused, telling him that his estate would soon be under their control. After that happened, the soldiers informed him, Hancock would have no say "and they would do as they pleased."[55]

Hancock went immediately to Gage, who told him that if he were insulted again, Hancock should send one of his servants to let him know and he would take care of it.[56] Hancock doubted the general could protect him. Two days later Hancock left town and set off for Concord, twenty miles away, where the Provincial Congress would now be holding its meetings. It would not be long before the countryside was unsafe for him, too.

CHAPTER 7

War and Attempts at Peace

Hancock thought he would feel more protected in the Massachusetts countryside than in Boston. The Provincial Congress, where he served as president, was meeting in Concord in March 1775. That it was assembling at all was risky: the Congress was formed outside the bounds of any British authority and its very existence explicitly violated the recently passed Coercive Acts. Hancock and Samuel Adams were staying in Lexington during Congress's session, commuting the five miles to and from Concord. When it adjourned at the end of March, Hancock and Adams remained in Lexington.

Hancock stayed at his cousin's house, which had previously been owned by his grandfather. An opulent, elegantly furnished mansion like his home on Beacon Hill, it was not. But it was familiar. The house was a two-story wooden structure whose front door skewed at an angle to the main road. It sat about a third of a mile from Lexington Green and Buckman Tavern, places where men met and drilled and drank; places that would soon become critical locations in American history.[1]

Upon entering the house's front door, there was a small entryway and staircase to the rooms upstairs. On each side of the foyer were rooms with windows that faced the road, perfect to receive the warming southern light. The Clarkes and nine of their children put aside their comfort to accommodate their esteemed cousin and his guests. Jonas Clarke and his wife, Lucy, offered the nicest room to Hancock—the downstairs parlor—a spacious place he shared with Samuel Adams. Aside from the bed, there was a fireplace, a wooden table, and a pair of chairs. Interior shutters brought in or shut out daylight. The bedroom directly upstairs from Hancock belonged to Jonas and Lucy, but they gave it up to the women in Hancock's group who had recently arrived: his aunt Lydia, and his fiancée Dolly Quincy.

A population with Puritanical roots and a deserved reputation for prudishness could be scandalized by Hancock and an unmarried woman lodging together, but it was not unusual in eighteenth-century New England for an engaged couple to sleep in the same house, so long as there was a chaperone. It was mostly accepted, too, that they would be sexually active during courtship. Hancock was likely relieved that he could respectably have the two women closest to him out of Boston and under his same roof.[2]

The houseguests jeopardized the safety of the home, however. As minister to Lexington's seven hundred residents, Clarke often heard the latest news and this night it was ominous: Hancock and Adams were the target of an upcoming raid by British soldiers. Quincy felt nervous, as did Clarke, who stationed at least eight men to guard his house. The rumor about kidnapping Hancock and Adams had merit—officials across the Atlantic were growing weary of Boston's leading rebels.[3]

Lord North, prime minister of Great Britain, believed that Hancock and Adams were zealots who only spoke for a small contingent of people, but he wanted to silence them anyway. The prime minister was troubled by Massachusetts's resistance to the Coercive Acts—especially the establishment of the Provincial Congress—and thought that if he could suppress those who he viewed as the vocal minority, he would stymie further trouble. He failed to realize that the resistance had spread far beyond Hancock and Adams. From 3,000 miles away and assured of his plan, Lord North directed General Gage to get his hands on the two men.[4]

Gage did not share the minister's concern and instead wanted to seize and safeguard colonial military supplies, including cannon that had been stolen under British watch and taken to Concord. His approach was more passive: take munitions, not leaders, so colonists could no longer rebel. Gage had tried this tactic—with mixed results—in September 1774 in Cambridge and in February 1775 in Salem. For this next raid, Gage was going to target Concord in the early hours of April 19, 1775.[5]

Colonial networks picked up on the general's plan. Because Lexington was on the road to Concord, some thought British soldiers might capture Hancock and Adams on the way. The leading Patriot who remained in Boston, Joseph Warren, called on Paul Revere to warn the two men that they were in danger. Revere rowed from the North End to Charlestown where he got on a horse. He had not gone far before two British officers charged toward him near a ghastly landmark: "where Mark was hung in chains."[6]

Mark had been enslaved by John Codman, who had died from poisoning in 1755. Mark and his accomplice, Phillis, stood on trial and ultimately confessed to petit treason. Not just murder, but a more serious charge. Under English law, their crime was a form of treason because Codman was Mark's master, so murdering him was akin to killing a king. (A woman in the eighteenth century could also be convicted of petit treason if she killed her husband, her sovereign.) Phillis was burned alive and Mark was hanged and then gibbeted. His body hung suspended in chains near Charlestown Common for over twenty years until it nearly disappeared, from the elements or birds—a reminder to enslaved persons and passersby of the barbarity of the institution.[7]

As Revere dodged his pursuers, Clarke's full house tucked in. Hancock and Adams shared a bed, which was not uncommon at this time — eighteenth-century Americans had different notions of privacy. Sometime around midnight Revere arrived at Clarke's house and demanded that the guards let him speak with Hancock. Clarke leaned out from the second-floor window and told him that they did not want to deal with someone this late at night. Also, could he quiet down? He was making a lot of noise.[8]

Revere exploded. "Noise! You'll have noise soon enough! The regulars are coming out!" The commotion between the messenger and minister woke Hancock, who seemed to recognize Revere's voice. Hancock would have folded the wooden shutters into themselves to open the window and peer out. Seeing Revere's familiar face, Hancock diffused the tense situation. He called, "Come in Revere, we're not afraid of you."[9]

Revere entered the home and likely found Hancock in a state of undress. When lounging at home, gentlemen strove for comfort more than the formality required from their restrictive clothing, including jackets and waistcoats. They removed their wigs — they had shaved heads underneath — and put on lightweight, silk caps. Hancock had a red velvet one that he wore with a linen cap underneath. The headwear would be accompanied by slippers and a silk or damask banyan, a Turkish-inspired robe. Hancock's gown was silk-lined and constructed of blue damask that he wore with red slippers that matched his cap. At that point in the night, the merchant also likely sported a five o'clock shadow — his beard came in easily.[10]

Revere disclosed the plan to the now-awake household: Gage's soldiers were on their way to Lexington — Hancock and Adams needed to flee. The house mostly acted quickly: the Lexington militia was called out and Hancock sent an alarm to nearby Concord. But Hancock did not hasten to leave. His military delusions seized him, and he began polishing his sword. Many witnesses said that the man whose military experience was limited to drilling the Cadets was eager to confront the redcoats. Surely, he did not think he would actually be allowed to go out and muster. Several men had been guarding the Clarke house so someone like Revere could not have access to him, much less British soldiers.

After lots of coaxing, Hancock eventually gave in and fled, but not before crowing, "If I had my musket, I would never turn my back upon these troops." He left in his coach and four with Adams, who did not even pretend to want to go to battle. He believed men could and should endanger themselves, but not men of wealth or status. Adams was not just being elitist here; he was reflecting eighteenth-century ideas about the perceived inherent differences between men who went to Harvard—like Hancock and Adams—and men who were farmers. Farmers could fight; Harvard men thought, philosophized, and created the ideas that spurned other, lower men to fight.[11]

The two men found safe shelter at a friend's house in Woburn, and once settled in, Hancock turned his mind to the salmon that he had left behind in Lexington. He sent his carriage back to fetch it.[12] The Revolutionary War was moments away from beginning, Hancock had fled from hundreds of armed soldiers who were believed to be after him, and he was concerned about his salmon. Salmon!

He was not terribly worried about his loved ones' safety either because he told them "to get into the carriage and come over" to Woburn. With the salmon, of course.[13] Hancock did not seem to grasp, much less appreciate, the gravity of the moment. In fairness, no one did. The outbreak of a battle in Lexington that morning—and the beginning of an eight-year-long war—was a surprise to all.

About 130 men had mustered at Lexington Green around one or two in the morning. These were not professional soldiers gathering, but a body of men who fought temporarily. Because the British troops had not yet arrived, their elected captain dismissed them, but told them to assemble if they heard the drum. Some went off to Buckman Tavern to warm themselves with drink and others meandered home.[14]

Revere, however, stayed busy. After being captured on his way to Concord, redcoats stole Revere's horse and he walked back to Lexington. He had a job to do for Hancock: move some of his most sensitive personal papers. They were stashed in Buckman Tavern and Hancock worried they would fall into enemy hands, so Revere and Hancock's employee, John Lowell, grabbed the trunk of correspondence. While moving it, the redcoats marched toward them. The militia was reassembling at Lexington Green when Revere and Lowell passed through lugging Hancock's trunk. They planned to conceal it inside the Clarke house.[15]

The redcoats arrived and their officer yelled, "Lay down your arms, you rebels, and disperse!" Revere heard a shot and turned to look back, seeing "the smoake in front of the Troops." It's unclear who fired first, but after the shot rang out, the British regulars fired several volleys, all without orders. The Lexington militia retreated.[16]

At the Clarke house, Quincy and Aunt Lydia had been watching the fight—the parsonage had a clear view of Lexington Green. Lydia poked her head outside and some bullets "whizzed by."[17] They came even closer to the action when two wounded men were brought into the Clarke house. In the end, eight colonists died in the bloodshed and seventeen were injured.

The real tragedy of the battle was that it did not need to happen. Hancock and Adams could have remained inside the home and been safe. The British troops were not in Lexington to capture them and had it not been for the alarm, the soldiers would have likely passed right by and gone to fulfill their mission to seize munitions in Concord.[18]

Later that morning, the British troops did continue to march to Concord and had another deadly confrontation with the colonists. Officers decided it would be best to return to Boston, but it would not be an easy trip. Men from over twenty neighboring towns were mobilizing, with more than twenty-one hundred colonists willing to take on the redcoats. The British retreat was a "continual Skirmish

Lydia Hancock.
National Portrait Gallery.

for the Space of Fifteen Miles, receiving Fire from every Hill, Fence, House, Barn, etc." As soldiers were being fired on with minimal opportunities to fire back, their humiliation continued.[19]

Colonists shouted at the retreating redcoats, "King Hancock forever!"[20] The derisive nickname had been appropriated by people in the countryside. As they shot to kill or wound the king's soldiers, the men of Massachusetts were both angry and upbeat, taunting their new enemies with a novel rallying cry.

Hancock may have avoided the fighting, but he still had his fair share of trouble that morning. He was settling in with the "nicely cooked" salmon when a man from Lexington came in and warned him that the British troops were on their way. Everyone jumped up from the table and moved quickly. His hosts wanted to hide Hancock's carriage, which was conspicuously parked in front of their house. The family's enslaved man, Cuff, moved it into the woods while Hancock and Adams fled to the "swamp and staid till the alarm was over."[21]

Once they thought the threat had abated, the two men trudged back to the house, where Hancock had another confrontation waiting for him. Quincy said she would be leaving for Boston tomorrow. Hancock said, "No madam, you shall not return as long as there is a bayonet left in Boston."

"Recollect Mr. Hancock I am not under your control yet. I shall go in to my father to-morrow," she replied.[22]

Boston was a miserable place in the spring of 1775. The harbor remained closed, so fresh food and supplies were scarce. The two thousand occupying soldiers were further dwindling the town's provisions.[23] Quincy returning to Boston would have been a mistake.

Instead, she went with her fiancé to Billerica, a town neighboring Woburn, where they stopped at the home of Amos Wyman. After settling in with many other people—several women and children from neighboring farms had also fled to the Wyman homestead in search of cover—and apprehending they were safe, Hancock and Adams turned to their grumbling stomachs. They had not eaten that day and asked their hostess for a meal.

She provided what she could: boiled salt pork, potatoes, and some brown bread. Served cold on a wooden tray. It would not be the salmon or fine meal Hancock had been thinking about for hours, but it satisfied him. Later, Hancock would send the Wymans a cow as a gift for their hospitality.[24] His long day was over, but the war was just beginning.

———

Despite sitting out the First Continental Congress, Hancock had agreed to attend the second gathering, happening in Philadelphia in the spring of 1775. As he readied to leave for Pennsylvania, he was still shaken by the recent battles and wrote to colleagues in the

Provincial Congress and made suggestions about fortifying and securing Boston but helplessly acknowledged, "You know better
what to do than I can point out." He also wanted intelligence about
the "conduct of the troops, from the 19th instant to this time, that we
may be able to give some account of matters as we proceed, and especially at Philadelphia." Massachusetts was developing a reputation among some colonies for being instigators and Hancock wanted
to share with skeptical congressional delegates any confirmation
that the king's troops fired first.[25]

Hancock got little information back and soon needed to leave with
the other Massachusetts delegates. The preferred way to go south
would have been by sea, cutting the travel time down by several days,
but the Port Bill made such an option an impossibility. If they had to
go by land, riding in a private carriage, especially with John Hancock,
was the most glamorous way to commute. Most women and men in
the eighteenth century walked where they needed to go. Horses were
expensive—both to buy and maintain—and many people could not
afford one. Paul Revere had needed to borrow a horse for his ride to
Lexington.[26]

One of Hancock's carriages survives today and its confined space
seems stifling, even though it represents some of the finest transpor-
tation in colonial America. When ordering his carriages from London,
John's uncle Thomas had demanded that they be better than the sorry
versions that were shipped to his neighbors, James Bowdoin and
Thomas Flucker. The seats should be covered with scarlet cloth, if
that was "most fashionable," and the coach customized with steps to
make it easier for the short-statured Lydia to get in and out. Hancock's
carriages were pulled by four or six horses maintained by liveried servants, some of whom were enslaved.[27]

While the carriage and its attendants belonged to the wealthiest
man in Boston with exacting taste, it would be no way to travel today.
Trekking by land in colonial times—even in a Hancock carriage—was
trying. A coach covered about four to five miles an hour and needed

to stop at regular intervals to change horses. There would also be lay-
overs at taverns for a meal or to sleep. The roads were bumpy and
unreliable—they could be muddy, have unexpected holes, or be
blocked by debris. Benjamin Franklin, who suffered from gout as
Hancock did, found traveling in a carriage extremely painful in his
advanced age because the bumps in the road exacerbated his condition. There were other annoyances: Silas Deane, a delegate from
Connecticut, complained to his wife that the roads were "sandy" on
the way to Philadelphia. He was grateful when "a Rain had laid the
Dust" because it made traveling more pleasant.[28]

The ride had its perks, though: attention. Lots of it. As word of the
Battles of Lexington and Concord spread throughout the colonies,
so did the recognition of Hancock and Adams. For nearly two hundred miles the delegates were escorted by armed guards, greeted by
local militia, and frequently huzzahed by townspeople. When the
group stopped in a town, they were welcomed by its residents and
then dined at a private home or tavern. At night, their lodgings were
under guard.

As the entourage inched closer to New York City, on both his left
side and his right, Hancock saw well-wishers, as many as seven thousand of them. The roads were "fill'd with people," which kicked up
dirt and caused "the greatest Cloud of Dust I ever saw." Hancock's
carriage—"of course being first in the Procession"—was swarmed by
men who wanted to unhook his horses and tow his vehicle a mile into
town. Hancock pleaded with the men not to carry him, "not being
fond of such Parade." He was pleased but had to refuse the men's of-
fers to act as beasts of burden in service of him. Hancock "Beg'd and
Intreated" that they stop, and he had to ask the other delegates to in-
tervene. The crowd eventually acquiesced, but Hancock "was much
Oblig'd to them for their good wishes and opinion."[29]

This reception clearly meant a lot to him—over half of a letter to
Quincy described the scene. This was not just Boston's rebels fawning
over him. It was people from other colonies as well. The crowd had

not offered to carry Samuel Adams into the city. Only Hancock. He summarized the day: "in short no Person could possibly be more Notic'd than myself."[30]

The delegates' arrival to Philadelphia was no less warm, as the people wanted to "Shew their approbation" for Hancock and his work in the Provincial Congress. As the delegates neared the town, they were met by companies of men on foot and on horses, all with swords drawn. People continued to join in the procession, "rolling & gathering like a Snowball." The commotion so startled Silas Deane's horse that he "was in fear of killing several of the spectators."[31]

A wartime spirit pervaded the capital city. Fife and drum sounded every hour and the residents' energy was as high as the Philadelphia temperatures. "A Martial spirit prevails" in town, with many of its male residents preparing for battle—even the usual pacific Quakers were drilling. Hancock must have been relieved to be in a town where none of the people carrying guns were redcoats. At least not yet.[32]

The men from New England found an urban center nearly double the size of Boston and far more adventurous. Philadelphia had a vibrant and permissive sexual culture where casual sex, and subsequent access to treatments for venereal diseases, was not taboo. With about twenty-eight thousand inhabitants, Pennsylvania's capital was the most populous and ethnically diverse town in the North American colonies. Most townspeople lived crammed along the Delaware River in a grid covering about forty blocks, part of Old City today.[33]

With his rising celebrity, Hancock was poised to make a difference. He was a newcomer to Congress, being in the minority of delegates who had not attended the First Continental Congress. One of fifteen rookies, he was in good company. Benjamin Franklin and Thomas Jefferson were also attending for the first time. The Second Continental Congress had an upgraded meeting location: the Pennsylvania State House, known today as Independence Hall. The First Congress had met in the smaller, nearby Carpenter's Hall.

Before it was Independence Hall and had its floors trampled by millions of annual visitors, it housed all three branches of Pennsylvania's government. A brick building completed in 1748, its interior and exterior symmetry are characteristic of the Georgian architecture of the time. One enters the first floor through a wide hall. The Pennsylvania Supreme Court met on one side and the state legislature on the other. It is here where Congress convened. It is a nearly square room, about forty feet by forty feet with wooden floors.[34]

The sixty-five delegates faced the president, Peyton Randolph from Virginia, who sat in front of a table on a raised platform, flanked by two fireplaces of hip-height. Randolph was used to being in charge: he had been president of the First Continental Congress and served in his home colony as president of the Provincial Assembly. But Randolph did not last long. As would be true throughout Congress's existence, delegates had other duties that sometimes summoned them back home. Virginia's royal governor, Lord Dunmore, called the Assembly into session just as the Second Continental Congress was beginning. Because provinces' needs were seen as more important than intercolonial issues, Randolph went home to preside over the legislature.[35]

The delegates changed course by looking to the northern colonies for their new president. The journal of the Second Continental Congress minutes said that after a motion, "John Hancock was unanimously chosen President." Hancock's wealth assuaged conservatives and his reputation for rebelling against imperial policies satisfied the more defiant delegates. He'd also served as president of the Provincial Congress in Massachusetts, the first political body to formally reject British rule. He had safe credentials.[36]

History is often comprised of small, seemingly meaningless moments that can sometimes, when reflecting back, show a path to something much bigger. This was one of those moments. Hancock's appointment passed with very little ceremony or acknowledgment.

But it would be the single most significant event in his career, and it ultimately made him famous.

―――――――

Both the colonists and the crown were stunned by the bloodshed in the Massachusetts countryside and made attempts to reconcile shortly after. In June 1775, Gage issued a proclamation demanding colonists stop war preparations. There was a reward for those who did: "I do hereby in his Majesty's name, offer and promise, his most gracious pardon in all who shall forthwith lay down their arms," but all must "return to the duties of peaceable subjects."

Two men, however, were not eligible for the pardon—John Hancock and Samuel Adams—because their "offences are of too flagitious a nature." Anyone who helped or conspired with them would not be pardoned either because they will be considered "rebels and traitors, and as such to be treated."[37]

Gage's proclamation made its way to Philadelphia and while there is no evidence of Hancock's reaction, we know how Samuel Adams took the news. "Gage has made me respectable by naming me first among those who are to receive no favor from him. I thoroughly despise him and his Proclamation. It is the Subject of Ridicule here." Adams believed that his reputation increased by being named.[38] And he was not a man who enjoyed the spotlight. But Hancock was, so surely he was proud to be identified by Gage. Only two people were excepted and he was one of them. His fame throughout North America was growing.

Gage was not the only person who wanted to reconcile. Many delegates of the Second Continental Congress—led by John Dickinson of Pennsylvania (the "farmer" who wrote pamphlets opposing the Townshend Duties)—urged a moderate approach, even after the king's troops shot men in Lexington and Concord. Congress approved a document of attempted reconciliation known as the Olive

The Second Continental Congress gathered in the Assembly Room of the Pennsylvania State House (Independence Hall). Hancock is seated at the table in the back of the room. Library of Congress.

Branch Petition, which pledged loyalty to the king but also blamed his officials for the violence in the Massachusetts countryside.[39]

No one from New England sat on the drafting committee for the petition, as the memories of British troops firing on their neighbors were still fresh. Nevertheless, every delegate signed the petition, including Hancock, whose ink was darkest, his signature largest, and his penmanship the most distinguished. King George III refused to even look at the petition. Hancock was not surprised—he seemed to expect the monarch's indifference.[40]

Congress sent the Olive Branch Petition asking for peace as it simultaneously prepared for war. And it had a lot of work to do.

Despite the efforts of Hancock and the committee of safety to procure provisions before fighting began, Massachusetts and the other
colonies were not ready for a sustained fight. Hancock explained,
"The unprepared State of the Colonies on the Commencement of
the War, and the almost total Want of every Thing necessary to carry
it on," made readying for war a huge task.[41]

Someone was also needed to command the men fighting and unite
the efforts of several colonies and interests. The congressional records
do not mention the nomination process for a general, but John Adams
did, which is characteristic of him. Adams usually wrote a lot about
many events, but some of his accounts are not trustworthy because
he often seemed to be correcting a not-yet-existent historical record.

According to Adams, many southern colonies were nervous about
naming someone from a northern colony to command an army comprised of men from New England. Southerners worried the region
might eventually try to take over the entire continent. Having the
troops led by someone from the south would balance the effort. John
Adams could not be sure "whether this Jealousy was sincere, or
whether it was mere pride and haughty Ambition, of furnishing a
Southern General to command the northern Army."[42]

George Washington, a delegate from Virginia and a veteran of the
French and Indian War, helped his nomination when he started
wearing his uniform to Congress. Washington wanted the position,
but eighteenth-century men were supposed to act disinterested and
be nominated because they were known to be the best man for the
job. To wear a uniform showed blatant lobbying to become general
and proved that Washington, like Hancock, understood the power of
clothing. John Adams, for one, was convinced: "Coll. Washington appears at Congress in his Uniform and, by his great Experience and
Abilities in military Matters, is of much service to Us." Washington
cared very much about how he appeared to the world and acted with
a purposefulness that bordered on calculated.[43]

Adams claimed that Hancock also "had an Ambition to be appointed Commander in Chief." Adams did not know if Hancock wanted the nomination as a recognition of his status, only so he could turn it down, or whether he would have actually accepted it. If Hancock did want the post, it would have been another time he felt overconfident about taking on enemy soldiers, just as he had in Lexington.

Adams gave Hancock rare credit admitting that "his Exertions, Sacrifices and general Merit in the Cause of his Country, had been incomparably greater than those of Colonel Washington." But if he genuinely wanted the job—not just the chance to reject it—Adams had several concerns, including "the delicacy of his health" and "his entire Want of Experience in actual Service."[44] That did not stop Adams from wanting Hancock to think he was going to nominate him, an event he documented in his diary.

Adams allegedly spoke to Congress about the army in Cambridge and Hancock "heard me with visible pleasure," because he thought Adams was talking about him. But when Adams "came to describe Washington for the Commander, I never remarked a more sudden and sinking Change of Countenance." Adams loved to make others look bad and he continued to describe Hancock's disappointment: "Mortification and resentment were expressed as forcibly as his Face could exhibit them." After Samuel Adams purportedly seconded the motion, "that did not soften the Presidents Phisiognomy at all."[45]

Hancock may have wanted the position, but Adams's notes about the nomination are not corroborated by any delegate or proceeding notes. The only record of the process stated that delegate Thomas Johnson of Maryland nominated Washington. There is no mention of either Adams cousin. The congressional journal noted that the delegates voted by ballot and Washington was "unanimously elected."[46]

Even though he was writing in a diary, ostensibly to record events and feelings from a particular day, Adams inscribed many of these entries later in his life. He wanted to put himself at the center of a decision that led to massive success—Washington's generalship. And while he was rewriting history, he wanted to embarrass Hancock.

He admitted "Mr. Hancock however never loved me so well after this Event as he had done before, and he made me feel at times the Effects of his resentment and of his Jealousy in many Ways and at diverse times, as long as he lived." Adams would not have known about any future resentment in 1775. Years later, Adams told this story to undermine the popular Hancock. He wrote that Hancock even "overacted his part" in being cordial and "professing his regard and respect to me." Hancock likely knew how little John Adams thought of him, as Adams was terrible at hiding his emotions, even when it was a politically or socially prudent thing to do. Hancock was better at being congenial, but the rift between the two would continue to widen in months to come.[47]

Even if he was a little obvious about his desire for the job, Washington was a fine choice for general and was far better suited than Hancock. Washington had actually been in battle and could help unify the war effort. Eliphalet Dyer, a delegate from Connecticut, wrote of Washington, "Tho I dont believe as to his Military, & for real service he knows more than some of ours, but so it removes all jealousies, more firmly Cements the Southern to the Northern."[48] Like many delegates, Dyer understood a regional balance in the military was necessary, even as he found Washington's military credentials unimpressive.

Washington wrote to his wife after his commission was confirmed. He told Martha he had no choice but to accept unless he wanted to bring "dishonour upon myself." Honor was everything to a colonial gentleman. Men needed to be acutely aware of their reputation and any perceived threat to their status. He claimed that "I have used every endeavour in my power to avoid it," but we know that to be untrue. He wore his uniform to the Congress, planting the seed in delegates' minds that he was capable and willing. The legend of Washington sacrificing his own self-interest for the common good begins here with his appointment to the Continental Army and only grew later in his life. A biographer explains, "Things seldom happened accidentally to George Washington, but he managed them with such consummate skill that they often *seemed* to happen accidentally."[49]

Before Washington arrived in Massachusetts to take charge of the army, war resumed on June 17, 1775. The bloodiest battle of the Revolutionary War took place in Charlestown, Massachusetts, across the harbor from Boston. Known today as the Battle of Bunker Hill, the colonists lost control of the hill they had occupied and suffered a devastating casualty, Joseph Warren.[50]

News reached Philadelphia a week later. John Hancock had written to Warren on June 18, 1775, not knowing that he had died the day before. The president begged Warren to send him letters. He never heard enough from the people in his life. "Do write me. We know nothing from our Friends in Boston . . . Yours without Reserve, John Hancock." Warren would not ever write Hancock back. The promising doctor was dead at the age of thirty-four. It was an enormous loss for all of the delegates from Massachusetts. Samuel Adams mourned, "I sincerely lament the Loss of our truly amiable and worthy Friend."[51]

Hancock did more than offer his regrets that Warren had been killed. He wrote to Washington that he was willing to "take the firelock & Join the Ranks as a Volunteer." The general politely declined, claiming he had no post "equal to Col. Hancock['s] Merits & worthy his Acceptance." Even if it was a bit disingenuous, there is an aspect of leadership in Hancock offering his military services. By brandishing his sword in Lexington to take on the redcoats and asking to serve under Washington, he understood the need for soldiers. He would later plead with colonies to send men to fight "in Defence of their Wives, their Children, their Liberty and every Thing they hold dear." Hancock could feel better about such a request—especially when much of the fighting fell to the poor and the young—knowing he, too, had offered his services. Other delegates from Massachusetts made no such offer.[52]

The distance he felt with his friends in Boston also extended to his loved ones. Quincy and Aunt Lydia were in Fairfield, Connecticut staying at the home of Thaddeus Burr, cousin to Aaron Burr. Hancock wrote to his fiancée a lot to check on her, tell her how much he missed her, and most urgently, asking her to write back.

Hancock pled, "use not so much Ceremony & Reservedness, why can't you use freedom in writing, be not afraid of me, I want long Letters." He questioned whether his letters were even read because he never received a reply. Clearly very lonely, he complained, "I have ask'd [a] million questions & not an answer to one." He wrote a few weeks later that "the contemplation of you ever gives me much pleasure."[53] More responsibilities may have been in front of him, but war did not stop Hancock from wanting to feel loved.

Another letter to Quincy included "a few little things in a paper box." Offering gifts was a primary way Hancock showed affection. He wished he could see the clothing on her in person, but "insist[s] you immediately wear all the articles" or send them back. He hoped his presents would be a form of connection for him and Quincy; as such, he took it as an insult if she did not wear the clothes.[54] He was so desperate to feel her affections, but she ignored him.

There may have been something else capturing her attention. Aaron Burr is best remembered as the man who shot and killed Alexander Hamilton in a duel. That Burr killed the leading member of the opposition party while vice president of the United States is extraordinary. His interactions with women are also easy to question. An acquaintance of Burr's said he "acted upon the principle that the female was the weaker sex, and that they were all susceptible of flattery."[55]

Many familiar with the situation in Connecticut thought Burr, who was "generally considered handsome," had grabbed the attention of Quincy while he was visiting his cousin. The two had "animated conversation" and Lydia worried about the relationship developing between the two of them. She never let them be without a chaperone, but that still was not enough—she needed Burr gone. Not wanting her nephew's marital plans interrupted, "it was probably through the aunt's influence that Mr. Aaron Burr's visit came to an abrupt termination."[56]

After delaying marriage for years, Hancock needed to act quickly. Congress adjourned for a five-week recess at the beginning of August. The president left Philadelphia and told Quincy he would ride to Fairfield as speedily as he could because "I am very Desirous of being with you soon."[57]

Hancock and Quincy wed on August 28, 1775. Hancock married a woman who had just a few weeks earlier been interested in another man and who seemed far less in love with him than he was with her. There would have been no lack of suitors for a man as wealthy and prominent as Hancock. But Quincy came from a good family and Hancock appeared eager to finally marry, perhaps after seeing his life unsettled so much with the onset of war.

Hancock's marriage came as a surprise to one man who knew him fairly well. John Adams found it one "of the most unlikely Things, within the whole Congress of Possibility" to "have really, and actually happened." It may have been Hancock's decades-long bachelorhood—or other activity lost to the historical record—that caused John Adams to believe a Hancock marriage might never come to pass. Yet, after years of courtship and romantic prospects, King Hancock had finally found his consort.[58]

Lydia stayed behind in Connecticut, but Hancock brought his new wife back to Philadelphia. Once wed, Quincy's last name became Hancock, and she will now be referred to as Dolly to avoid confusion with her husband, who would open the next session of Congress as a newlywed and the president of a tenuous government. He was on the cusp of the most important moment of his life.

CHAPTER 8

Declaring Independence

When John Adams wrote to his wife, Abigail, in December 1775 and asked her to join him in Philadelphia so that "We will be as happy, as Mr. Hancock and his Lady," he had it wrong. It was just Hancock who was satisfied. The recently married Dolly was frustrated and distraught while away from her home and family. Adams could not see Dolly's distress, though, because she was a woman and he cared little about her thoughts, explaining, "She avoids talking about Politicks. In large and mixed Companies she is totally silent, as a Lady ought to be."[1]

Until the Hancocks were able to move into their own house, the newlyweds had to share a boarding house in Philadelphia with dozens of other delegates. Dolly was the only woman joining a husband, and she had little downtime because she always had to project the image of a proper woman and wife. Adams praised, "Among an hundred Men, almost at this House she lives and behaves with Modesty, Decency, Dignity, and Discretion," but the pressure on Dolly must have been exhausting.[2]

Dolly lived in a patriarchal world where wives were legally and financially dependent on their husbands and lacked the opportunities that men had to express themselves. It was only later in her life—long after Hancock had died—that Dolly publicly shared that she had been very unhappy during her time in Philadelphia. Living there was safer than in Boston, but her circumstances were difficult.[3]

For months, she lacked the type of real connection that was essential in the more isolated, private sphere of women. Aunt Lydia had stayed in Connecticut and Dolly felt little companionship with her husband—a man she seemed lukewarm about and who worked a lot. While Dolly made some new friends among Quakers, they could not match her desire for splendid entertainment. The war also forced an austerity that disappointed her. A ball in honor of Martha Washington had to be canceled because of the optics of hosting an elegant party during these "troublesome times." Fortunately, when Dolly learned she was pregnant in the spring of 1776, her older sister, Katy, came to help, which would have, no doubt, been a comfort.[4]

Dolly also had to assist her husband with his job. She "was busy all the time" toiling long nights to help with the more mundane tasks of his presidency. Hancock signed all important congressional paperwork, including officer commissions, and then his wife took over. She trimmed the edges off the bills of credit that had been issued by Congress and placed them and officers' appointments in saddle bags to be sent to various army stations. It would be long and tedious work for both of them, done by candlelight.[5]

Her husband's spirits, in contrast, were noticeably high upon returning to Philadelphia after his wedding. He had the fellowship of men and meaningful work. In addition to moderating every congressional meeting as president, he was chosen to chair the marine committee and threw himself into the job of setting up a navy. His experience in shipbuilding helped and he was aggressive about constructing vessels. He was also cajoling colonies to raise soldiers to help the military campaign.[6] And when he returned home after such work, he would have been glad to visit with his wife.

Hancock marked the happy transition of becoming a husband with a portrait—two of them, actually. As he had in the past, when he commissioned a painting for himself, he also had one made for someone else. This time, it was of his new bride. He called on Philadelphia artist Charles Willson Peale to paint miniatures of each of them. Hancock's measures a tiny 1.5 inches by 1.2 inches. These were meant to be intimate pieces of jewelry—Hancock could carry around a small picture of his beloved and Dolly had one of him.[7]

While Dolly's likeness by Peale does not survive, Hancock's image is striking. His greenish-gray eyes stare directly at the viewer. Instead of the bobbed wigs from his earlier years, he wears one with rolls over the ears. As usual, his clothing serves a deliberate purpose: it displays his elite status and, thus, his power. His maroon coat is tinged with brown and has gold embroidered details on the lapels

John Hancock miniature
by Charles Willson Peale.
RISD Museum.

and at each of the buttons. A tight, immaculate, lacy cravat covers his neck. His prominent eyebrows anchor his face and the blushed cheeks against his fair skin show a wealthy, vibrant thirty-nine-year-old man.

The vitality shown in the portrait faded within months. As 1775 turned to 1776, his workload became too much—Hancock was toiling "both Day & Night." Congress met six days a week (excepting Sunday) and nearly all delegates worked long hours. These responsibilities increased when other delegates were absent—a problem that frequently plagued the Continental Congress—because more work fell on those present, especially the president. "The great & important Business in which he is constantly Employed and the almost immense number of letters which he is constantly receiving" made Hancock's job especially demanding. Congress had appointed him a private secretary, but even with that help, the responsibilities took a toll on his health, which was sensitive to the stresses of work.[8]

Hancock began to feel "exceedingly ill" with a cold and fever and his gout cropped up again. Gout, considered an affliction of the wealthy because it frequently befell those who ate rich foods and consumed excessive alcohol, would plague Hancock for most of his later life and eventually severely limited his mobility. Benjamin Franklin, a fellow sufferer, imagined a conversation between himself and gout, asking what he had done to deserve such pain. Madam Gout replied, "you have ate and drank too freely," as she chided him for his "insuperable love of ease." Franklin did not walk enough and relied too much on a carriage to get him where he needed to go, Madam Gout explained. The admonishments could have been directed to Hancock, who had an appetite for rich food and madeira.[9]

With sparse downtime to rest and recover, it was no surprise that he was unwell. His "delicate constitution," as John Adams put it, could not handle such rigors. "I have been much hurried . . . very little time to my self," Hancock explained, also complaining that his eyesight had begun to deteriorate. One delegate acknowledged

Hancock's immense job: serving as president of Congress was "abundantly sufficient to employ the time of any one human being."[10]

Over the past twelve months, Hancock's life had been threatened by soldiers as he assumed the presidency of an illegal government. He had fled his hometown and narrowly escaped the opening battles of war. He moved to Philadelphia where he was elected to the highest-ranking political office in North America. He worked around the clock running an ill-prepared government at war. Hancock put it to his friend bluntly, "I think I have suffered enough in the common Cause."[11] Identifying anyone as involved as Hancock in the resistance efforts of the previous decade who also took on such a leadership role in the new government is challenging.

Hancock's daily aggravations were made worse by his old rivals from Massachusetts. General Gage lumping Hancock and Samuel Adams together as traitors ignored the two men's very real ideological differences. The divide grew so much that by the beginning of 1776, both John and Samuel Adams were plotting against Hancock and his allies. They were furious that Hancock was not ready to support colonial independence from the crown, something they were eager to make happen.

For his part, Hancock had decades of proof that being a part of the British Empire was financially lucrative. He had traveled to London the decade before, which deepened his overseas friendships and business connections; he even considered courting the daughter of one of them. Hancock, and affluent men like him, had many incentives to continue to work with London, especially when there was no certainty that independence would protect their significant means. The Adams cousins, in sharp contrast, had far less at stake. At the time, they had never traveled to England, nor was their property anywhere near the value of Hancock's. Rupturing with Great Britain would cost them little.

Hancock was not alone in being hesitant about independence. Other moderates in Congress still had faith that the king would try to find a diplomatic solution to what they thought was a bad miscalculation by him and his advisors. At the beginning of 1776, the people of Massachusetts also did not favor separation. Of the colony's five delegates, three of them wanted to wait on independence, including Hancock's confidant, Thomas Cushing, and Robert Treat Paine. The Adamses were so determined to push through their idea, however, that they managed to have Cushing replaced by Elbridge Gerry, a man who also wanted to formally break from the empire.[12]

"Some here who are not very friendly to you & I," Hancock admitted to Cushing. Hancock knew that the Adamses had schemed to have his friend voted out and assured Cushing that the conspiring would not "pass over unnotic'd." When Cushing returned home to Massachusetts, Hancock wanted details on local politics. "Give me all news, & by every Oppor[tunit]y," he requested. This was one of the few times that he openly acknowledged his political rivals and asked for updates about them. Spare no details, he said, and "Be superior to the Arts and Cunning of Designing Men." In particular, Cushing was to keep his eye on James Warren, who served as the president of the Provincial Congress and was a close friend of Samuel Adams.[13]

Cushing was an able agent. He confirmed Hancock's suspicions about behind-the-scenes plotting. "Soon after I arrived here, I found you, as well as myself, had been placed in a disagreeable light and measures taken to hurt our influence," he explained. He did not need to identify who was behind the attacks, "as you are well acquainted with their names & Characters." Cushing warned of "low, dirty, and sly insinuating arts and machinations" and advised that they both stay on alert.[14]

Installing Gerry did not tip the balance in Congress, and the colonies were no closer to casting off their connection to the mother country. Samuel Adams became antsy, griping, "Every Day's Delay trys my Patience." His growing frustration with Hancock was obvious to others. John Adams acknowledged there was an "Alienation" between the two men. Samuel Adams, harsh and unrelenting, "spoke of [Hancock] with great Asperity, in private Circles."[15]

Unlike Cushing, Hancock was too popular to unseat for his temperate views and he found moderate and conservative allies in Congress. These included John Dickinson and the prosperous merchant Robert Morris — they both hailed from Philadelphia — and Benjamin Harrison from Virginia, who had "courted Mr. Hancock and some others of our Colleagues." If the colonies cut ties with Great Britain, these men of great property had a lot more to lose than John or Samuel Adams. They were reluctant, taking their time, and grasping for other solutions.[16]

Hancock's new friends annoyed John Adams, especially when, as Congress's president, Hancock elevated them. Instead of always playing the role of moderator, Hancock sometimes joined into the congressional debate. Those instances were called a committee of the whole. The president would appoint someone in his place — typically Samuel Ward from Rhode Island, who John Adams described as having a "zealous Attachment to Mr. Samuel Adams." When Cushing was voted out, Hancock replaced Ward with one of his own allies, Benjamin Harrison. John Adams cried foul, considering the substitution "an indolent, luxurious, heavy Gentleman, of no use in Congress."[17]

Harrison was a rotund man with a sense of humor to match his size, even teasing the lithe Elbridge Gerry about the potential repercussion for the treasonous act of declaring independence, something the new representative from Massachusetts had been pushing for. Harrison joked that he had an advantage over Gerry "when we are all hung for what we are now doing. From the weight of my body I shall die in a few minutes, but from the lightness of your body you will dance in the air an hour or two before you are dead."[18] Literal gallows humor.

The Adams cousins' plotting in Congress did little to effect change compared to a popular pamphlet. In January 1776, Thomas Paine, an

English immigrant (and no relation to Robert Treat Paine), published *Common Sense,* in which he rejected the idea of colonial reconciliation with Great Britain. He supported independence from the mother country and a union of the thirteen states. This was a radical proposal, as many colonists were proudly British and had sufficient reverence for royal institutions, even as they disagreed about how to best be ruled under them. Paine also argued that the separation could only be achieved militarily and that the colonies would not succeed without the help of France and Spain. Help from these foreign countries was a big ask, as France, in particular, was a decades-long enemy with deep Catholic roots—something that worried many of the Protestants living in the colonies. Recent military failures in Canada showed that assistance was desperately needed, though, and many colonists enthusiastically embraced Paine's ideas.[19]

The congressional delegates responded in a mixed fashion: some were threatened by the changes Paine called for and others were slow to realize the pamphlet's broad impact. One of the few who mentioned Paine's work was Hancock. He sent Cushing a copy of the pamphlet "which makes much Talk here" with the note that he was enclosing it "for your and Friend's Amusement."[20] Hancock was still reluctant about independence, but events were closing the gap for him.

Parliament's recently passed Prohibitory Act was one provocation. The law allowed the British navy to seize American ships and any property on board. Some colonists referred to it as the "piratical Act, or plundering Act" because of its broad allowances. It essentially amounted to an act of naval war, and many saw it as the last step toward independence. Even the moderate Hancock could see it plainly: "The making all our Vessells lawful Prize don't look like a Reconciliation."[21]

Paine's pamphlet and the Prohibitory Act were not the only factors that moved people closer to independence—it was the king himself. The same day *Common Sense* went on sale, colonists learned that

George III had rejected Congress's Olive Branch Petition and declared the colonies in open rebellion. The conciliation that moderates had so badly hoped for was not happening. The king rebuffed colonial efforts at diplomacy, accusing them of wanting to establish an "independent empire." Independent was the king's word. Paine's word. Not Congress's word or Hancock's. Yet.[22]

While Hancock was in Philadelphia, his hometown drastically changed. Gage's fortifications on the town's neck had been matched by a barricade set up by provincial soldiers. The town was under siege, trapping the redcoats and Loyalists on the small peninsula. Thousands sympathetic with the Patriots fled if they could, leaving nearly all of their possessions. Several hundred others remained in town and competed for scarce resources. Boston was "Shockingly Defaced," as soldiers frequently tore down homes, bridges, and fences—including Hancock's—to use for fuel.[23]

Before he left for Lexington in the spring of 1775, Hancock had appointed a man he sometimes worked with, Isaac Cazneau, to look after his property. Cazneau hid some of the "Best Furniture," packed away the china and glass, and moved Hancock's books and papers from his counting house. Still, Cazneau could not protect everything. Even though Gage and his replacement, General William Howe, had ordered their soldiers not to plunder and steal, the command was never fully obeyed. Hancock's cellar was raided—gallons and gallons of cider and fine wine were gone. Kitchen furniture, a servant's bed and blankets, cords of wood, and a surplus of charcoal were all stolen from his house, as was a "Great Settee" and a backgammon table. The red velvet interior of one of Hancock's carriages "was torn out & carried away."[24]

Hancock's residence was occupied by General Henry Clinton—Howe's second in command. Clinton helped himself to Hancock's property, even summoning Cazneau to the home to show him where he could access more of it. Upon arriving, Cazneau saw Hancock's glassware and china out in the open. The very same ones he had squirreled away. Clinton demanded that Cazneau show him any other "Hiden Treasure" and berated him for concealing it. Another time, Clinton wanted Hancock's personal papers, which he was sure Cazneau stashed behind a locked door.[25]

Much of Hancock's property throughout Boston also suffered. One of his tenements was nearly taken over by "Officers Soldiers and Whores" who damaged the floors and staircases in the building, "to say nothing about Nastiness." Hancock's stable and coach house were repurposed as a hospital. A ship of his was methodically destroyed from the mast to the lower decks. The window shutters from his stores were stolen and the doors and locks removed. A surplus of salt was also swiped, one of the most valuable assets that Hancock lost. A cannon ball went through one house, but miraculously, "not otherwise much damaged." Hancock's name, which had been carved in the cornerstone of Brattle Street Church in recognition of his recent generosity, was "mangled out with an ax" by soldiers.[26]

To liberate the town from British occupation, newly appointed General Washington wanted the Continental Army to attack Boston, a strategy that Congress would have to approve. In Philadelphia, they met as a committee of the whole so Hancock could take part in the discussions. After "serious Debate," Hancock reported that if "a successful attack may be made on the troops in Boston, [Washington] do it in any manner he may think expedient, notwithstanding the town and the property in it may thereby be destroyed." With this resolution, Hancock could lose more than anyone. Despite that, "Mr. Hancock spoke heartily for this Measure."[27]

There is no doubt that Hancock knew what was at stake for the townspeople broadly and him specifically. The home his uncle built four decades earlier could be destroyed and all his possessions gone. Despite this, Hancock hoped for the general's success: "I most heartily wish it, tho' individually I may be the greatest sufferer." Reportedly, Dolly was quite upset when she heard what her husband authorized, but she was powerless to take a stand.[28]

Instead of the sanctioned frontal assault of the town, Washington's team decided to occupy a hill that looked down on Boston, the one-hundred-foot-tall Dorchester Heights. To avoid being spotted, Washington's men transported cannons at night. When morning broke on March 5 — the anniversary of the Boston Massacre — officers in Hancock's upstairs chamber used Uncle Thomas's telescope to see the hills across the harbor occupied with artillery trained down on Boston. Howe considered a frontal attack up Dorchester Heights but ultimately decided against it — the memories of the bloodshed on Bunker Hill still fresh on his mind.[29]

Howe was beat. He told Washington he would retreat and not burn the town down if his troops were allowed to leave safely. Washington agreed. Approximately one thousand Loyalists and the last of the British troops evacuated Boston on the morning of March 17, 1776, never to return. Dorcas Griffiths, the widow Hancock allegedly had a liaison with, was among the departed. Evacuation Day, as it became known, was a triumphant moment for the Patriots and Boston. After fifteen months under siege, Boston would never again be occupied by redcoats.

Back in Philadelphia, Hancock heard that "the Villains have done great damage" to his town, but Washington assured him that his house and its valuable effects were not completely destroyed. Cazneau, however, provided an itemized list of the damages, including the cost of repairs and money for lost rent. It totaled over £4000, a considerable sum. Some items did survive, including Hancock's portraits. "Your & Mr Adams Pictures is safe," Cazneau reported of the Copley paintings.[30]

Hancock had been willing to sacrifice his home in Boston to rid it of redcoats, but he faced another pressing threat in Philadelphia — one that was invisible. The pathogenic enemy of smallpox was devastating the capital city. The disease was so persistent from the summer of 1775 to 1776 that Hancock advised one officer who was marching with his battalion to "avoi[d] Philada. On Acct. of the small Pox." While the fatality rate fluctuated, it could be as high as 30 percent in North American towns.[31]

Delegates to Congress were afraid of catching the virus in the infected town but also afraid of variolation, or inoculation. Inoculation—different than vaccination—was a risky procedure because the patient would have a live virus implanted in their body, and after an incubation period, would develop a (hopefully) milder case of the disease. In addition to pox spreading on your body, a patient could have high fevers and pain. No doubt all patients experienced fear as a side effect, too, because a small percentage died from smallpox after the procedure. If you survived, you were immune for life.[32]

It was a privilege to decide whether or not to be inoculated. Variolation was mostly a procedure for the wealthy: it was too expensive for the lower orders to pay the doctor's fee and sacrifice up to two weeks of work as they recovered.[33] It's not clear when Hancock was inoculated, but by 1776, he and his pregnant wife most definitely felt immune to the danger. He kindly invited people to stay with him during their inoculations and recoveries, which would expose his house to the virus. He would not have done so if he had not felt protected.

General Washington and his wife were traveling to Philadelphia after the evacuation of Boston, and Hancock—no doubt eager to thank the general for preventing the total ruin of his hometown—invited both to stay in his house. Washington had smallpox when he was a young man visiting Barbados, so he possessed lifelong immunity, but Martha, "not having had the Small Pox," intended to be inoculated in the city. Hancock promised Washington that he and Dolly would go to all lengths to ensure they had a comfortable stay. He graciously offered "free use of my house, it is large & very Commodious." The Hancocks were living in a house with many amenities

Arch Street in Philadelphia in 1799. Hancock stayed on the same block
as the church with the slender steeple.
Library Company of Philadelphia.

and a block away from Benjamin Franklin "in an airy, open Part of
the City."[34]

Washington was cool in his reply, as usual. He talked mostly about
military business and concluded "with particular thanks to you for
the politeness of your Invitation to your House."[35] He neither accepted nor denied the offer.

The evasion only encouraged Hancock, who obsequiously reiterated the desire to host him and his wife. "Mrs Hancock will esteem
it an Honour to have Mrs Washington inoculated in her House . . . I
flatter myself she will be as well attended in my Family." In addition

to Dolly caring for Martha, the Hancocks' team of servants in Philadelphia would also help. "It will be entirely in your Power to live in
that Manner you should wish," he promised. A man as wealthy as
Washington was used to being waited on, Hancock knew. "In short,
Sir, I must take the Freedom to repeat my Wish that you would be
pleased to condescend to dwell under my Roof," Hancock pled.[36]

His entreaty was ignored. Neither Washington nor his wife would
stay with Hancock.[37] It was not the first time that Washington denied
an offer from Hancock—to serve under his command months earlier
was the first—and it would not be the last. But Hancock continued
to extend hospitality.

"I have a Bed for you," was his motto for friends and rivals. He also
volunteered his home in Boston to the family of John Adams, a man
who was actively insulting and working against him. Hancock heard
that Abigail and her children were traveling to Boston to be inoculated and suggested they make use of his house, the fruit in his garden,
and his servants. They instead stayed at a friend's during the procedure
and recovery, a time when Abigail blithely went out in public despite
being highly infectious.[38]

Some would accept Hancock's offer. That summer, a minister was
inoculated at Hancock's residence and convalesced there. Dolly's
sister, Katy, also underwent the procedure and had a more severe
breakout of pox, but she recovered well. Hancock's commitment to
combatting smallpox continued for another decade. Later, he would
pay for other family members and servants to be inoculated and recover at a Boston hospital created specifically for that purpose.[39]

If he could not host the Washingtons, Hancock was determined to
show his affection in another way: a portrait. Hancock called on Peale
again. Washington accepted this gift, and the artist depicted the general against a backdrop of tattered Boston, a symbol of his recent victory over the British troops.[40] Hancock was consistently openhearted
with his peers, even those who treated him coldly. He made them

feel welcome and appreciated, but he wanted attention and connection in return, which some, like Washington, never gave.

———————

Amidst the constant stress of work, Hancock suffered another blow.
In April 1776, Aunt Lydia passed away suddenly. "I am greatly
Distress'd," the nephew wrote to a friend about his primary nurturer
and supporter. Lydia's death impacted many people beyond Hancock,
whose assets would grow considerably. Her will had been made out
in 1765—the year after her husband died—and she gave nearly the
entire estate to her nephew, including the mansion on Beacon Hill
and all of its furnishings.[41]

Lydia also "manumit and sett free" the enslaved women and men
she purported to own. Like her husband's freeing of Cato at age thirty
only if he behaved himself, Lydia had contingencies, too. Such pro-
visional freedom was not uncommon. Violet, a "Negro Girl," was not
to be freed until the age of twenty-one, provided that she comported
herself in a way pleasing to her new enslaver. Upon manumission, she
was to be given a small sum of money and furniture for a room. An
older woman, Agnis, was to wait a year after Lydia's passing to be freed.
Hannibal was to be manumitted without a waiting period and given
a bit of money, as was Cato.[42]

Since Lydia's will was written eleven years before she died, it may
be that Violet and Cato had reached their age of freedom by the time
she died in 1776. No matter what, Agnis had to serve another year
under Hancock, as her term length was defined by the death of Lydia.
Perhaps Violet and Hannibal ended all connections to the Hancocks
after being freed, but Cato, like other freed slaves in Boston, worked
for his former master as a paid servant for at least another decade. This
probably had less to do with Hancock being fair or compassionate,
and more about racism making it difficult for former slaves to find
good work.[43]

Manumission could have a dark side because some slaveowners freed slaves past their prime working years to avoid paying for their care in old age. To stop this practice, Massachusetts passed a law at the turn of the eighteenth century that required slaveowners who freed slaves to also put up a bond to the town. The fee was hefty and out of the range of many. Lydia knew the rules and directed Hancock, as executor, "to give such Security to the Town of Boston as the Law requires upon the Manumission of Negroes."[44]

By manumitting her slaves, Lydia shared a mindset with other New Englanders who thought of black servitude as finite, even as they bequeathed slaves in their wills. She had inherited slaves from her husband, but decided that the lifelong servitude stopped with her. Slaveholders often thought of their legacy as they drafted their wills and wanted to seem benevolent. Yet, by liberating slaves after her death, Lydia was implicitly acknowledging that they wanted to be free.[45]

Hancock also knew firsthand that enslaved women and men sought freedom. Between 1773 and 1777, Black Bostonians, both free and enslaved, filed four petitions for emancipation directed to the House of Representatives and the governors of Massachusetts. One directly called out men like Hancock: "We expect great things from men who have made such a noble stand against the designs of their fellow-men to enslave them." Enslaved men and women understood the changing political landscape and used the same language of their oppressors. Hancock was a member of the House when three of these petitions were filed and he sat on a committee to consider two of them. The legislature ultimately passed a bill to ban the slave trade, but it died with Governor Hutchinson.[46]

As never before in the colonies, the American Revolution brought public criticism about the immorality of slavery. In Hancock's circle, James Otis; Josiah Quincy, a cousin of Dolly's; and Abigail Adams recognized the incongruence of fighting for liberty while enslaving people. "It allways appeard a most iniquitious Scheme to me-fight ourselfs for what we are daily robbing and plundering from those who have as good a right to freedom as we have," Adams wrote. Those in London saw it too. An English writer famously asked, "How is that we hear the loudest yelps for liberty among the drivers of negroes?"[47]

Lydia and her nephew needed to reconcile the cognitive dissonance of considering themselves caring masters who eventually freed slaves with the reality of enslaving people they knew did not want to be. Hancock was often tentative on matters of principle, and this was no exception. To justify enslaving people, he and his aunt, like others, considered slaveholding to be protective and acceptable because it was part of the social order. They lived in a hierarchical world with few completely independent people, and those who had such status, were usually white men. Dolly knew this as a recent wife, children felt it with their parents, and apprentices with their masters. But no one sat at the bottom of the social order more than enslaved Black persons. Black women had it worse because they were considered twice inferior, owing to their skin color and their sex.[48]

One Black woman, however, forced Hancock to recognize her intellect. In 1761, a girl around seven years of age was brought from Africa to Boston and purchased by John and Susannah Wheatley. They called her Phillis and taught her to read and write in English. She was a quick study and began composing poetry, including a piece on the repeal of the Stamp Act and the death of eleven-year-old Christopher Seider at the hands of a customs official. She called the boy a "young champion." Wheatley was politically savvy, writing about the same issues that dominated the political sphere of Hancock and others like him.[49]

She compiled a book of poems that she wanted to get published. Skeptics, rooted in an ideology of Black inferiority, required that white men attest that she was the true author of the poems. Hancock was one of those who signed his name, sanctioning that Wheatley's works were her own. Her volume was published in London in 1773, making her the first female African American to publish a book of poems. The front of the book included the attestation from Hancock and other prominent men from Boston, including then-governor Thomas Hutchinson and lieutenant governor Andrew Oliver, and Samuel Cooper, Hancock's minister and the man who baptized Wheatley.[50]

While Black women and men in British North America fought for complete independence, many white men clamored for political independence. By early June 1776, John and Samuel Adams were anxious because separation did not have more support among delegates. Samuel Adams wrote, "You know my Temper. Perhaps I may be too impatient."[51] Fortunately for him, his friend and ally Richard Henry Lee put forward a resolution for independence on June 7 and forced a debate on the matter.

One reason to declare independence would be to gain crucial allies. Recent military failures in Canada showed that the colonies could not win a war without the help of European powers. The colonies were simply not equipped to withstand a long conflict against the most powerful army and navy in the world. The declaration was less about a break from England, and more of an impassioned plea to France and Spain for help.[52]

Motivated by their devastating loss in the French and Indian War the decade before, and wanting to support the enemy of their enemy, both European powers had been sending arms and financial aid since before the fighting began in Lexington in 1775. Americans now wanted a more formal alliance and needed to officially break with the British Empire to get it. They had to show they were serious about becoming their own nation, not just seeking changes within the colonial system.[53]

On July 1, the day the debates about independence began in Congress, Hancock joined the committee as a whole and his friend, Harrison, stepped in to moderate. At the end of a tense day, nine colonies—including Massachusetts—favored independence. That was enough to move forward, yet Congress wanted all thirteen to agree so the decision seemed unified. The discussion continued the following day, when twelve colonies supported the measure. New

York—whose largest city had many inhabitants fiercely loyal to the monarchy—abstained. The motion went forward without them. The next two days were spent changing the language, which hurt the feelings of the author, Thomas Jefferson, but the document was finally confirmed on July 4.[54]

Hancock authorized the declaration with his signature and little fanfare. But he understood its import, calling it "the Ground & Foundation of a future Government." Initially, his whole heart had not been behind the idea of independence, but he went along, as did most other moderates who had opposed the measure but eventually signed. Independence had not been possible without them.[55]

July 1776 was a turning point in Hancock's political life. Once he endorsed independence, he went all in on the Patriot cause. His temperament was still inclined to moderation, which would help the war effort and the new nation, but he could no longer be considered indifferent or wishy-washy to the Revolution. And he was optimistic about the future. Hancock sent a copy of the declaration to a friend, confident that it would lead to Americans as "a free and happy people, totally unfetter'd and Releas'd from the Bonds of Slavery."[56]

We know that declaring independence did not make all people equal, or free everyone from slavery, but it did lead to a critical ally. France's military would not arrive in time to stop British troops from coming dangerously close to Philadelphia in late 1776, however. Hancock and his family would soon be fleeing British soldiers for the second time in two years.

CHAPTER 9

The Art of Popularity

In late 1776, Hancock found his circumstances "really distressing." General Howe and his troops were moving closer to Philadelphia and Congress wanted to relocate operations a hundred miles south to Baltimore. Hancock was concerned about the move because his wife had just given birth; his daughter, Lydia Henchman Hancock, named for his beloved aunt, was born in November 1776. At nearly forty years of age, Hancock was a first-time father. But just a month later, because of his duties as Congress's president, his family would have to travel with "a little Infant just Breath'd in the World." They would be on crowded roads with loads of clothing, papers, and "considerable Effects."[1]

Baltimore may not have had soldiers nearby, but it was still an uncomfortable place to stay. One congressional delegate called the town of about five thousand people "the Damdest Hole in the World." Over the past thirty years, the town had grown quickly from an outpost of about two hundred people and its infrastructure had not kept up. It lacked the proper accommodations for such distinguished visitors. Delegates maligned the town as "infinitely the most dirty Place I was ever in." The roads were muddy and the water was brackish.

Worse still: "there is not even a Tavern that we can Ride to for Exercise and amusement within 15 miles of the Place."[2]

Delegates' dissatisfaction grew when they saw the prices in the ill-prepared town. Say what you will about their water and roads, but Baltimore's townspeople understood basic laws of supply and demand. Renting a horse was expensive and "every article of provision-cloathing and the common conveniences of life are 100 percent higher in this place than in Philadelphia," one complained. Most delegates stayed at boarding houses that were "an infinite Expence."[3]

Hancock, however, "keeps an House by himself," but he was not living in luxury. When he, his family, and his servants had first arrived in town, they stayed with a local merchant for ten days and "were Treated by him & his Lady with the utmost Civility." That warm hospitality ended when Hancock set up his own residence. He moved into a house: "the only one I could get, in a Remote place among Whores & Thieves." The dwelling was small, overpriced, and had "just Furniture sufficient to live tolerably decent." He was not exaggerating about being among thieves: within two days of being in this new residence, the Hancocks were robbed.[4]

Hancock had another unexpected visitor in Baltimore. Stephen Hall was a tutor at Harvard College and had been sent to collect property, including papers and notes, that belonged to the school. In 1773, Harvard had asked Hancock to be its treasurer and he had grossly neglected his duties. Despite the college's president imploring Hancock not to risk the college's money and records by bringing them to the Continental Congress, Hancock did. He returned most of the money to Hall—the entire balance would not be collected until after Hancock's death—but Hancock had failed to send the tutor home with the one thing Harvard wanted most: his resignation. His pride got in the way of admitting the job was too much for him at this time. After making many attempts with Hancock, Harvard was forced to elect another treasurer months later.[5]

After three stressful months of meeting in the marsh masquer-
ading as a town, Congress decided it was safe to return to Philadelphia. Hancock called on one of his new friends to help. Robert
Morris was a merchant and the wealthiest man in Philadelphia—he
and Hancock shared privilege and moderate political views. Morris
would draw criticism during the war because his wealth grew through
profiteering so much that he accumulated the largest fortune in the
United States.[6] Nevertheless, Morris was one of the few people Hancock trusted.

The friendship blossomed through their letters. Hancock hoped
they could talk not "only in the Commercial & publick Line, but in
a solid, friendly & free intercourse." Hancock really appreciated his
new confidant, especially because Morris could procure smaller items
for him that he could not find in Baltimore, including writing paper,
sealing wax, and quills, and could act as his liaison in Philadelphia.
Hancock had sent someone else to scout out a "suitable house well
furnish'd" for him—he wanted to avoid a repeat of his dismal lodging
in Baltimore—and asked Morris to accompany him in case a second
opinion was needed. Hancock was grateful and informed Morris "that
hereafter I shall take the Liberty of a Friend" and "shall be ambitious
of being Reckoned among the list of your Real Friends."[7]

The anticipation of the two men reuniting in Philadelphia excited the convivial Hancock, who wanted them to drink, eat, and socialize together—some of his favorite things. He hoped "to Take you
by the hand; my Friend, it will give me pleasure to see you." Friendships between men in the eighteenth century were often emotionally
intense and could be expressed physically, including by holding
hands. While some male confidants became sexually intimate, it was
not unusual for men to express love and affection without any erotic
undertones. Morris was equally looking forward to Hancock's arrival: "I hope soon to take you by the hand & pass that social hour
that gives an honest soul more real joy."[8]

Despite his promise to help, the Hancocks' move from Baltimore was delayed when Morris could not provide wagons on time. Annoyed with Morris for not securing provisions, Hancock set off without Dolly and baby Lydia, traveling "Thro' much bad Road" and "Cutting thro' the Ice" to cross the Susquehanna River. He mostly stayed in decent taverns or boarding houses, which was anything but certain in colonial America where the quality of taverns varied considerably. Lodging in a tavern overnight got you a meal and Hancock filled himself. "Boil'd Beef, Roast Turkey, Ham, Roast Beef, Green Sallad, Goose Berry & Apple Tarts, Cheese, Apples &c. Baltime Punch, Wine &c.," were among his choices. There was one problem, though: "The Turkey was so tough that I broke out one of my Teeth."[9]

If an affluent person lost a tooth in the eighteenth century, it could be replaced with ivory, human teeth, or bones, which were held together by wires connected to neighboring teeth. Still, the replacement would not be a perfect match in size, shape, or color. It would be jarring for us in the twenty-first century to see the revolutionary leaders smile because their mangled teeth would not match the formality of their wigs and fine clothing. Washington's teeth troubles are well known—he had just one surviving original tooth when he became president and had to rely on dentures made from ivory, human teeth, hippopotamus tusks, and reshaped cow and horse teeth.[10]

With one fewer tooth for the time being, Hancock continued his travels when his luck with boarding houses ran out. He had to sleep "in the common Room" with other men, instead of having a bed of his own, which went to a husband and wife. Shared accommodations among men were not uncommon—even for elites who could pay for a private bed—because country taverns often lacked space. He joked with Dolly that if she were with him, "I should be better off. I am sure in point of Beds I should." He longed for his wife, and not just so he could get better sleeping arrangements. He admitted that in spite of the company of people around him, "I however lead a doleful lonesome life."[11]

Dolly and Lydia would soon join him in Philadelphia, which energized Hancock. He prepared his wife for the travels, including warning her about Howe's troops, seedy boarding houses, and smallpox. The unpredictability and violence of war was always lurking for the Hancocks at this time. There was also a question about where young Lydia would be inoculated. Hancock decided it would happen as soon as they arrived in Philadelphia, so as not to slow their leaving Baltimore. Clearly missing Lydia and showing affection in the way he knew how, he sent his daughter a sash but was not yet able to get his hands on "a gold or silver rattle."[12]

Before departing, Hancock wanted Dolly to offer gifts to those who had showed them kindness in Baltimore—he reminded her in two separate letters about it. And if she should encounter someone helpful on the road, "order a handsome Dinner and I beg you will pay every Expence." She was not to accept money in exchange. Among white women and men, Hancock moved through the world generously and expected his wife to do the same. Also important for the gourmand, Dolly was to pack up the house, buy some parsnips to carry with her, and bring "all the wine, none to be got here." He asked her to keep him apprised of their progress, leaving "Pen, Ink & Paper sufficient; if not, purchase at any price."[13]

For a man who had been very slow to get married, he took to family life and found comfort in the domestic world. It warded off some of his loneliness, especially after the death of his aunt less than a year before. In every letter, Hancock asks about his firstborn, imploring Dolly to "Take precious care of our dear little Lydia." He looked forward to reuniting with his family and promised his wife, "I shall have Fires made & everything ready for yor Reception."[14] This tenderness and care makes the events of the summer all the more heartbreaking.

The beginning of August was brutally hot in Philadelphia, with a heat wave lasting two weeks. "The Air of the City has been like the fierce Breath of a hot oven" and people rushed to the town's water pumps to relieve themselves. Even in the shade, one could not escape the heat. John Adams complained that the weather "exhausts my Spirits, and takes away all of my Strength of Mind and Body."[15]

The spirits in the Hancock house were also exhausted—not from high temperatures, but from tragedy. Hancock's first and only child, Lydia, had died. There is some indication that the child was not doing well in Baltimore, as a doctor had attended her there. Once she and Dolly were back in Philadelphia, Hancock sent for another doctor. A woman staying above the Hancocks also helped them care for the infant, but these efforts could not save her. The exact date and cause is unknown, but by August, she had passed away. Both of Hancock's beloved Lydias—his firstborn daughter and his adoptive mother—had been taken from him within seventeen months. The grief would have been total.[16]

Hancock reached out to a leading cabinet maker in Philadelphia, David Evans, and asked for the saddest of orders: "a Mohogany Coffin 2 foot 6 inch Long." He also commissioned artist Charles Wilson Peale, who had painted him, Dolly, and Washington the year before, to create a posthumous miniature of Lydia. When Peale painted dead or dying children, he relied on the portraits or features of their parents. This technique is obvious when seeing Lydia, who appears like a young version of her father. She has the same grey eyes and similar nose and lips. She is wearing a purple sash, which may have been the gift from Hancock. In the background, Peale painted a weeping willow and urn, common mourning symbols. This miniature would serve as a memorial for their child whose life was cut short.[17]

After a difficult move to and from Baltimore and with the memories of her daughter hanging thick in the stagnant Philadelphia air, Dolly went back to Boston. Hancock did not know it then, but his wife was pregnant with another child, so it was best for her to be at home. He, however, had to remain stoic and continue his duties as president, all as troops lurked nearby.

Philadelphia felt so vulnerable to attack in the summer and fall of 1777 that Hancock resorted to sleeping with his clothes on in case he

Lydia Hancock miniature
by Charles Willson Peale.
RISD Museum.

needed to flee. "The Enemy are within 26 or 30 miles of us," he worried. The uncertainty of Howe's location put the town in a constant
state of anxiety with "Alarms began & continued Day & night."[18] It
was enough to shred a man's already frayed nerves.

In the middle of one night, an express letter from Washington arrived for Hancock advising that Congress evacuate Philadelphia. It
was not the first time a messenger had interrupted Hancock in the
darkest hour of night and told him to flee — Revere had done that two
years earlier. His past experience and being already dressed helped
him to act quickly. He raised the alarm for the rest of the town and
then "Rous'd the Members," who were staying in boarding houses
throughout town.[19]

Hancock then "fix'd my Packages, Papers, &c in the Waggons and
Sent them off, about 3 oClock in the morning I Set off myself." The

roads were filled hundreds of other fleeing civilians—children wailed, women scattered, and wagons rattled against an undercurrent of terror. The delegates hustled westward and eventually settled in York, Pennsylvania, while Howe and his troops took over Philadelphia shortly after. In contrast to Baltimore, York was "pleasant enough," but the workload was exhausting.[20]

Congress had set a new schedule with two sessions a day. A bell called them to convene at ten in the morning and they met until one. Hancock took his midday meal at a tavern before the second session began at four and continued until nine in the evenings, "which is too much." His only private moments came in the evening when he also had to attend to presidential matters. "I cannot stand it much longer in this way," Hancock assessed.[21]

The constant work was no way for someone predisposed to sickness to live. Not surprisingly, he started to feel unwell. Before leaving Philadelphia, Hancock had gone riding in the rain, which gave him "a Touch of the Cholick" and caused him considerable worry. In addition, his gout had returned—"my old disorder"—and he frequently wrote to Dolly complaining that he was exhausted or ill. His body was feeling the effects of three arduous moves in the middle of a war, the death of his only child, his wife's departure, and seemingly unending work.[22]

Hancock hoped his wife might comfort him during this trying time. He never lost hope that she would write despite her past epistolary silence. He promised that for every letter she wrote him he would write a letter back. This proposal for equal correspondence did not sway Dolly: within two weeks he chided her for not sending "a single word . . . I expected oftener to have been the object of your attention."[23] They were both mourning the loss of their first child, but Dolly did not find solace in or share her grief with her husband.

Hancock found other ways to console himself. Ever the epicurean, Hancock turned to food and wine. He asked Dolly to procure an item he did not have access to that he craved: pickles. In two separate letters, Hancock mentioned pickles to his wife and hoped she would send some to him—a request she ignored. Hancock's "hope to get them" drove him to send someone else to buy them. He also asked Dolly about cherries, hoping that she'd "feasted on them" and wished he could have some of his own.[24]

To get wine, he turned to his friend Robert Morris, who remained behind in Philadelphia when Congress moved to York. Hancock did not want to deplete Morris's stock, but asked if he could "spare me a little Madeira." Hancock connected with people by hosting, so he said he would take the wine at any price. This was a risky offer given Morris's shrewd ability to profit during wartime shortages, but the president confided, "I feel awkward not to have it in my power to ask a friend to take a Glass."[25] For most of his life, Hancock had been able to host people and treat them to alcohol. War should not stop that.

On the morning of the Battles of Lexington and Concord, Hancock had been concerned about salmon. Two years later, in the midst of severe wartime shortages—the Continental troops were just a few months away from the devastating hunger and cold of Valley Forge—the president was worried about nonessential provisions. It showed his privilege and desire for some normalcy. He was consoled by food and hospitality during war, but they would not be enough to keep him going.

———————

"My constant application to Publick Business both in & out of Congress, has so impair'd my Health, that some Relaxation has become absolutely necessary," Hancock wrote to Thomas Jefferson in the fall of 1777. Hancock had been going so hard for so long as president that he finally hit a wall. "I am wore down," he explained. He announced to Congress in October that he was returning to Boston for a time to tend his health and "my own Private Affairs." Hancock did not know it, but he was leaving the highest political office in which he would ever serve.[26]

Hancock departed right before two monumental events for the nascent United States. The first was the news of General John Burgoyne's surrender in Saratoga. Supplied with arms and ammunition from the French, the Continental Army overpowered British forces. Burgoyne's defeat was so devastating that Hancock used the officer's name as a synonym for a sound thrashing. "If we can Burgoyne this Army it will be a fine Affair," he wrote months after Saratoga. After this decisive victory, France decided to formally help the war effort, even as Spain remained reluctant. No longer would France simply provide supplies; they were also going to send troops and their navy.[27] Hancock would come to play a key role in nurturing this tenuous alliance.

The departing president would also miss Congress finalizing the Articles of Confederation. The effort to write them began in the summer of 1776 and Hancock moderated many discussions and disputes about representation and how the states would vote. He boasted, "The Confederation will soon be Ratified, & a new Congress will bring on the Conclusion of my Plan." He felt no need to stay an extra two weeks to see it finalized—he was that eager to leave—but it was meaningful to finally have a document to send to states for review.[28]

Eight states approved the Articles in July 1778, but the unanimous approval of all thirteen states would not happen for another three and a half years, in March 1781. That the Articles took so long to be written and then ratified should have been (and was for some) a signal that the thirteen states would have a difficult time uniting under a central government.

On his last day in Congress, Hancock gave a farewell speech thanking his fellow delegates for their kindness and expressing hope that he had done his job well. A delegate from New York motioned for Congress to give formal thanks to Hancock for his service, but another delegate moved that "it is improper to thank any president for the discharge of the duties of that office."[29] Two votes were taken on the matter and ultimately, one more state voted to thank Hancock than to not. He received a cursory note a couple weeks later.

His fellow delegates from Massachusetts—Samuel Adams, John Adams, Elbridge Gerry, and Samuel Lovell—had all voted against thanking him. Samuel Adams was annoyed because no other president had "made a parting Speech or receivd the Thanks of Congress" and claimed that such a gesture was "unprecedented, impolitick, dangerous." It was not unusual for Congress to offer thanks, though, as Adams alleged. Twice in one year Washington received appreciation for his "distinguished exertions," and Benedict Arnold was also offered thanks from Congress. Denying him any gratitude showed the tension some in Massachusetts still felt toward the popular Hancock and the pettiness of those politicians.[30]

With the president's resignation settled, Hancock needed the help of Washington to travel comfortably back to Boston. He told the general that the journey home may be risky "passing thro' some Tory Towns," and asked him to provide an escort. Washington recommended Hancock avoid travel at this time, but if he insisted on leaving, the general would supply a guard. Except Washington could spare few horses or men because of the war, so Hancock must excuse "the escort being so small." Washington sent a dozen dragoons—mounted infantry—and an officer.[31]

If Samuel Adams had not wanted to thank Hancock for his service as president, he certainly did not want him escorted back to Massachusetts. "I have not seen nor heard of any Dangers on the Road that should require Guards to protect one," he sniped. He felt Hancock wanted the attendants just to get the attention of "honest Country Folks" who responded to such a display with "gapeing and staring." Another observer scoffed, "I verily believe that the President, as he passes through the Country thus escorted, feels a more triumphant Satisfaction than the Col. of the Queen's Light Dragoons attended by his whole Army and an Escort of a thousand Militia."[32]

John Adams also did not approve, especially when he heard that members of Hancock's escort had not paid their bills on the road. A story came to him about Loyalists who had been kicked out of taverns after speaking ill of Hancock. They "now scoff at the [taverners] for being imposed upon by their King, as they call him." The tavern keepers had defended King Hancock—their regal leader—but his traveling party had allegedly cheated them.[33]

The military resources may have been better allocated elsewhere, but Hancock understood that grandeur and ceremony connected people to their leaders. He had witnessed that in London in 1760. His travel, like his clothing, communicated social authority in a way that words could not. His enemies mocked and loathed him for his supposed frivolity—fashion was often derided as feminine, insignificant, or trivial—but Hancock knew that appearance mattered. Traveling from Pennsylvania to Massachusetts in such a visible way would further boost Hancock's national profile. The Adamses and their allies, though, had not yet recognized the importance of courting public opinion. They could not see what was clear to an enemy officer: a public image must be cultivated. He said of Hancock, "he who desires to advance in popularity must understand the art of making himself popular."[34]

Hancock made a triumphant return to Boston—cannon fired, bells rang, and a militia company mustered to meet him. Rival James Warren—the man who had helped oust Hancock's friend Thomas Cushing from Congress—was unimpressed and scoffed that Hancock travels with "the Pomp and retinue of an Eastern Prince." An alternate perspective of Hancock's entourage came from a prisoner of the Continental Army, who would have been more inclined to hate Hancock than Warren. He said that Hancock's reception that day showed him "worthy of the position he holds as the first man in America."[35] Just as the British officer understood Hancock's appeal more than Warren and the Adamses, so, too, did the enemy prisoner.

Even though Hancock had told Congress he was taking a "leave of absence for two months," he was in no rush to return. He needed to get used to the changes at home. His family's mansion had been occupied and abused by General Clinton and it was devastatingly empty without Aunt Lydia. That is, until a joyful new addition arrived: Hancock and Dolly welcomed their first son in May 1778. Expectedly, they named him John, like the three first-born Hancock sons before him. His middle names were an homage to a man his father admired, the general of the Continental Army.[36]

Once he felt that Dolly and John George Washington Hancock were well, Hancock returned to Congress, but he would soon find that the job was not worth leaving his family. Hancock would not serve as president because his replacement, Henry Laurens, did not accede the position back. Hancock saw the insignificance of simply being a delegate in Congress, which had a problem with especially spotty attendance over the past year. Some states sent no representatives at all. Given the delegates' lack of commitment, Hancock's devoted service as president for two years and five months stands out. He was the longest-serving president of the Continental Congress.[37]

As a delegate, though, Hancock was bored with the work and worried about being away from his family, especially "little John." His anxiety is understandable given his daughter Lydia had not made it a year. He was concerned, too, about Dolly's health. He sent visitors to be with her, encouraged her to ride horses to help her feel better, advised her to keep a nurse to attend her, and "pray her to take great care of the little fellow."[38]

When Dolly did not respond, Hancock threatened that his health would suffer if she did not write back. He even offered to pay for news. "I would have hir'd any one to have sent a few Lines just to let me know the State of your health." Hancock counted the number of letters he sent while receiving nothing from her. "It really is not kind, when you must be sensible that I must have been very anxious about you & the little one. Devote a little time to write me," Hancock pled. Dolly sought no consolation from her husband when their first child passed away and she seemed content to be away from him when their son was born.[39]

Hancock decided to leave Congress because to stay "would prejudice my health exceedingly." Before he left, the war required that he move one more time. Congress relocated back to Philadelphia in June 1778 after Howe and his soldiers evacuated. Hancock found the town stifling hot and filled with "an amazing Quantity of Flies," so much so that "there is no Eating or drinking without their Company." The flies probably came from the direction of the State House. Howe and his men had used it as a hospital and military executions had taken place behind it. Adding to the macabre scene, soldiers had dug a pit nearby where they put the dead bodies of horses and men.[40]

Hancock had one thing to look forward to in Philadelphia—he was on a committee to plan the anniversary of independence, fitting for the first man to sanction it and a consummate host. The festivities took place at City Tavern, a two-story brick building that opened in 1773 and was one of the town's most popular taverns. The second floor was the best place to entertain because there was more space. Windows looked out over Second Street, bringing in the summer sunlight, which made the narrow room feel bigger. Hancock may have chosen to have the men gather in a nearby room and then, after conversation, draw a curtain to have the guests view the elegantly arranged food. John Adams attended a party at City Tavern that had such a presentation and he had been impressed.[41]

Party goers saw two tables extending the length of the room flanked by two additional tables set at right angles. About eighty men crowded in for an "elegant and well conducted" event. At the head of the table, there was a large, baked pudding decorated with symbolic images, including a man holding "the Declaration of Independency." Eighteenth-century desserts were ornately decorated and arranged so they could be displayed and leave an impression with guests. As people enjoyed the midday meal, an orchestra played clarinets, French horns, violins, and instruments resembling oboes and violas.

After eating, thirteen toasts rang out to the United States of America and the friendly European powers. Later that evening, as remains the case nearly 250 years later, there was a fireworks display.[42]

This "Celebration Day" was filled with touches of Hancock: music, toasts, and fireworks. He came from Boston and the traditions of the Sons of Liberty—a group that understood the importance of commemorating revolutionary events to fortify people's morale. Shortly after the successful party, Hancock left for home because of "His own Want of Health & the dangerous Illness of his Lady."[43]

Hancock had been in Boston to delight in his growing son and dote on his wife for just two weeks before setting off on another trip. Only something special could take him away—he finally had the opportunity to serve in the military. When he pulled out his sword in Lexington and when he volunteered to serve with Washington, he had been denied. Now he was going into battle as an officer. Two years earlier he had been named major general of the Massachusetts militia and he was ready to prove his rank.[44]

French military forces arrived in the summer of 1778 and their services were needed right away. Washington hoped the French navy, led by Comte d'Estaing, could help liberate Newport, Rhode Island, which had been occupied by British soldiers since 1776. Washington also sent the nineteen-year-old French officer, the Marquis de Lafayette, to serve. Major General John Sullivan was heading the efforts and requested five thousand militia members from New England further support his troops. Thousands heeded Sullivan's call, including Hancock. "It seems as if half Boston was here," noted Paul Revere, who came with the town's artillery train.[45]

Sullivan and D'Estaing disagreed about strategy, though, and any attack was delayed. Then a severe storm blew through—heavy rain and thunder pounded Newport for three days. Hancock wrote home frequently, begging Dolly for updates about his beloved son. He was proud to be on the battlefield and had so much to share with her about the experience he was finally getting to have, even if little of military consequence was happening.[46]

After the hurricane cleared, Hancock rode through the camp to check on his men who were "in better Spirits than I expected." But D'Estaing was discouraged. His fleet was badly damaged and he wanted to sail to Boston to repair the ships. Sullivan, Hancock, and others tried to convince him to stay, telling him that his honor depended on fighting. He could not be persuaded and was offended that they would suggest anything about his character. Sullivan was furious and some worried that this could rupture the new and very fragile alliance with France. D'Estaing sailed from Newport and Hancock's opportunity for combat left with the fleet, never to return. He would prove to be more helpful with the French military on the home front than on the battlefront.[47]

Two seemingly contradictory facts can both be true. The French alliance was critical to the United States winning the war, and many colonists—especially those in Boston—hated the French. Great Britain and France had been warring in North America since the late 1600s, aided by their tenuous alliances with Native tribes. Much of the Hancock fortune had been made supplying the British army with provisions to combat the French. And just the decade before, colonists had fought against France—proportionally, Massachusetts sent more men to battle in the French and Indian War than any other colony.[48]

The fear of France was worse in Massachusetts because most of the European country's inhabitants were Catholic. The province, by contrast, had been founded by Puritans who wanted to purify the Anglican church from the rituals they found too Catholic—a dangerous religion that ultimately seemed loyal to the pope, not the state. Recall that every year Boston celebrated Pope's Day, when rival street gangs would try to capture each other's pope. And destroy it.

All in commemoration of a failed attempt by Catholics to blow up Parliament.

Many in New England felt further betrayed by D'Estaing for pulling out of Newport, leaving thousands of their militia without protection. Even Paul Revere distrusted the European nation—and he was half French. Paul's father, Apollos Rivoire—who later anglicized his name to Paul Revere—was a Huguenot (French Protestant) who had immigrated to the colonies to escape violent persecution by the Catholic king, Louis XIV. The silversmith admitted that "I was as much prejudiced against them" but acknowledged "that prejudice arose from our connection with Brittain." Echoing Revere's disdain, Benjamin Franklin was prescient about the potential for tension between the French and Bostonians. "Every means should be used to cultivate this new friendship, and wear off antient prejudices. I find our common people and Sailors are might ready to resume them."[49]

As Franklin predicted, there was trouble early on. Local ship workers initially refused to fix their ally's damaged ships and the influx of thousands of soldiers led to a shortage of food. A "most uncommon hot and dry season" hurt crop output, bread was expensive, fruit was difficult to find, and cider—a staple alcoholic beverage for the hard-drinking town—was not being produced. The demand from French sailors "enhances the price of every article of life scarce before but now incredibly so," explained Abigail Adams.[50]

The French military set up a bakery in Boston to serve their troops, but did not share its bread with hungry civilians. Tensions boiled over when about fifty men assaulted the bakers with clubs. Two French officers intervened to try to break up the fight and one of them was mortally wounded in the scuffle. Many worried that this could end the alliance because he was an officer from a well-connected family. Conflicting reports put blame on sailors who were stopped in port, Bostonians, and a privateer ship filled with British deserters.[51]

In the interest of defusing the situation, D'Estaing accepted that it was British deserters, exonerating Bostonians and blaming their common enemy. Washington was relieved that the admiral believed that story and advised, "All possible means should now be taken to cultivate harmony between the people and seamen."[52]

Hancock stepped in with his hospitable diplomacy. He had no prejudice against the French or was savvy enough to compartmentalize it. One of D'Estaing's first stops was to dine at the mansion on Beacon Hill, where he would be a frequent visitor during his stay. Hancock spoke very little French—he likely relied on the French-English dictionary he had on hand—but his sumptuous hospitality communicated for him. Hancock was the closest thing to an aristocrat in Massachusetts and he fit in well with the officers who expected their hosts to be refined in dress and manner and provide fine entertainment. Lafayette admitted that Hancock "did much to distinguish himself by his zeal" for hosting. Lafayette thought Hancock vain, but he understood the sway of the "all-powerful" merchant. Once Bostonians saw how Hancock treated these new allies "they I hope will do the Same," Lafayette said.[53]

Even when they strained his patience and resources, Hancock took "unwearied pains to promote a good understanding with the French officers." While dining at the Hancock mansion, Lafayette noticed a portrait of Washington and asked Hancock if he had a copy that he might have. Hancock did, but he intended to give it to D'Estaing—gifting portraits, we know, was a way Hancock showed his respect or affection. He assured Lafayette he could procure another for him.[54]

Hancock's generosity was tested when he invited thirty officers for breakfast and D'Estaing brought 150 men instead. Hancock only realized the number of people attending when he saw the men "bedizzened with lace" advancing up Beacon Hill. Fortunately, the man who loved to entertain had earlier added a one-story space to his house that functioned as a ballroom or dining hall. The Hancocks had the room to host D'Estaing's party crashers, but did not have enough food. Hancock hollered to Dolly to have the servants prepare 120 additional meals. And do it in the time it would take them to walk up the incline to their house and amidst severe food shortages.[55]

Dolly had to rely on her neighbors to help with this near impossible task. The servants were sent to Boston Common to milk townspeople's cows that were grazing there. These were not communal cows, but Dolly was not troubled by that—she was desperate. She also went to neighbors' houses and pled for any cake they may have. The servants could barely set the desserts down before the midshipmen pounced on it. The fruit from Uncle Thomas's cherished orchards were also wiped clean by the Frenchmen.[56]

Dolly's efforts made an impression, so much that when the Marquis de Lafayette returned to Boston decades later, he made special note of her. In 1824, cities throughout the United States feted the Continental Army's last living general. Boston was no exception: they erected arches, decorated their streets, organized dinners, and held a parade that stretched for three miles. Seventy thousand spectators lined the streets and perched on "every roof, window, balcony, and steeple." One balcony in particular caught his eye: that of Colonnade Row, where Hancock's widow sat. Lafayette ordered his carriage stopped. "Rising, he placed his hand over his heart and made a profound obeisance, which was gracefully returned."[57]

D'Estaing reciprocated the Hancocks' hospitality by inviting Dolly and her friends on to his ships, where they spent the day. They were treated to a ceremonial *feu de joie*, a rifle salute, which Dolly had unwittingly set off by giving the troops the signal to fire. She was "stunned by the noise," but found D'Estaing an elegant man. Abigail Adams and her friends were also welcomed. Adams dined with the French at least three times during their stay. Without seeming to recognize the irony of invoking and appreciating monarchial trappings, Adams noted that while on the French ships, "An entertainment fit for a princiss was prepared."[58]

The entertaining on both sides seemed endless. Hancock at this time "always kept open house" with frequent French visitors. "His

House is full from morning till Night" and the pressure of cooking for so many people took its toll on one of Hancock's servants. She was "worn out" and could not pluck every feather off every turkey to be served.[59]

At one meal, the cook's sloppiness and exhaustion were visible on the table. Feathers were stuck to the poultry. Mortified by the oversight, especially among French noblemen, Hancock set out to teach the cook a lesson. Shortly after, he told her to roast an entire turkey with the plumage intact. The cook roasted the bird on the spit, where it eventually caught fire. As the feathers burned, they "popped off with such a noise" and emitted a foul odor that enveloped the house. The staff was bothered by the smell and smoke, but the master of the house airily claimed he could not smell anything. The cook learned her lesson and plucked those turkeys clean, even when she had to cook two or three of them each night.[60]

Hancock's efforts went further than entertaining the French—he also used his influence to soothe tensions with Bostonians. D'Estaing acknowledged that the French owed a lot to Hancock who "restrained the people" and patrolled the streets at night to prevent trouble. Hancock could not stop all fights, as some continued to break out, but "without that, we would have had to take refuge on board our vessels and not leave them." Hancock helped turn around the town: "The disposition that at first appeared to Cast an Odium on the Count and to discredit our New Allies seems to have entirely subsided and has been succeeded by the most perfect good humour and respect shown them."[61]

After staying a couple of months, the French were ready to depart. To send the allies off in style, Hancock arranged for a "Grand Ball" to be held in Boston's Concert Hall. The cost of the event was estimated at £1500, a large sum of money that Hancock would have footed.[62]

Hancock heard that people were denouncing him for his extravagant entertaining, but even frequent critics of Hancock had to admit that his efforts helped bind the two countries. Abigail Adams—who took after her husband in disliking Hancock—conceded that he and another general "have done their part" in entertaining the French. James Warren also remarked on Hancock's role: "General Hancock has made most Magnificent Entertainments for the Count and his officers, both at his own and the public Houses." Warren frequently denounced Hancock for being extravagant and showy, but this was precisely what had been necessary to win over the French.[63]

For all of his efforts, Hancock received a high honor. He was adopted by the allied nation. D'Estaing concluded of his host: "I have named the honorable general John Hancock a patron of the French. He became one, and he served as one during our stay in Boston." Hancock helped secure the alliance that became crucial to winning the Revolutionary War. He did so using the tools of soft power: shaping others' attitudes and earning loyalty with hospitality and generosity, rather than coercion or fear.[64]

The day after the French fleet sailed away, a "Good Deal of Snow fell," ushering in one of the coldest winters in Boston in decades.[65] It was a good time to recover, especially after two difficult years in his personal and political life. Hancock's gout had flared up during the French visit, so the chilly season was a chance to hibernate, heal, and figure out ways to make his political enemies irrelevant.

CHAPTER 10

Traitor to His Class

As early as 1760, when he was a twenty-three-year-old in London, Hancock used clothing to "Appear in Character." What he wore expressed the way he thought about himself and how he wanted others to view him. One day in October 1780, appearing in character was of paramount importance. Hancock did not outfit himself in the heavily embroidered jackets that he often favored. Instead, he wore a "suit of crimson velvet, plain."[1]

He intended to look simpler and more like a man of the people on the day he would be inaugurated their first governor. The colony had dozens of governors before him: Bernard, Hutchinson, and Gage, most recently, but they had been appointed by the crown. With Massachusetts no longer under royal control, Hancock was the first to be chosen by the people.

After independence, former colonies worked to write and approve constitutions to replace the crown's authority. Experimenting and improvising as they went, states grappled with how power would be distributed and what character their leaders should have. It took a few years for Massachusetts to establish a new government. Two failed attempts led to a constitutional convention in 1779 attended by some of the state's most familiar names, including Hancock and the Adams cousins. John Adams wrote most of the constitution that was narrowly approved in 1780. It received most of its opposition from counties in the west—a harbinger of trouble to come.[2]

The Commonwealth of Massachusetts's constitution laid the foundation for political office and suffrage. A governor and bicameral legislature would be popularly elected annually, but not everyone could serve. Officeholders must have assets—the executive branch required the largest sum. And not everyone could vote. If you were a white man with enough property, you were able to cast a ballot, but you would need more property to vote in 1780 than had been required under the British Empire. Lots of Massachusetts men, then, would continue to be victims of taxation without representation. They could have participated in Stamp Act riots, defended the countryside during the Battle of Lexington, or fought in the war for independence and been no better off in terms of suffrage than before. John Adams got his wish for a small electorate, but many towns in western Massachusetts simply ignored this property requirement.[3]

The first gubernatorial election had come down to two men: "It is thought that Mr. Bowdoin or Mr. Hancock will be chosen governor." There were no political parties in Massachusetts at this time and no formal campaigns, so people voted for who they trusted and felt could do the job. John and Samuel Adams, as well as their ally James Warren, wanted James Bowdoin to win, as did many elites who thought he was more financially conservative.[4]

On paper there was little difference between Hancock and Bowdoin. Both were Harvard-educated merchants and among the wealthiest men in Massachusetts. Bowdoin loved wine and entertaining as Hancock did, which led to similar health problems. They were neighbors on Beacon Hill, and both attended and donated to Brattle Street Church. During the 1760s and 1770s, they had served on the General Court.[5]

But only one had been dubbed King Hancock and he cruised to an easy victory. At this time, credentials in the recent revolutionary

struggle helped public officials get elected and Hancock's far exceeded those of Bowdoin, as did his vote total. Despite knowing of
Hancock's immense popularity, Samuel Adams was surprised by the
margin by which Hancock won. "I confess I did not foresee that
Boston would have been so united as I find they were," he wrote.
Adams was out of touch with his hometown, which cast nearly
93 percent of their ballots for Hancock.[6]

Statewide, Hancock received an astounding 91 percent of the vote
and even Mother Nature cast a late ballot for him on inauguration
day. Autumn weather in Massachusetts is often a trick or a treat. One
day the sky is clear, leaves are bursting with color, and crisp air revi-
talizes the spirit. The following day could be gray with downpouring
rain and the ground papered with soggy leaves, portending winter.
October 25, 1780, however, was "remarkably fair and pleasant." The
morning "was ushered in by the ringing of bells, firing of cannon, and
other public demonstrations of the public rejoicing."[7]

Lucky Bostonians caught a glimpse of their governor in his inau-
gural suit and you can still view the jacket today. The original is in
storage at the Old State House in downtown Boston, but a replica is
part of their permanent exhibit. Even without embroidery, the coat still
conveyed his elite status. The coat had a short, standing collar, with
room at the neck for his cravat. Nine flat, crimson buttons extended
past his hip. The coat would have hung to near his knees. There were
wide cuffs on the sleeves and likely a matching waistcoat underneath.
His look would have included knee britches and silk stockings. No
shoes of Hancock's survive, but we can imagine that his shoes were the
fanciest a man could wear, including silver shoe buckles adorned with
paste stones and heels up to an inch tall. Higher-heeled shoes for men
declined in popularity around the middle of the century, yet men in
the 1780s still added a little height to project authority.[8] Becoming the
executive of Massachusetts was certainly a day for heels.

Dressed and ready, he took his carriage from Beacon Hill to
the Town House, a very short ride. The walk from his mansion to the

capitol building would take about seven to eight minutes at a leisured pace. The return trip would last a few minutes longer, accounting for the steep incline. Taking the carriage was necessary for Hancock because he was often in pain at this time, and it ensured he arrived without dust or mud on his shoes.

Once in the Council Chamber, he spoke briefly to the two houses of the General Court and then stepped out on the second-floor balcony to the adulation of his supporters. He was sworn in "before a great concourse of people." The Declaration of Independence was first read here to the women and men of Massachusetts, so it was a fitting place for its most notable signatory to stand. Cannon boomed and the militia gave a rifle salute, filling the air with the smell of gunpowder and optimism.[9]

Hancock then attended a sermon at Brattle Street Church given by his friend, Samuel Cooper, followed by a party at Faneuil Hall "where an elegant entertainment was provided." As was customary at such gatherings, they drank thirteen toasts, each followed by a cannon firing. The food and merriment continued until sunset. While most seemed pleased with their new governor, others stewed.[10]

Samuel Adams took issue with the "Pomp & Parade" on inauguration day because it violated the "sober Republic Principles" he expected of the new state. He, like many other Americans, believed the commonwealth demanded public virtue, an ideal wherein citizens sacrificed their private desires for the public good. Adams feared Hancock's frivolity because "publick Liberty will not long survive the Loss of publick Virtue." Despite a mutual friend trying to patch things up between the two around this time, Adams would not reconcile.[11]

His ally James Warren further decried the inauguration: "All ranks of people in the capital are intoxicated" by "Balls, public and private entertainments, and feasts." Warren had credited Hancock's ostentatious hospitality with helping to win over the French. It served a purpose, but only for a time. Now he wanted the "hardy and sober manners of a New-England republic" with its citizens seeking virtue over luxury, and its leaders embodying industry, frugality, and simplicity. These were traits Hancock never had, and 91 percent of the propertied, white men in Massachusetts did not care.[12]

John Adams and James Warren both married smart and politically curious women who were also concerned about Hancock. Abigail Adams wished she was allowed to vote only so she cast a ballot against Hancock, and her friend, Mercy Otis Warren, despised him. Mercy was the wife of Warren and sister to the firebrand James Otis. She would become the first American woman to publish political works in her own name—including a history of the American Revolution. She was not impressed with Hancock, referring to him as "the Guilded puppet" who had "become the Idol" of town with his demagoguery and materialism. He resembled less of a king and more of a deity, who received Americans' "Highest Instances of Worship." She was especially concerned after seeing his inauguration: "Addresses, Assemblys, Entertainments and Balls have ushered in the Happy Era of Republicanism." She, like Adams, thought that Massachusetts and the nation would not be able to survive under such excess.[13]

Hancock's critics were writing at a time when the Revolutionary War was still raging and with no assurance that Washington, his weary troops, and their French allies would win. Instead of focusing on their common enemy—the British armed forces—Samuel Adams and others attacked Hancock, so dangerous was he to Massachusetts. This was not uncommon. There had been no long-term plan for how to govern after independence, and internal divisions surfaced among many politicians in Massachusetts and other states.[14]

The feelings among some for Bowdoin and against Hancock could be so virulent that John Adams likened it to famous European family feuds, wondering, "is not the History of Hancock and Bowdoin the History of the Medici and Albizi." The difference was that it was less a rivalry—a match between two equals—and more a one-sided feud because Hancock kept winning. He secured the governorship for the next five years despite his enemies' suspicions and frequent criticisms.

He was clearly the people's choice, so much that even frequent critic James Warren admitted, "The chief magistrate possesses a popularity and influence never exceeded if known in any other country."[15] Hancock was their king for as long as he wanted to be.

———

Hancock did not have an easy job before him as governor. Ruling Massachusetts from 1780 to 1785 meant dealing with two related issues: war and severe financial troubles. After crucial support from the French army and navy, British general Charles Cornwallis surrendered in Yorktown in 1781 and the Treaty of Paris officially ended the war in 1783. Eight years of fighting led to a devastated American economy, which states tried to improve by printing currency. The value of paper money then plummeted and the cost of consumer goods skyrocketed, leading to hyperinflation.[16]

In the midst of this pecuniary crisis, Americans were expected to cover the costs of the Revolutionary War. Two decades earlier, Parliament had similarly passed taxes to recoup the expenses of the French and Indian War. But the weak Articles of Confederation prohibited Congress from imposing taxes, so legislators could only bill each state. Adding to the burden, these payments had to be in hard money, not the circulating paper currency.[17]

Many states, including Massachusetts, levied heavy taxes to pay their share. Americans must have considered the irony that they fought to be free from arbitrary taxation only to be hit with higher taxes after imperial rule ended. Two-thirds of the tax revenue paid off bonds, which were payments to soldiers and others who serviced the government during the war. Yet, many of these notes ended up in the hands of speculators who purchased them for a depreciated price, banking on the government paying them back at face value. Those in Massachusetts who sold the bonds below market were often poor Revolutionary War veterans from the west who needed whatever money they could get in the moment. Those who bought them were typically from the east, including the shrewd speculator, Abigail Adams. Veterans, then, were paying higher taxes to enrich people who had not stepped on the battlefield.[18]

By 1783, nearly two-thirds of Massachusetts towns were delinquent in their tax payments. The economic distress was especially acute in the countryside, where at least 85 percent of the state's citizens lived on small, family-run farms. The tensions in western Massachusetts reached such a pitch that a minister gained a following by calling for revoking and replacing the 1780 constitution. He was jailed for his seditious ideas, but men took axes and broke him out of jail. Smaller revolts followed the next year, with men rebelling against tax collectors. Hancock heard about the mounting troubles in the west with alarm. The urban center of Boston also saw their lower and middling sorts grow poorer. Sympathetic to his constituents' plight, Hancock was lackadaisical about tax collection in his five years as governor. This helped his popularity, but the state's balance continued to increase.[19]

The financial crunch also affected Hancock, who was on the front lines of debt collection as both a creditor and debtor. The governor enlisted a business associate, William Hoskins, to belatedly dun debts as old as 1771. Those who owed Hancock told Hoskins they could not pay because wartime suspended their work, they held worthless paper currency, or both. One whaler in Nantucket detailed the desperate situation: "People in general are poor among us, having lost a good deal of their property & have had but small ways & means to get anything during the Continuance of the war." Another man was embarrassed for not paying on an old obligation, but cited similar problems: "I am exceedingly ashamed to be called upon for a Debt so long standing nothing could excuse such a neglect in me but the unavoidable misfortunes which has attended me at Sea and thro' the various changes of Currency during the late War."[20] Hancock heard directly from the people about the financial problems that plagued them.

For a time, then, Hancock accepted repayment in valueless paper money instead of requiring gold or silver, as other creditors did. He even said he preferred the paper bills. This was an incredible gift to those in his debt. His reasons were likely twofold: generosity based on understanding the dire circumstances of Americans, and self-interest to preserve his good name. One man wondered whether Hancock accepted paper money because "he takes his dues at that rate; or to become popular, and obtain votes at the choice of governor next May?"[21]

Hoskins was diligent in his pursuits, even chasing down Hancock's colleagues, including James Otis and James Warren. The latter owed Hancock money from "years back." Warren requested that Hancock dismiss the interest on his debt, a bold request given the way he frequently attacked the governor. Hancock graciously agreed to waive the interest, even though it "was not altogether pleasing to him." Hoskins was typically patient with those who owed Hancock, but he asked for Warren's "Immediate Compleating the Remainder."[22]

Hancock, too, faced pecuniary problems. He was in arrears on taxes for land throughout New England. He had inherited vast holdings from his uncle, and some were ultimately seized to pay his debts. Hancock simply lacked the time and vigor to focus on his varied business affairs. A man hired to help him revitalize the House of Hancock told him his "attachment to the public is too Detrimental to your private Interest."[23] But politics were not always occupying the governor's energy either.

The constitution gave the governor broad power, but Hancock rarely used it. He did not want to support or enforce unpopular laws, so he let bills, especially those regarding taxes, languish on his desk. One of them was called an impost tax—a duty on imported goods— which Congress supported but could not levy. The matter went to the states to decide and collect.[24]

Hancock was against the impost, but his General Court approved it. He could veto the bill or, if he did nothing for five days, it would become law automatically. Five days ticked by, and Hancock ignored it. When the bill became law, Hancock objected that it had not been "Constitutionally pass'd" because one of the five days was a Sunday. Hancock wanted some tax like the impost because it "would be very Beneficial to the Commonwealth," but did not want to approve a bill that would exacerbate his constituents' financial problems.[25]

Hancock pulled the same stunt five months later. This time, the issue was a state excise tax. The governor was hesitant, but the Court passed the bill. Hancock waited over five days without sending his objections, so it, too, became law. A sometime ally of Hancock, James Sullivan, was annoyed with this behavior. It made the governor look feckless and such antics "weaken our government exceedingly."[26]

Avoiding burdening his citizens with taxes was one motivation for his conduct, but Hancock's body was failing him, too, which made it difficult to do any work. Hancock explained that he had "taken such cold as to give me such a nervous pain in my head as has confined me to my chamber unfit for business for several days past." Excuses like this abound in his correspondence. Illness hindered him from being his full self, and he could no longer write on his own. "He has not been able to hold a pen" in weeks, so many matters of the state were ignored.[27]

In 1782, one politician even predicted Hancock's impending demise, speculating that "from present appearances . . . death will in the course of this winter turn the attention of the partisans to a new object." The gout swelled his legs so much that he could not wear his customary elegant attire. He was a "thin person, stooping a little, and apparently enfeebled by disease." He was just forty-three when he became governor, but his health had deteriorated so much that he "had the appearance of advanced age."[28]

Weakened by illness and discouraged by the financial problems facing him and the state, he considered retiring as governor in 1783. "I am really worn out with public business," he explained. He stayed on that year but wanted to focus more on his family. "I have a fine little boy," Hancock bragged. By 1785, his poor health and the citizens' rising dissatisfaction caused him to get out while he could. With a shrewd eye to the challenges facing the state, he retired before his term was up. Lieutenant governor Thomas Cushing stepped in as executive and then battled James Bowdoin in the first gubernatorial contest that did not include Hancock. Cushing narrowly lost and Massachusetts became Bowdoin's burden.[29]

Retiring as governor did not keep Hancock out of political consideration, though. Later that year, Hancock was elected to the Continental Congress, where he last served in 1778. Even though he had recently "Recover'd from a late very severe fit of the Gout," he accepted the post. He began making arrangements for his stay in New York, the new US capitol, but before he left Boston, he stepped down, begging off for health reasons. Unable to write the resignation letter himself, Hancock's clerk claimed his boss's "disorders at present [are] wearing no appearance of leaving him soon."[30] He likely would not have liked serving in Congress anyway, as its attendance remained as sporadic as in 1778.

Hancock had made a lot of sacrifices for the public good over the past twenty years and his health suffered as a result. Even John Adams acknowledged how tirelessly the governor had worked and all that he gave up as a result. Beginning with his election to the legislature in the 1760s, Hancock worked "to the end of his life." His "mind was soon engrossed by public Cares, Alarms, and terrors; his Business was left to Subalterns; his private Affairs neglected so."[31] For nearly half of his life, Hancock had been a public figure and leader. He had earned the downtime.

With more opportunity for leisure, Hancock threw himself into making his home—where he was spending a lot of time—more comfortable. One project included updating his furnishings. The house had not changed since his uncle built it, so the furniture "is much worn & stands in need of a Recruit." He wrote to a longtime employee who was in London and requested the most fashionable pieces. He wanted the parlor room—where he would receive visitors—to look presentable, but not extravagant. He sent the dimensions of the parlor room, its windows, and two bedrooms. Much of the style was left to those overseas, but he had some specifics. No yellow. The room above the parlor was decorated in that color and he did not want any more of it. Also, the curtains should "be made to draw up" and should be of the same fabric as the window cushions, chairs, and sofa. He also refreshed the floor coverings because "[t]he British Officers who possess'd my house totally defac'd & Ruin'd all my carpets." All of these efforts were done with his son in mind, who Hancock knew "will want it."[32]

He did not stop there. Like any redecorating project, changing one or two rooms made other parts of his home in need of a refresh, too. He ordered six dozen pewter plates, along with "oval or long dishes for Saturday's Salt Fish." His weekly salt fish dinners were elaborate affairs and he wanted appropriate serving dishes for the guests who may stop by. All of the dishes were to be engraved with his crest. Hancock owned an "elegant" and valuable set of fine china, but the sound of utensils on it was too grating when he felt unwell. Hancock told his household staff that they were only to serve food on the pewter.[33]

One afternoon he was convalescing upstairs while friends downstairs were having dinner. Hancock's ears filled with the sound of the forbidden dishware. He called Cato, the servant previously enslaved by his aunt and uncle, into his bedroom and asked if he had heard the sound of china.[34]

Cato said that, yes, they were using china, but only to serve the cheese. The rest of the food was being served on pewter. Hancock ordered Cato to put the cheese on a pewter plate instead "and bring the china one up to him." Cato made the swap and brought the offending dish upstairs. Hancock told him to throw it out the window.

Not wanting to smash the plate, Cato intended to give it a gentle toss. Since he could not move easily, Hancock would be unable to check if the dish actually broke. Cato threw it on "a slanting bank of grass" where it landed safely in one piece. Hancock likely heard a thump, but not the telltale sound of broken china. Dissatisfied, he told Cato to go outside and "smash the plate against the wall."[35] Hancock's home needed to be a place of refuge from so many things: the pressures of politics, unhappy citizens, and china.

The comfort of his refurbished home was not enough to assuage the utter despair he felt in January 1787. His eight-year-old son, John George Washington Hancock, fell while ice skating. The fall caused him to pass away shortly after, likely from a head injury.[36] At fifty, Hancock would not father another child, ensuring he would have no heirs. No more John Hancocks would descend after him. No son would inherit the new furniture he bought. Even in a world that was more familiar and accepting of childhood mortality, this loss of his only remaining child is difficult to comprehend.

An elegist expressed the despair that Hancock and Dolly must have experienced. It was not just the death of a boy, but a son who showed promise, would have immense opportunities, and could continue his family's good name. "This amiable child gave every indication of future eminence; and while his sweetness of temper, his strength of memory, and brilliancy of genius, led his parents to hope, that he would be . . . eminently useful in the world." As he did with the people he cherished, Hancock commissioned a miniature portrait of his son to accompany that of his departed daughter Lydia.[37]

Hancock wanted an understated funeral, which was appropriate given the dire circumstances of the state and the unrest in the countryside. John George Washington's coffin was transported in the Hancocks' carriage with his grieving parents riding in a coach behind. Friends followed in their vehicles. The boy's body was interred at the Granary Burying Ground in the Hancock family tomb, visible from their home.[38]

Weeks passed before Hancock could reply to friends who sent their respects. When ready to resume correspondence, he explained his

John George Washington
Hancock miniature.
RISD Museum.

silence: "you will excuse my dwelling upon the Melancholy Subject." For a man who loved sending and receiving letters, not writing
back showed the dark days he faced. "My situation is totally deranged
by the untimely death of my Dear and Promising boy," Hancock
offered.[39]

Traveling had been a way Hancock enjoyed himself in the past, so
friends recommended he and Dolly take a trip. As soon as the roads
were in suitable traveling conditions, they intended to leave the mansion that carried the weight of their son. The couple planned to go to
New York and Philadelphia because "the obtainment of health is now
my pursuit." He asked Henry Knox, who was stationed in New York,
to set up elegant arrangements for him "in an Airy place."[40]

Even in the midst of grief, Hancock still knew how to request the
best. He was going to be traveling with three servants and wanted a
"handsome, well-furnished chamber" for he and Dolly and "a decent

parlor or two parlors." It was clear they would be entertaining while there, which would do the inherently social and hospitable man some good. It also must have been a relief to have his wife with him during this period, something he had not had after the death of his daughter. They set off in March and were gone for several weeks.[41] It was an opportune time to get away because the strain of taxes and debts in Massachusetts eventually buckled.

Throughout the 1780s, men in western Massachusetts had sent petitions pleading for financial redress from the crushing taxes, but they received no help. Instead, Bowdoin—who won reelection in 1786 when Hancock did not run—increased the tax burden. On top of that, Bowdoin blamed his own constituents for the state's debt problem. Calling them extravagant and wasteful, he advised them to adopt more industrious habits: simplicity, frugality, economy. As one of the largest securities holders in the state, Bowdoin had a vested interest in the people of Massachusetts remitting taxes because that money would pay off bonds and benefit him.[42]

Some in western Massachusetts rightfully believed Bowdoin did not respect or understand them. A man in Springfield—a town ninety miles west of Boston—wrote that those in government thought of the people in the countryside "as the Ragamuffins of the Earth, poor illiterate Rascals who owed more than they were worth." Yet, the farmers were not trying to avoid paying debts and were not living luxuriously, as Bowdoin suggested; they simply wanted tax relief.[43]

When their appeals went nowhere, the men set up conventions. They employed the same methods—petitions, intimidation, and meetings—that helped achieve independence ten years earlier. The conventions had little effect, so "popular odium against Government now ran high." The situation escalated when armed men in western towns—many of them veterans of the recent war—intimidated the courts into closing. They reasoned that if the courts could not hold sessions, men would not have their property auctioned off or be hauled into jail for nonpayment of debts. They had successfully shuttered them in 1774 and the tactic was effective again in 1786: judges backed down and the courts stayed closed for months. This resistance became known as Shays's Rebellion, a misnomer because Daniel Shays, a poor Revolutionary War veteran, did not organize the actions—it was mostly a decentralized effort—and had been drawn in reluctantly and identified as the leader by the opposition.[44]

Fueled by misunderstandings, self-interest, and contempt, Bowdoin and his legislature passed several harsh and overreaching laws to stop the protests in the west. They suspended some civil rights, including the writ of *habeaus corpus,* which meant a sheriff could detain anyone he thought was threatening public order. They also instituted a riot act which exonerated sheriffs who killed anyone accused of rioting. A supporter of Bowdoin remarked on the severity of the governor's tactics: "for fear that Capt. Shays should destroy the Constitution they violated it themselves."[45]

Bowdoin sought more than just laws to control the situation. He also wanted to militarily "suppress all such violent and treasonable proceedings," and had support to do so. Samuel Adams—a state senator and advisor to Bowdoin—urged the governor to take a hard stand against the protestors, believing them traitors and insurgents. The radical who whipped up violence in the streets a decade earlier was now condemning it. If it seems hypocritical, it was.[46]

Adams had a problem with the farmers' conventions, believing they had a purpose ten years ago (when he was the one calling them), but now, when there are "annual & free Elections of the People, we are safe without them." To Adams, annual elections—in which only propertied, white men could participate—solved every problem. "The next Elections will set all right," he reasoned. Any sort of popular uprising was now unnecessary.[47]

To suppress the resistance, Bowdoin raised an army of over four thousand men. They mostly came from the east because many in the west were unwilling to take up arms against men they agreed with, or at least sympathized with. Bowdoin had not received the legislature's approval or financing for this military action, so he asked wealthy Bostonians to put up funds for the army's expenses. The governor paid one of the largest sums, and two men who participated in the Boston Tea Party—one of the most flagrant acts of property destruction a decade earlier—also gave to the cause. Notably absent on the list of subscribers was John Hancock.[48]

The militia marched west to Springfield. On January 25, 1787, government troops fired a cannon to break ranks. The rebels scattered and three men were killed. Another confrontation happened a few weeks later, but shortly after, the rebellion in western Massachusetts petered out. Participants' punishments ranged from fees, collection of arms, and suspension of voting rights, which many hoped would silence future opposition. It would not, as Bowdoin would see. The worst offenders went on trial and eighteen men received death sentences.[49]

Fortunately, financial relief followed the rebellion. The General Court reduced court fees and proposed a cut to the governor's salary. Surely a man who touted thrift as much as Bowdoin would appreciate this cost-saving measure. Predictably, he vetoed it. The most significant help, however, came in the spring of 1787 with the gubernatorial election. Adams was correct that the annual election would help set things right, just not in the way he hoped.[50]

Those sympathetic to debtors came out on election day in record numbers and, for the first time in state history, voted out an incumbent governor. Bowdoin received 5,150 votes to Hancock's 17,040. Just three months after his son died, Hancock was back in power, even sweeping every vote in three towns. The voters also sent more newcomers to the Senate than any other time in the previous decade and only 26 percent of the representatives in the House remained. The election was a clear referendum on Bowdoin's and the legislature's handling of the resistance.[51]

Hancock had no problem winning across Massachusetts, but his popularity dropped in Boston, where much of the state's moneyed interest lived. The elites who touted the virtues of frugality and simplicity wanted those traits embodied by the masses, but expected the men in government to protect their considerable property. A traitor to his class, Hancock often sided with the poor and middling, so he and Bowdoin received nearly the same number of votes in their hometown — a steep decline from Hancock's 93 percent of Boston's vote in 1780.[52]

A partisan of Bowdoin's claimed in a local newspaper that Hancock had disproportionate support from Boston's "Labourers, servants, &c," while Bowdoin did better among "Merchants and Traders" and "Independent Gentlemen." Bowdoin had the backing of a wealthy and supposedly more respectable crowd, while Hancock was most popular with working men. This was meant as an insult to Hancock and sounds extraordinary today, when most politicians claim to be fighting for the poor or middle class. But Hancock's connection to and genuine courtship of those beneath him was new in America.[53]

A defender of Hancock fired back in the newspaper's next issue and recategorized the voters, claiming that "Usurers," "Speculators," and "Persons under British influence" cast ballots for Bowdoin, who also received a single vote from "Wizards." The greedy and magical sided with Bowdoin. Hancock, by contrast, swept all votes from "Friends to the Revolution." The legacy of resistance and rebellion meant different things to different people but for the majority of white men in Massachusetts, it was Hancock who upheld the principles of Revolution, not Bowdoin or his allies.[54]

After being elected, Hancock demonstrated how well he understood the people. He agreed to the salary reduction that Bowdoin had rejected. He also issued full pardons and reinstituted the citizenship of the rebellion's participants, except for two men who were also accused of breaking into houses. This may have been for self-preservation, as many feared attacks on government officials if participants were executed. But according to the governor, the pardons were intended "to restore the publick tranquility, to conciliate the affections of the people, & to establish peace in the State."[55]

For most of his life, Hancock was a man who avoided extremes. In 1787, his moderation enormously benefited him, the western rebels, and the state. He lamented the rebellion but told the General Court, "I am persuaded you will join with me in the sentiment that this unhappy occurrence cannot be considered as a certain mark of the indisposition to good order & government." He was optimistic that people would respect the new government and knew that healing the rift, not widening it, was good for the state. It helped that his legislature approved measures for debt relief—they imposed no taxes that year.[56]

Hancock and the tax reprieve were the salve the state needed. Even his critics softened a bit. James Warren was disappointed in Bowdoin and unhappy that Hancock was now the state's executive, but conceded, "I do not regret the change so much as I once should." Christopher Gore, future governor and one of the men who donated to suppress Shays's Rebellion, admitted that Hancock as executive "will at least tend to the peace of Massachusetts."[57]

Others outside the commonwealth were not as charmed. The debt relief in Massachusetts concerned powerful men who saw the masses get what they wanted through protests and elections. These elites would upend the existing government to stay in power and better control those beneath them.

CHAPTER 11

Defending Massachusetts from the United States

The church floor on Boston's Long Lane was packed with convention delegates. The second-floor galleries held hundreds of spectators from Massachusetts, Rhode Island, and New Hampshire—all had arrived at least an hour before the session began to secure a seat. Where it could find space, anticipation also filled the room. After missing the first three weeks of debates, the convention's president, Governor Hancock, was finally going to attend.[1]

When the doors opened, Hancock appeared. Those who had not seen him recently, or ever, must have wondered if it was actually him. There was no velvet coat or his signature embroidery—instead, he was "wrapped in his flannels." He did not look frivolous and vain, as critics often accused him of being, but old and feeble. Furthering the shock: Hancock was "thence carried into the Convention by several young gentlemen." He was unable to walk on his own at this time and regularly had two servants carry him. It was a devastating contrast from the man who had always dressed in the finest clothing and projected a noble air. Despite Hancock's weakened appearance, his arrival created a buzz and "diffus'd much pleasure in the Gallery & below."[2]

The governor claimed that only "the greatness of the emergency" brought him from his sick bed. He assured the attendees that he had been following the convention's proceedings via newspapers and friends. The question being debated was one of the most significant in our nation's history and one Hancock could not sit out: whether or not Massachusetts should ratify the US Constitution.[3]

A new government structure had been proposed after conservative men across the United States worried that state governments had become too responsive to common people, especially after Shays's Rebellion and Hancock's reaction to it. Dozens of elite men met in Philadelphia in May 1787 to revise the Articles of Confederation, but they soon changed course and started over, writing an entirely new governmental framework. Its creators sought to take power back from the people and states and put it in the hands of a small group of wealthy men who would run a central government. There, they felt, power was safest.[4]

The most prominent revolutionaries from Massachusetts did not attend the Constitutional Convention. Hancock skipped it, likely because he was busy as governor and beholden to his gout. Samuel Adams did not attend either, having concerns about its authority. John Adams was in Europe. The four delegates from Massachusetts represented the monied interests of coastal inhabitants. One of them, Elbridge Gerry, was forthright about how he felt about letting ordinary people have power. James Madison, the architect of the Constitution, summarized Gerry's political beliefs: "Democracy, the worst he thought of all political evils." This attitude tracks with the political practice named for him: gerrymandering.[5]

To stack the deck in favor of ratification, the proposed Constitution would not be voted on by the state legislatures—which would deny this attempt to take away their powers—or by the people. Instead, special ratifying conventions with select delegates would decide. The framers also unilaterally determined that only nine states needed to approve the Constitution, thereby ignoring the Articles of

Confederation, which required the consent of all thirteen states to change a law. They also claimed that the state ratifying conventions could only vote to approve or deny the suggested Constitution. Delegates were essentially deciding between it and the broken Articles of Confederation.[6]

Before the Massachusetts convention convened in January 1788, four states had already approved the Constitution, and Connecticut ratified the day their convention began. Federalists—the name given to those who supported the Constitution—were more than halfway to the required nine states before Massachusetts weighed in. But Hancock's home state was not just one more vote. It had strong revolutionary credentials and clout; as a result, it was considered a swing state—if the Constitution was ratified there, it would likely prompt other states to do the same.

Over fifty newspapers throughout the United States covered the Massachusetts debates—no other state received as much attention. New Hampshire's convention was waiting to deliberate until it heard its neighbor's choice, and Federalists James Madison and George Washington worried that New York would also be affected by the decision of Massachusetts. Washington acknowledged that it could sway Virginia, too: "There is no question however but the decision of other States will have great influence here; particularly of one so respectable as Massachusetts."[7] The state and its governor were on the national stage.

Given that the Constitution still governs the United States today, we can look back on the debate about its ratification and feel convinced that it was the right government at the right time. Psychologists identify a tendency called "hindsight bias" wherein people see the results of a past event as predictable or logical. With this thinking, outcomes seem more likely to have occurred than they actually were, and other perspectives and alternatives are ignored or dismissed as irrelevant to the final outcome. When evaluating history, and especially a revolution, it is natural to succumb to hindsight bias and believe that everything transpired the way it should have or that the outcome was inevitable. But this ignores the complex reality of 1788. The country's proposed government structure was unpopular among many Americans, and prominent men — including the future first president — were anxious that it would not pass.[8]

The delegates in Massachusetts were pretty evenly split for and against the Constitution, with a slight majority opposing ratification. Until the governor arrived, "the balance of power was each day vibrating, as the mercury in the thermometer." In some ways, the fight over the Constitution mirrored the divisions exposed by Shays's Rebellion a year earlier. Those in the west mostly opposed the new government while those who railed against Hancock's moderate approach to the rebellion were in favor.[9]

Citizens with concerns about the proposed government were branded Anti-Federalists. They included farmers and the middling sorts of Massachusetts who worried that the Constitution did not assure them of their rights. It spelled out the power of the government, but neglected to do so for its citizens. They were further concerned with the three-fifths rule, which gave slave states greater representation. It also seemed that the Constitution would create and empower an aristocracy because the president and senators were indirectly elected, served long terms, and had no term limits. (It was not until the Seventeenth Amendment passed in 1913 that senators were elected by popular vote, and we still use the electoral college to select our presidents.)[10]

Delegate after delegate agreed: the side Hancock landed on would be victorious. "If he should come out full in favour of [the constitution], it is the general opinion that his popularity will draw a large majority in its train," one man noted. While no one knew for sure, the common belief was that Hancock "wavers" between both sides and feared that the Constitution would take away some of his authority as the governor of a sovereign state.[11]

Before the convention broke for lunch, Hancock excited the "uncommonly crouded" room when he told them he would speak that

afternoon. Later, the spectators and delegates sat "in the most profound silence" as the most popular man in New England mustered
his energy to weigh in. The charisma and vitality were gone from the
man who captivated his audience on the anniversary of the Boston
Massacre fourteen years earlier, but people still hung on his words.
There was so much riding on the frail man before them. Not just what
he thought about the Constitution, but how it might influence other
delegates' decisions. All of these factors "conspired to render the scene
as interesting and affecting as possible."[12]

Hancock opened his speech by acknowledging the "diversity of
sentiment" among the delegates and said he strove to understand
everyone's perspective. As he continued, Federalists must have been
nervous, even as they had left little to chance.[13]

Fearing defeat, they had caucused after hours "as hard as in convention," including going to Hancock's house and proposing a bargain. If he supported ratification, he could also offer amendments to
the Constitution. No one from any state had done that yet. The Federalists knew that if the influential Hancock suggested changes, it
might assuage the middling and lower orders' concerns.[14]

The Federalists thought they had convinced the governor, but
one of them remained uncertain because Hancock's "character is
not entirely free from a portion of caprice."[15] That afternoon in the
overstuffed church, people on both sides wondered: which way
would he go?

After a few introductory remarks, he got to it. Hancock had decided
to support the Constitution, but to "remove the doubts, and quiet the
apprehensions of gentlemen," he wanted to make changes. Charac-
teristically, he had chosen a moderate path. He split the difference
between support for and opposition to the Constitution. He would
vote to ratify, but not in its current form. He read nine amendments
aloud and concluded "with the sincere wish, that it may have a tendency to promote a spirit of union." Hancock's amendments focused
on the power of the states, which would be stripped by the Constitu-

tion as it was currently written. Specifically, he wanted states to have any powers that were not explicitly given to Congress. He also wanted to prevent Congress from directly taxing the people before state legislatures had the opportunity to raise the money on their own. Hancock likely provided some input on the proposed changes but was not the mastermind behind them.[16]

After Hancock spoke, "the opposition despaired of success."[17]

The vote to ratify took place a few days later. Spectators arrived at nine that morning and once again jealously guarded their seats. During the two-hour afternoon break, "such was the anxiety of the minds of the people" that the galleries remained full during the entire adjournment. One spectator sent a boy to a nearby shop to buy his midday meal of gingerbread and cheese to avoid giving up his spot.[18]

Just before the vote, the governor, wrapped in flannels, was carried up the aisle and made one of the most significant speeches of his life. He wanted to calm his constituents before the divisive vote. He would not offer any new ideas to the debate, which "is quite exhausted," but he hoped to prevent discord. All sides, he acknowledged, wanted a new government structure to "save our country from ruin." Hancock then reiterated that he thought the Constitution should be approved along with his suggested amendments. No matter which side prevailed, however, "there can be no triumph on the one side, or chagrin on the other." If the Anti-Federalists were defeated, they must unite under the new government, and the Federalists must recognize that others will not be happy with the decision. All delegates, spectators, and citizens should "sincerely lament the want of unanimity" and "strenuously endeavor to cultivate a spirit of conciliation."[19]

Throughout the American Revolution, Hancock had excelled at bringing people together. He could genuinely offer such sentiments for unity because he was able to find merits on both sides. Even Elbridge Gerry, a frequent detractor of Hancock, admitted the value of his opinion because he took "a fortunate middle course between the violence of opposing factions." To soften divisions, Hancock relied on his reputation as a moderate and the social influence he earned over the past twenty-five years. "We must all rise or fall together," Hancock proclaimed.[20] With that, the vote began.

"The Desition of so important a Question as the present you might have heard a Copper fall on the Gallery floor," a participant noted. The only sounds were the yeas and the nays called out by the delegates. While his constituents looked on, Hancock gave his yea. When all the votes had been cast, the Constitution squeaked by with 187 for and 168 against. A difference of 19 votes.[21]

Without Hancock, the Constitution surely would have been defeated, for he had "an amazing influence over a great number of wavering Members." But even Hancock's input had its limits, as the vote was decided by just 5 percent of the convention attendees. For those he did sway, his support and the proposed amendments "furnished many with Excusces to their Constituants." They could justify to the men back home that they voted in favor because Hancock had supported it.[22]

Some Anti-Federalists internalized Hancock's message about accepting the results. Five of them gamely pledged to support the Constitution going forward. One said that not only would he accept it, but he would urge his constituents to do the same. The Federalists would not be as gracious in victory.[23]

What had been a very narrow win was celebrated in Boston as if it was a triumph for all people. "The moment the *Ratification* was declared outdoors, the whole of the Bells in Town were set a Ringing & a general Joy & Congratulation took place throughout the Town," one supporter of the Constitution observed. Thousands of people flooded the streets and cheered so loud that someone speculated—if the wind had been blowing right—"it must have reached your ears in New York."[24]

For two days, the party continued and included a parade. Hancock was pulled in his carriage, not by his own horses, but by thirteen tradesmen who "expressed their love and respect for a man who ever loved and respected his country." In 1775, on his way to the Second Continental Congress, men had similarly offered to pull him. Then, he begged them not to carry him, but this time he allowed them to do so. "Governour Hancock has gained himself immortal Honor," one observer noted.[25]

Not for the first time in his life, Hancock was feted with a version of Yankee Doodle. The author credited him for the passage of the Constitution:

> Then 'Squire Hancock like a man,
> Who dearly loves the nation,
> By a concil'atory plan,
> Prevented much vexation.
>   Yankee doodle, &c.
> He made a woundy Fed'ral speech,
> With sense and elocution;
> And then the 'Vention did beseech
> T' adopt the Constitution.[26]

After Massachusetts's convention, six of the seven states yet to ratify also suggested changes before approving the Constitution. The proposed amendments eventually became the Bill of Rights, some of the most recited and cherished of American liberties. Freedom of speech, press, religion, and assembly do not reflect the framers' ideals, though. The men at the Constitutional Convention in Philadelphia had not felt it necessary to include them. Rather, it was the men who opposed the Constitution who bestowed Americans with such freedoms.[27] This very much includes Hancock.

Hancock had his own reasons to support the Constitution. First: he likely wanted to further his legacy, which was already tied to the Declaration of Independence. An adversary admitted his name could only be enhanced by a connection to the Constitution. "The fame of having given his official sanction to the declaration of his country's independence, might be added that of securing for it a permanent constitution of government," Gerry predicted. He could also hope to win back some support from Federalists, who had pledged their loyalty: "Hancock will hereafter receive the universal support of Bowdoins Friends." But Hancock did not need Bowdoin's allies so something else must have helped persuade him. There was some speculation that holdouts like Hancock could have been bribed, but there is no evidence that Hancock took money for his vote.[28]

The most likely reason is that he wanted to be president of the United States. When the Massachusetts Federalists lobbied him, "We tell him that if Virginia does not unite, which is problematical that he is considered the only fair candidate for President." Virginia was facing strong opposition to the Constitution and if they did not ratify, Washington—the favorite for the job—could not become the chief executive. Other accounts said that Hancock wanted to be second-in-command. Either way, Hancock had been wooed on the promise of a top national office.[29]

As talk of the presidential election heated up, Hancock did one of the things he did best: courted public opinion. In August, he and Dolly traveled throughout Massachusetts, New Hampshire, and Rhode Island and were celebrated along the way. A New Hampshire newspaper reported that Hancock "appears to be selected by the united voice of the Continent . . . for the second seat in the new Federal Government." Wherever Hancock went, there was "a deal of stirring in the Streets." Hancock was one of the most famous and popular men in America and would have had no trouble securing votes outside Massachusetts.[30]

The flaw in Hancock's plan was that Americans did not—and still do not—directly elect the president and vice president. In the first presidential election of 1789, there was not even a popular vote. Voters selected electors who then cast ballots for president. Hancock could have the backing of ordinary Americans, particularly in New England, but if he lacked support from those in the electoral college, his candidacy would not go very far.[31]

No matter what Federalists had promised, most politicians deemed Hancock unsuitable for a national office because of his poor health. "I cannot believe that the Governour would under his present want of health leave this government even if he should be elected second in the new one," a Hancock rival wrote to Washington. Benjamin Rush, who served with Hancock in the Second Continental Congress, predicted John Adams would win the vice presidency because "Mr Hancock['s] frequent indispositions alone will preclude him from that mark of respect from Pennsylvania."[32]

A statesman from Massachusetts believed "there certainly will be a division of the votes between Mr Hancock & Mr Adams" for vice president. That person had miscalculated—it was the rare election when Hancock got trounced. Washington was unanimously elected president and John Adams's thirty-four votes handily beat Hancock for vice president, who received only four electoral votes—none of them from Massachusetts. He had been betrayed by the Federalists who had pledged their support. Years later, John Adams claimed, "Mr Hancock was ambitious of being President or Vice President," but smugly admitted, "I stood in his way." Such gloating was possible not because the people preferred Adams over Hancock, but because of the system created to select the nation's executives.[33]

———————

Hancock may not have been elected to national office, but Federalists could do nothing to stop his popularity in his home state, even as they tried. Hancock's reign would continue, with a critic derisively but aptly resurrecting his nickname, referring to him as the "Massachusetts King." In the gubernatorial election in the spring of 1789, Hancock easily defeated Bowdoin, securing 81 percent of the vote. He consolidated his power even more over the next few years. No

Federalist would serve as governor as long as he was alive. There was one influential party in the state, and it revolved around Hancock.[34]

One way Hancock had gained such popularity over the years was his skill at getting ordinary people on his side. Buying dinners, accepting worthless paper currency on debts, and pardoning rebels all contributed to this. But he also was able to connect personally and meaningfully with people far beneath him in the social hierarchy. He had emotional intelligence, to use a modern term. A French visitor dined at Hancock's house in the late 1780s and remarked on Hancock's ability to relate to those beneath him. "He has the virtues and the address of popularism; that is to say, that, without effort, he shews himself the equal, & friend of all."[35]

Hancock's people skills were unrivaled and unusual. Typically, a man of his stature would not socialize with the lower orders. But, as the foreign guest noted, the governor—representing the highest political office in the state—would not simply talk to men of the lower class, he had genuine friendships with them. One such associate was a hatter, someone stations beneath Hancock, but "who appeared to be in great familiarity with [the governor]." The hatter dined at Hancock's mansion amidst men who were wealthier and more refined than he. This man's presence was noteworthy to the French visitor because his native country's aristocracy did not deign to mix with commoners.[36]

The hatter mentioned, no doubt, was Nathaniel Balch. Hancock had known him for decades and over the years, the two became close friends. Hancock liked Balch's sense of humor and lighthearted disposition. It was a mutually supportive relationship. At least once, Balch attended a General Court meeting so he could see Hancock give a speech. The governor also stopped into Balch's hat shop to chat with him and other workers and clients, sometimes discussing politics and other times, exchanging jokes. If a government post came up that would benefit one of them, even if they were not ideally suited, Hancock would appoint them. A common tool for the wealthy or powerful to employ, his patronage sometimes offended his rivals, but the governor used his clout to help those who needed it.[37]

There were other benefits to being friends with Hancock. After the Constitution was passed, the governor wanted to mark the moment with another portrait and, as usual, he gifted one to someone else in his life. This time, it was for Balch, who could not pay for a portrait on his own. A story about the paintings demonstrates Hancock's jovial spirit with the hatter.

According to Balch family tradition, the governor joked to his friend, "Come up and see a Savage I have locked in my garret." Balch dutifully followed Hancock back to Beacon Hill, likely imaging any number of ferocious animals being kept in captivity. Instead, they went upstairs and found the self-taught painter, Edward Savage, working on a portrait for Hancock. He would also paint Balch.[38]

Savage's likeness of Hancock is different than previous portraits: it is his only full-length depiction and Dolly appears with him. It is also massive: seven and a half feet tall and nearly five feet wide. Dolly is demure, seated in a chair looking out of frame, but Hancock stands, staring directly at the viewer, the dominant presence. The smug look from years earlier is gone, but other accessories remain. He is wearing the same embroidered jacket and matching waistcoat that he wore in his Peale miniature. This was clearly a favorite of his and Savage's portrayal captures its full glory, with the gilding shining brightly and the jacket extending to his knees. A tight white cravat at his neck, navy knee britches, stockings, and golden-buckled shoes complete the outfit. Further sign of his gentility sits near his waist. His golden watch chain and trendy breloques—trinkets that include a watch key—peek out. The watch would be kept in his fob pocket, a discreet spot in the breeches' waistband, but the chain was intended to be noticed. His wig is in the style he favored later in his life, with rolls over the ears. Savage betrays none of Hancock's illnesses—the governor's face has matured, but he looks vital and composed.[39]

John and Dorothy Hancock. The American University Museum, Washington, DC.

Hancock was at the peak of his power in Massachusetts when he gained a most unlikely political ally: Samuel Adams. In 1789, his old adversary was elected lieutenant governor. Adams, who had recently lost statewide elections, realized if he was going to be relevant, he needed to reconcile with Hancock. The duo continued to win the offices of governor and lieutenant governor for the next three years. During that span, Hancock grew more suspicious of the federal government and protective of states' rights, as did Adams. This cause helped unite them.[40]

Today, the term states' rights evokes the Confederacy's justification to preserve slavery by seceding from the Union, but in the late eighteenth century, it had no such connotation. In 1789, even after the passage of the Constitution, states still considered themselves "seperat Republicks," according to Hancock. Americans in the 1780s and 1790s associated themselves first with their home state, not the country. The war and new national government had not united citizens under a common American identity. That would not come until much later.[41]

Because each state had different climates, people, religion, and "habits of life," Hancock believed each needed some sovereignty. Hancock acknowledged the importance of the central government but claimed that it could not exert force over him as an officer of Massachusetts. He felt no obligation to follow a law Congress passed regarding the governors, for example, "because I am not in my official capacity amendable to that Government." His state was his top priority and authority.[42]

Hancock's tension with a national government had begun before Massachusetts ratified the US Constitution. In the early 1780s, thirty-four slaves from South Carolina were captured by privateers and brought to Boston. Hancock hired two of the women to work in his home and a free Black man on the same ship, James, also came under his employ. The slaveowner, however, wanted to retrieve his property and enlisted the help of the South Carolina governor, Benjamin Guerard.

In 1783, Guerard wrote to Hancock demanding the previously enslaved men and women be returned to South Carolina, accusing the
governor of violating the Articles of Confederation by not protecting
a slaveowner's property. Hancock would not deliver the enslaved
women and men back to South Carolina and many of the captives
remained free in Massachusetts.[43] The governor was following the
trend in his state of weakening the institution of slavery.

The state constitution's pronouncement that "all men are born free
and equal" had prompted legal challenges to bondage almost immediately. In 1781, an enslaved woman named Mum Bett successfully
sued for her emancipation. Two years later, an enslaved man, Quock
Walker, won his freedom from the Supreme Judicial Court. This decision is often heralded as the death of slavery in Massachusetts, but
many slaveowners had been emancipating women and men for years
prior. Hancock's aunt Lydia's will from 1765 exemplified this bottom-
up emancipation: she was the one who chose to manumit—it had not
been required by the courts. Some slaveholding persisted through the
end of the decade, but it petered out enough that in the first national
census of 1790, Massachusetts was the only state to report having
no slaves.[44]

In 1788, Hancock worked with Prince Hall, a free Black man
and abolitionist, to keep men of African descent safe from slavery.
In a terrifying episode, three free Black men had been kidnapped
in Boston and were going to be sold as slaves in Martinique. Hall
petitioned the governor to prevent their sale and Hancock successfully coordinated with governors in the West Indies to stop
anyone from purchasing the abductees. The men were eventually
returned to Boston and Massachusetts abolished the slave trade
shortly after.[45]

Hancock's mind had clearly shifted about slavery, which likely
came, as many of his ideas did, from the changing perspectives of the
people around him. He may have also done his own reading on the

subject. His library contained a work entitled "Essay on Slavery," which was likely the 1773 pamphlet arguing that slavery was inconsistent with humanity and Christian scripture. Born into a family of slaveowners and benefiting from the practice for years, at some point in his life—most likely in the late 1770s—Hancock enslaved no women or men.[46]

Despite gains in Massachusetts, Black women and men were still considered second-class citizens. Hospitality, we know, was a way that Hancock connected with people and bridged divides. He enjoyed hosting different classes of men, foreign allies, and late in his life, Black men. In 1792, a newspaper reported, "in the true spirit of liberty and *equality*," Hancock held a ball in his home for the free Black men of Boston. Black women were surely in attendance too. It is easy to imagine the sumptuous food, plentiful drink and toasts, and lively company—characteristics of Hancock's parties. It is difficult to imagine, however, other leaders opening their homes to entertain Black men, especially in the name of liberty and equality. Politicians might have opposed slavery, but that did not mean they promoted equality between the races.[47]

As such, some found this event disgraceful. An anonymous critic from Connecticut mocked Hancock for his "Equality Ball" and derided it in a poem, especially poking fun at the Black men for their "graceful tricks, and winning ways." A later illustration of the event portrayed caricatured Black women and men dancing while dressed in genteel clothing. The governor clasps hands with a Black man, Cuffey, who told Hancock he was happy to see the governor because of Hancock's love for Black people. A white man behind them holds his nose. The cartoon's attempted humor lay in the incongruity of people of color being dressed and entertained as equal to whites. The governor was similarly mocked around this time for buying his Black servant a "suit of scarlet broadcloth and a large wig" because a finely dressed man of African descent was absurd to many. When the servant

Cartoon poking fun at Hancock's "Equality Ball."
Library Company of Philadelphia.

led "gouty" Hancock into church, the deacon and parishioners laughed "heartily," so ridiculous was the sight.[48]

Not everyone was appalled by Hancock hosting well-dressed Black men and women in his home. A Boston newspaper came to Hancock's defense: "They say, 'He gave a Ball to the BLACK of the town of Boston!' Stupendous CRIME!"[49]

Of course, hosting a ball did not mean the Black women and men in Boston were treated equally. Nor did it ease the legacy of slavery in Massachusetts or within Hancock's own household. Yet in a very small way, Hancock tried to lead by example. He had changed his mind about slavery and hoped others might take cues from how he treated an oppressed and marginalized group. He had done something similar with the French military—a group vastly more privileged, but whom Bostonians were also openly prejudiced toward. Hancock did not influence with political tracts, laws, or newspaper articles, the way other politicians might. He had no gift for that. But he knew how to throw a party.

_____

By the late 1780s, life improved for many in Massachusetts and Hancock's job as governor was admittedly pretty easy. He and his legislators "have little more to do than to improve & enjoy that general tranquility & those scenes of Public prosperity." The economic slump of the early 1780s had ended and nearly all citizens saw their finances stabilize. The assumption of the state debts by the federal government in 1790 greatly benefited elites, especially Massachusetts bondholders, but ordinary taxpayers were also helped because the state tax bill they had previously been responsible for paying was no more. Taxes dropped overall.[50]

Hancock had the time to advocate for causes that meant something to him, including the education of young people and more humane treatment of criminals. Harvard deserved financial support from Massachusetts, but so did the teachers in free public schools, he argued. This way "children of the poorer will have equal advantages with those of the richer part of the Community." He also called for a revision of the cruel punishments from the colonial era, including the public whipping post and the branding of bodies. Hancock did not believe that such measures actually prevented crimes or helped keep people safer.[51]

Another policy of his was less popular—Hancock cracked down on stage performances. An illegal theater had begun operating in Boston and while the governor was undecided about Massachusetts's current law prohibiting "stage plays," he was furious at its "most open breach." He forced its closure mid-performance. Many elites supported Hancock for standing up to the performers who were flagrantly violating the law, but the many people who enjoyed the entertainment were angry at Hancock. The Massachusetts legislature ultimately voted to allow theaters, even though the governor never formally signed it, nor rejected it—one of his old tricks.[52] The show would go on.

Hancock made another misstep when he insulted one of the only men in America more popular than him: the newly elected president of the United States. In 1789, George Washington was taking a good-will tour of the thirteen states now under his purview, including traveling to Boston for the first time since British soldiers evacuated in 1776.[53]

The consummate host, Hancock invited Washington to lodge with him. Just as he had in Philadelphia, Washington declined Hancock's offer. The president wanted "to avoid giving trouble to private families," so he planned to turn down all invitations to stay in citizens' residences. Rejected, but not defeated, Hancock asked Washington to join him at his home for a midday meal on the day he arrived. Washington accepted.[54]

Even though the day was cold and damp "with a raw northeast wind," Washington found his reception in Boston "in every degree flattering and honorable." A parade was organized, with an estimated 24,000 people in attendance, much more than the town's population. "The Streets, the Doors, Windows & Tops of the Houses were crouded with well dressed Ladies and Gentlemen," Washington noted. The demand to see him was so great that even inanimate objects wanted a glimpse. A poet remarked, "You would thought the very windows mov'd/To see him as he pass'd."[55]

The procession ended at the State House where a temporary arch had been constructed in his honor, designed by the young architect Charles Bulfinch. Washington passed through the arch, which he found "handsomely decorated," and received three hearty huzzahs from the crowd. A choir sang an original ode to him, military companies volleyed three times, and fireworks shot off. The tribute meant a lot to Washington, for he detailed it in his diary that day. But he still felt he had not been honored enough.[56]

Conspicuously absent from the welcome celebration was Hancock. Taking this as a slight, Washington reneged on his plan to eat at the governor's that day. There was no ambiguity as to why he skipped: he expected Hancock to call on him first. When the governor did not, Washington would not visit him: "Having engaged yesterday to take an informal dinner with the Govr. to day (but under a full persuation that he would have waited upon me so soon as I should have arrived) I excused myself upon his not doing it."[57]

Washington was a man with a strong pecking order. He believed his position as president was superior to Hancock's as governor, so he should be shown proper respect. But he had an equally fussy counterpart in Hancock, who keenly felt his own rank among elite men. The president of Harvard had to apologize on one occasion for a seating arrangement because Hancock had felt entitled to a better place than the Marquis de Lafayette.[58]

Washington had always gotten the better of Hancock, though, and his upper hand continued. The president sent a message expressing annoyance that Hancock had not called on him. Hancock dispatched Samuel Adams and a few other men to Washington to apologize for him not being there, blaming his poor health.[59]

The president rejected the excuse: "I informed them in explicit terms that I should not see the Govr. unless it was at my own lodgings." He and Hancock sent notes back and forth before the governor eventually offered to visit Washington, claiming that he "hazards every thing as it respects his health, for the desirable purpose." Hancock was not feeling well, having "the gout in his foot and hands, and could not move." Washington told Hancock he could come by, but "he most earnestly begs that the Governor will not hazard his health on the occasion." Washington extended no grace to Hancock.[60]

"Enveloped in red baize," Hancock took a short carriage ride to Washington's lodgings and was carried into the house by servants. He assured the president that it was only his sickness that had kept him away. Years later, Hancock's widow, Dolly, claimed that when Washington "saw them bringing up a helpless man in their arms" he realized how sick Hancock was "and burst into tears." Washington's hardened response hints that Dolly's account was more wishful than true.[61]

Washington was still ruminating about Hancock after his visit. He suspected that Hancock "expected to *receive* the visit from the President, which he knew was improper."[62] Washington had won and still, even in his diary, he could not be good-natured to the man who relied on servants to help him move.

This match of wills was likely based, in part, on Hancock's jealousy of the man he named his son after. Washington had been selected general of the Continental Army and president of the United States, positions some alleged Hancock had wanted. Hancock liked to feel accepted and seen and Washington consistently failed to give him such attention. Further, Hancock was used to receiving all the adulation in Boston, and Washington had received a parade, an arch, and several balls. The governor wanted to best him for once.

Hancock was also very ill at this time. Any person struggling with their health would have taken one look at the raw conditions on the day of the parade and decided to stay indoors. It was a prudent decision— many in Boston, including the president, were afflicted with a cold after the visit. It became known as "Washington influenza."[63]

But there was also a lot more to this conflict. Hancock was playing out in a small way what he and the country were grappling with on a larger scale: the supremacy of state government versus federal government. Hancock felt that as the dignitary of the state, the president should pay him respects when visiting Massachusetts. By wanting the president to call first, he was defending his state from an overreaching central government.

Today, we take for granted knowing that the US president is the ultimate authority in the country. For most of the previous nine years, though, Hancock had been ruling his own sovereign republic of

Massachusetts and did not believe the president should occupy a higher station than he. Americans had no experience with a powerful national government and no knowledge of the country's future political norms. Hancock relied on the past (and his ego) to guide his actions.

Maybe he also claimed to feel sicker than he was as a ploy to get Washington to call on him, but he truly was not able to function well. Shortly after Washington left town, Hancock invited sixty people to his home to celebrate Harvard's graduating class. He could not mingle freely with his guests or share the same table with them. Rather, he "dined at a small table by himself, in a wheel-chair, his legs swathed in flannel." He gamely navigated the party with his limited mobility. "He wheeled himself about the general table to pay attention to his guests, and to take part in the conversation," a graduate reported.[64]

An accident that day showed that he had not lost his ease as a host. At the center of Hancock's table stood an epergne: a cut glass, ornamental centerpiece that had a central bowl with smaller dishes radiating from it. They typically held nuts, fruits, and sometimes pickles, one of Hancock's favorites. "When the animation of the company was at its loudest," one of his servants, James—perhaps the same free man Hancock hired from South Carolina a decade earlier—removed the elegant centerpiece and it crashed to the ground in "a thousand pieces."[65]

A hush fell over the guests, who were unsure how the governor would react to the destruction of an expensive object and the disruptive sound. Any servant could also recall Hancock's peevish reaction to hearing food served on china.

"James, break as much as you please, but don't make such a confounded noise about it!" Hancock exclaimed "good naturedly."[66]

James and the attendees were relieved. Everyone laughed and forgot the awkward moment as the broken glass was removed. The merriment continued "as if nothing had happened."[67] Being able to

entertain and socialize surely kept his spirits up in the dark years of
his illness, especially as his body continued to weaken.

In the summer of 1793, Hancock's health was in a bad state and declining rapidly. "I have never more devoutly wished for mens sana in
corpore sano than at the present moment," the governor wrote to
Samuel Adams. Translation: a healthy mind in a healthy body. While
he had some moments of recovery—including hosting a ball with invitations "made on a liberal scale" in Concord in late 1792—Hancock's
gout made him frail, caused a lot of pain, and prohibited him from
readily moving on his own. His illness would take his life far sooner
than his contemporaries. Hancock died at fifty-six, while his widow
and Samuel Adams lived into their eighties. John Adams made it to
ninety.[68]

On September 18, 1793, Hancock appeared in public for the last
time. He was carried into the State House that afternoon and told
his General Court that he did not have enough strength "to speak so
as to be heard." The secretary had to read his remarks. The issue that
brought him from the comforts of home involved the federal judicia-
ry's influence over states. He asked that citizens monitor the national
government to prevent any encroachments on the state's power because
it would be easier to prevent a new law or precedent than to have it
repealed after it had taken effect. He was praised for his "attention, anxiety, and alacrity to support the Sovereignty of the Commonwealth."[69]

At the speech's conclusion, Hancock apologized for not being able
to address them on his own. In a weakened and emotional tone, he
admitted, "I feel the seeds of mortality growing fast within me."[70]

Those who heard this candid admission and had seen Hancock's
health decline over the past several years must have felt the end was
near. It was a sober moment. "The fall of a pin might have been heard,
such a death-like silence" pervaded the House chamber.[71]

Three weeks later, there was a promising sign of a turnaround. Hancock "appeared more alert than for many days before," which encouraged his friends and loved ones. One day later, on October 8, he was again declining. He felt fine that morning until about seven o'clock "when he suddenly felt a difficulty in breathing." A doctor was sent for but could only offer temporary respite. Within an hour, the sitting governor passed away.[72]

An amateur poet had anticipated this moment a few years earlier. He mused about the way the governor would be remembered after his passing, composing these lines: "For Deeds so Generous and deserv'd Renown / Thy Worth Oh Hancock claims a heav'nly Crown."[73] His reign as King Hancock would continue, even after death.

Remembering Hancock

Those who lived in Boston at the time of Hancock's death could not ignore his funeral. On October 14, 1793, the town's bells tolled at sunrise for an hour "without cessation." At noon, military corps from neighboring towns gathered in front of Hancock's mansion—the place where he had entertained shoemakers, hatters, Black women and men, and French aristocrats, and where he retreated from politics and business when he felt ill.[1]

Prominent citizens also assembled in front of the house, including politicians, Harvard professors, judges, and ministers. Walking four astride, they planned to accompany Hancock's coffin for a mile and a half through Boston's streets, passing meaningful locations from his political life. Dolly joined them, as did many men who had worked alongside Hancock, including vice president John Adams and lieutenant governor Samuel Adams.

Shops had closed at one o'clock and remained shuttered until the funeral was over. Not that people were going to do much shopping on this solemn day. The streets were lined with thousands of mourners—more "than we ever remember to have seen on any occasion." The narrow and winding streets had earlier been cleared of any carriages and obstructions that could hinder the procession.[2]

The man who understood how to garner attention and meet a moment warranted the "Pomp, Ceremony, and Honors" that he received in death. At three o'clock, military companies on horseback began the procession, making their way from the top of Beacon Hill down through Boston Common.[3] In this public park, Hancock had built his popularity and visibility as a leader. He offered wine and a fireworks display to celebrate the Stamp Act repeal and drilled his newly uniformed Corps of Cadets until they transformed into a disciplined group. Here, he had won people over with his congeniality and generosity.

The procession continued through the park until it arrived at the neck of Boston, which Hancock had traveled over many times to come home, especially triumphant when he returned as president of the Continental Congress. The caravan continued to the site of the Liberty Tree as the "dead march" played on muffled drums draped in crepe.

The storied elm had been chopped down by British soldiers during their occupation of Boston in 1774, but the morning of Hancock's funeral, a Liberty Pole had been erected where the mighty tree had grown. The pole was fifty feet tall with a gilded eagle at the top, covered in black: a "monument of the affection of the town of Boston, for the man, who so ably defended the rights of his country."[4] Hancock had waited here for tax collectors' resignations—successfully with Andrew Oliver and less so with Richard Clarke. As the Adams cousins passed by, they may have recalled sharing drinks and toasts with Hancock under the tree's shade.

Continuing from the neck and down the main street, the procession passed Old South Meeting House. In 1773, Hancock had gathered here with thousands to protest the Tea Act and, just a few months later, had stirred a large crowd with his tribute to the Boston Massacre. In this building, he had become one the town's most visible symbols of resistance. The procession continued toward the docks, where spectators saw flags at half mast, including on Castle William and the ships in the harbor.[5] At the waterfront, young Hancock had stared down customs officials and been huzzahed by the crowds, who had found a new hero.

Spectators in this part of town would have seen a tribute at Hancock Tavern, a watering hole opened by a husband and wife a few years earlier. The tavern's sign had Hancock's likeness on it, but on that funeral day in October, it was draped in mourning crepe, which "arrested the attention" of observers.[6]

The cortege wrapped around the Town House—where Hancock had toiled as a colonial legislator and where, on its balcony, he was sworn in as the first governor of Massachusetts after a landslide victory. The ratification of the US Constitution had also been announced here while Hancock absorbed his constituents' cheers. Inside, the governor had frustrated radical politicians, ignored unpopular legislation, extended healing after Shays's Rebellion, and advocated for the rights of states.

Houses and streets on the route were "thronged" with people as the procession made its way to the final stop: the Granary Burying Ground. Seventy-one-year-old Samuel Adams, who assumed the governorship after Hancock's death, was exhausted by this point. Aides tried to "support his debilitated frame," but he ultimately bowed out and returned home. The cemetery on Tremont Street was where Hancock had, with a heart heavy from unexpected losses, intombed two of the people closest to him: his uncle Thomas and his beloved son. His body would now join theirs in tomb number sixteen, on the west side of the cemetery. His coffin was lowered and a volley of three shots rang out, but otherwise "the most solemn silence and attention pervaded."[7]

Because of the popularity Hancock enjoyed during his lifetime and the name recognition he has among Americans today, it may be surprising that in 1809, just sixteen years after his death, John Adams decried America's neglect of its history, lamenting that "Samuel Adams and John Hancock are almost buried in oblivion." He was not wrong. Immediately after the American Revolution, there was an intentional forgetting of the radical and turbulent events that men like Hancock and Adams had participated in. Politicians grew increasingly uncomfortable celebrating the violence of the Revolution, especially when it could be used to inspire rebellions like those in western Massachusetts in 1786–1787. Washington was celebrated as a hero, but few other leaders were acknowledged.[8]

Such neglect was also true for physical objects from the Revolution, including the Declaration of Independence. For decades, the sole original copy—the one with all of the signatures—had suffered terribly, being almost burned in the War of 1812 and shuffled insecurely to several different sites. Such wear is visible on the battered document displayed at the National Archives in Washington, DC.

Things began to change in the 1810s when the country took a growing interest in its revolutionary past and reached a pinnacle with the fifty-year anniversary of independence. By 1826, the declaration had taken on a sacred quality. As public excitement grew, prints were made of the engrossed declaration for the first time. Previously, the only available copy for the public to see was the printed one, which had Hancock's typeset name at the bottom. It was not until 1818 when Americans—aside from the fifty-six men who put their names down—saw this version and the signatures.[9]

Hancock's fame benefited enormously from this new attention, especially as printers competed to sell commemorative copies of the signed declaration. One printer asked Thomas Jefferson's opinion on his design. The aging former president looked at an early draft and suggested that the three men pictured at the top—he, Washington, and Hancock—be reordered. "Were I to hazard a suggestion it should be that Mr. Hancock, as President of the Congress should occupy the middle and principal place." This would have bumped Washington out of the center. The printer kept the general in the middle, but Hancock's image still sat next to two revolutionary luminaries.[10]

As Americans were increasingly exposed to Hancock's signature, his bold penmanship sealed him a place for posterity. In the 1820s, a multivolume biography of the declaration's signatories was published and the author noted that Hancock's signature "has contributed, in no small degree, to the extension of his fame." More than a century later, it continued to enchant. Writing in 1930, an author critical of Hancock conceded that signing the declaration "has made his name known to every generation of school children ever since." This persists today. If you look up John Hancock in the dictionary, signature is the second definition.[11] One can easily ask an American to "put your John Hancock on this line" and expect them to sign their name.

The Declaration of Independence may have been saved after decades of abuse, but the careless way it was handled mirrored other overlooked relics from the founding generation that are lost forever. Hancock's name recognition could not save his house, for example, which was demolished in 1863.

He had unwittingly contributed to the mansion's destruction by inexplicably dying without a will. For a man of his means who inherited his uncle and aunt's sizeable fortune because they had created wills, to die intestate prompts questions. If he knew the end of his life was near, as he admitted two weeks before he passed, why had he not protected his assets? Did he naively think that because he had been sick for so long that he would not actually die at that time? After the tragedy of losing both of his children, Hancock may also simply have not cared what happened to his property.

After wrangling with probate courts, Dolly was named the administratrix of the estate and received the bulk of the property. It was considerably less than what Hancock had received from his uncle three decades earlier. Nevertheless, Dolly got busy. Less than two weeks after Hancock's death, and continuing for the next several years, she auctioned off Hancock's goods and sold some of the family land to

Massachusetts—lawmakers planned to build their new state house on top of Beacon Hill. Dolly moved on from Hancock in another way. Despite some relatives' concern that she would marry so far beneath the station of her first husband, in July 1796, she wed Captain James Scott, one of Hancock's most trusted and loyal employees.[12]

After Dolly's death, the estate passed down to relatives and by the early 1860s, they wanted to sell it, offering both the land and house to the state at a below market rate. Massachusetts did not purchase either; instead, two wealthy men bought the land to build townhouses. Before the developers knocked the house down, descendants tried to give it and many of its furnishings to the city "as a memento of our colonial and revolutionary history." The city would simply need to raise funds to move the structure elsewhere.[13]

To fund relocating the mansion, Boston's City Council tried to justify the house's significance. They claimed that Hancock had intended "to give the whole property . . . for executive purposes," even alleging, "The minutes for his will to his effect were under his pillow when he died." Sources from 1793 suggest nothing like that. Perhaps Hancock had expressed that he wanted his estate given away for the public good, but if he had said anything to that effect, his wishes had been coldly ignored. The City Council did not raise enough funds to move the house.[14]

Citizens, too, rallied to protect it, but there were no local or national organizations committed to preserving old buildings in the 1860s. Federal protection of historic landmarks was not established until the first decades of the twentieth century, so any preservation relied on grass roots efforts. A poster implored: "BOSTONIANS! SAVE THE OLD JOHN HANCOCK MANSION," but such efforts were unsuccessful. After a final auction of its furnishings, the house was "ruthlessly swept away." The only indication that the mansion once stood on Beacon Hill is a small plaque outside the State House gates.[15]

According to historian Michael Holleran, the destruction of Hancock's house was the "catalyst" for future preservation efforts. People no longer trusted the government to preserve monuments that meant something to them and Bostonians busied themselves saving extant revolutionary sites, including the Old South Meeting House and Old State House. Hancock's funeral procession passed both buildings and today they anchor Boston's top tourist attraction, the Freedom Trail. They would not be standing without ordinary citizens' conservation efforts.[16]

Americans' interest in honoring Hancock's generation continued to grow into the late nineteenth century when more attention was paid to founders' burying places. Massachusetts paid for a memorial to mark Hancock's grave, which had sat unremarkable on Tremont Street for one hundred years. At the monument's unveiling in 1896, a journalist noted that even though it was set many feet back from the street, "it can be readily seen by the hurrying passer-by."[17] That remains true—Hancock's face is engraved at the top of the marker as he looks out over the other graves and the millions of tourists who annually visit.

Hancock's name continues to live on in ways that have nothing to do with his life or politics. A Boston-based insurance company named itself after the merchant and in 1949, they commissioned a building called the John Hancock building. A couple decades later the company's taller and sleeker skyscraper went up a block away and took the name. When it was completed, it was—and still is—the tallest in New England. Chicago, too, boasts a John Hancock skyscraper.[18]

If Hancock knew that he would remain famous into the twenty-first century for little else than tall buildings and his signature on the Declaration of Independence, he would surely take the tradeoff. For decades he worked in service of Massachusetts, the North American colonies, and the United States, and sacrificed his health and wealth to do so. Many men of the founding era who similarly toiled are known only to specialists, but otherwise forgotten to popular memory. To be remembered at all—much less for something positive, like unparalleled penmanship—would be worth it to a man who craved people's affection.

Hancock would also no doubt be pleased to know that John Adams had been wrong about him one last time. Late in his life, Adams—who never fully understood Hancock's political approach or popular appeal—recalled the man to a friend, saying: "His Life will, however, not ever be written."[19]

ABBREVIATIONS

AFP	Adams Family Papers
BC	*Boston Chronicle*
BEP	*Boston-Evening Post*
BG	*Boston Gazette*
BLSC	Baker Library Special Collections, Harvard University
BPL	Boston Public Library
FCCC	First Corps of Cadets Collection
FO	Founders Online
GB	GenealogyBank.com
HD	Harbottle Dorr Newspaper Collection, Massachusetts Historical Society
HFP	Hancock Family Papers
HGARC	Howard Gotlieb Archival Research Center, Boston University
HL	Houghton Library, Harvard University
JAD	John Adams Diary
JRD	John Rowe Diary
MHS	Massachusetts Historical Society
MHS-C	*Collections of the Massachusetts Historical Society*
MHS-P	*Proceedings of the Massachusetts Historical Society*
NA	National Archives, London
NEHGR	*The New England Historical & Genealogical Register*

NOTES

PROLOGUE

1. Robert Treat Paine diary, July 4, 1776, Robert Treat Paine Papers, MHS online; Richard Beeman, *Our Lives, Our Fortunes, Our Sacred Honor: The Forging of American Independence 1774–1776* (New York: Basic Books, 2013), 413–414.

2. Larrie D. Ferreiro, *Brothers at Arms: American Independence and the Men of France & Spain Who Saved It* (New York: Alfred A. Knopf, 2016), xvii, xxiv. J. L. Bell dates the beginning of the spectacles myth to 1841: "The Legend of John Hancock's Signature," *Boston 1775* (blog), August 1, 2016, https://boston1775.blogspot.com/2016/08/the-legend-of-john-hancocks -signature.html.

3. Pauline Maier, *American Scripture: Making the Declaration of Independence* (New York: Alfred A. Knopf, 1997), 150.

4. Worthington C. Ford, et al., eds., *Journals of the Continental Congress, 1774– 1789*, vol. 5 (Washington, DC, 1904–1937), 590–591; Maier, *American Scripture*, 3–7.

5. Tamara Plakins Thornton, *Handwriting in America: A Cultural History* (New Haven, CT: Yale University Press, 1996), 12; Richard L. Bushman, *The Refinement of America: Persons, Houses, Cities* (New York: Vintage Books, 1992), 92–96; National Archives Museum, *Founding Documents* exhibit, Washington, DC; Ben Blatt, "Was John Hancock's Signature Too Big? Or Was Everyone Else's Too Small?," *Slate*, August 5, 2014, https://www.slate .com/articles/news_and_politics/history/2014/08/john_hancock_s_declara tion_of_independence_signature_was_it_too_big.html.

6.   John Adams autobiography, "March 15, 1776," FO.

7.   Robert McCluer Calhoon, *Political Moderation in America's First Two Centuries* (New York: Cambridge University Press, 2009), 5.

8.   Calhoon, *Political Moderation*, x, 5–6.

1: THE EMERGENCE OF JOHN HANCOCK

1.   William M. Fowler, Jr., *The Baron of Beacon Hill: A Biography of John Hancock* (Boston: Houghton Mifflin, 1980), 1–8. The section of Braintree where Hancock was born is now Quincy.

2.   Fowler, *Baron*, 10–11.

3.   Mark Peterson, *The City-State of Boston: The Rise and Fall of an Atlantic Power, 1630–1865* (Princeton, NJ: Princeton University Press, 2019), 9–10; Thomas H. O'Connor, *The Hub: Boston Past and Present* (Boston: Northeastern University Press, 2001), 6–11.

4.   W. T. Baxter, *The House of Hancock: Business in Boston, 1724–1775* (Cambridge, MA: Harvard University Press, 1945), 75–77; Samuel Adams Drake, *Old Landmarks and Historic Personages of Boston* (Boston: J. R. Osgood & Company, 1873), 338–340.

5.   "Hancock House, Boston," *The American Magazine of Useful and Entertaining Knowledge* 1, no. 2 (October 1, 1834): 81–82.

6.   Abram English Brown, *John Hancock: His Book* (Boston: Lee and Shepard Publishers, 1898), 238–239; Harlow Giles Unger, *John Hancock, Merchant King and American Patriot* (Edison, NJ: Castle Books, 2000), 20–23; Baxter, *House*, 67–69, 75–76, 184; Walter Kendall Watkins, "The Hancock House and Its Builder," *Old-Time New England* 17, no. 1 (July 1926): 13–19.

7.   Thomas Hancock to James Glinn, December 20, 1736, Series 1, Thomas Hancock Papers, Letterbook (business), 1750–1762, HFP, BLSC; Baxter, *House*, 67–69; "Hancock House, Boston," 82.

8.   Wendy Warren, *New England Bound: Slavery and Colonization in Early America* (New York: Liveright, 2016), 116, 126; Jared Hardesty, *Unfreedom: Slavery and Dependence in Eighteenth-Century Boston* (New York: New York University Press, 2016), 73–74, 113–114; Jared Ross Hardesty, *Black Lives, Native Lands, White Worlds: A History of Slavery in New England* (Amherst, MA: Bright Leaf, 2019), 57, 76–79.

9.   Gordon Wood, *The Radicalism of the American Revolution* (New York: Vintage Books, 1991), 11, 20–31, 44–56; Ross, *Black Lives*, 50–52; Hardesty, *Unfreedom*, 81–84, 102, 114.

10. John Hancock to Ebenezer Hancock, December 27, 1760, *MHS-P*, vol. 43 (Boston: Massachusetts Historical Society, 1910), 194.

11. Baxter, *House*, 4–6; quote on 5.

12. Baxter, *House*, 6–7, 39–40; Fowler, *Baron*, 10–15.

13. Fowler, *Baron*, 34–35.

14. Baxter, *House*, 100–107; 141–142; Alan Taylor, *American Colonies* (New York: Viking, 2001), 424–428.

15. Baxter, *House*, 69–74.

16. Baxter, *House*, 84–86; quote on 114–115.

17. Wood, *Radicalism*, 76; Jill Lepore, *Book of Ages: The Life and Opinions of Jane Franklin* (New York: Alfred A. Knopf, 2013), 84; Gary B. Nash, "Urban Wealth and Poverty in Pre-Revolutionary America," *The Journal of Interdisciplinary History* 6, no. 4 (Spring 1976): 574; Fowler, *Baron*, 33.

18. Gordon S. Wood, *Power and Liberty: Constitutionalism in the American Revolution* (New York: Oxford University Press, 2021), 151–155.

19. Arthur Meier Schlesinger, *The Colonial Merchants and the American Revolution, 1763–1776* (New York: Longmans, Green and Co., 1918), 29–31, 110–113.

20. Arthur Wellington Brayley, *Schools and Schoolboys of Old Boston* (Boston: Louis P. Hager, 1896), 29–30, 33–34.

21. Brayley, *Schools and Schoolboys*, 33; Fowler, *Baron*, 21.

22. John Hancock to Mary Hancock, May 1, 1754, box 1, folder 1, John Hancock Collection, 1754–1792, UAI 50.27.73, Harvard University Archives.

23. Unger, *John Hancock*, 45; Fowler, *Baron*, 28, 30–31.

24. Fowler, *Baron*, 32–33; Thomas Hancock to Barlow Trecothick, May 19, 1760, Thomas Hancock Papers, Letterbook (business), 1750–1762, HFP, BLSC.

25. Thomas Hancock to John Hancock, July 5, 1760, Thomas Hancock Papers, Letterbook (business), 1750–1762, HFP, BLSC; George F. E. Rude, *Hanoverian London, 1714–1808* (Berkeley: University of California Press, 1971), 64–79; Stephen Inwood, *A History of London* (New York: Carroll and Graf Publishers, 1998), 41–46.

26. Richard Thompson Ford, *Dress Codes: How the Laws of Fashion Made History* (New York: Simon & Schuster, 2021), 355–367; Malcolm Barnard, *Fashion as Communication*, 2nd ed. (London: Routledge, 2006), 59–67.

27. Thomas Hancock to John Hancock, July 5, 1760, Thomas Hancock Papers, Letterbook (business), 1750–1762, HFP, BLSC; John Hancock to Thomas Hancock, January 14, 1761, *MHS-P* 43: 196–197.

28. John Hancock to Ebenezer Hancock, March 31, 1761, *MHS-P* 43: 199; Rae Katherine Eighmey, *Stirring the Pot with Benjamin Franklin: A Founding Father's Culinary Adventures* (Washington, DC: Smithsonian Books, 2018), chapters 9, 10.

29. John Hancock to Daniel Perkins, October 29, 1760, *MHS-P* 43: 193; John Hancock to Ebenezer Hancock, March 31, 1761, *MHS-P* 43: 198.

30. Barlow Trecothick to Thomas Hancock, February 12, 1761, Thomas Hancock Papers, Foreign Letters from London, 1761 February to August, HFP, BLSC; Wood, *Radicalism*, 38–39.

31. Barlow Trecothick to Thomas Hancock, February 12, 1761, Thomas Hancock Papers, Foreign Letters from London, 1761 February to August, HFP, BLSC.

32. Thomas Hancock to John Hancock, March 16, 1761, Thomas Hancock Papers, Letterbook (business), 1750–1762, HFP, BLSC; Baxter, *House*, 149–150.

33. John Hancock to Daniel Perkins, October 29, 1760, *MHS-P* 43: 193.

34. John Hancock to Thomas Hancock, January 14, 1761, *MHS-P* 43: 194, 197; John Hancock to Daniel Perkins, October 29, 1760, *MHS-P* 43: 194; Thomas Hancock to John Hancock, March 16, 1761, Thomas Hancock Papers, Letterbook (business), 1750–1762; Barlow Trecothick to Thomas Hancock, February 12, 1761, Thomas Hancock Papers, Foreign Letters from London, 1761 February to August, HFP, BLSC.

35. Benjamin Bussey Thatcher, *Traits of the Tea Party; Being a Memoir of George R. T. Hewes* (New York: Harper & Brothers, 1835), 53.

36. Edmund S. Morgan and Helen M. Morgan, *The Stamp Act Crisis: The Prologue to Revolution* (Chapel Hill: University of North Carolina Press, 1953, 1995), 21–22; Woody Holton, *Liberty is Sweet: The Hidden History of the American Revolution* (New York: Simon & Schuster, 2021), 52–57.

37. Fowler, *Baron*, 46; Fred Anderson, *Crucible of War: The Seven Years' War and the Fate of Empire in British North America, 1754–1766* (New York: Vintage Books, 2000), 588–603; Brown, *John Hancock*, 55–58; Cornelia H. Dayton and Sharon V. Salinger, *Robert Love's Warnings: Searching for Strangers in Colonial Boston* (Philadelphia: University of Pennsylvania Press, 2014), 19.

38. Richard R. Beeman, "Deference, Republicanism, and the Emergence of Popular Politics in Eighteenth Century America," *The William and Mary Quarterly* 49, no. 3 (July 1992): 411; "John Adams to William Tudor, June 1, 1817," FO.

39. Thatcher, *Traits*, 52–53; William Sullivan, *Familiar Letters on Public Characters* (Boston: Russell, Odiorne, and Metcalf, 1834), 12–13; Kimberly S. Alexander, *Treasures Afoot: Shoe Stories from the Georgian Era* (Baltimore: Johns Hopkins University Press, 2018), 110–111.

40. Thatcher, *Traits*, 53–54; Hardesty, *Unfreedom*, 74.

41. Wood, *Radicalism*, 20–33.

42. Thatcher, *Traits*, 54; Wood, *Radicalism*, 29.

43. Thatcher, *Traits*, 55.

44. A Private Letter from New England, December 30, 1777, in *Letters of Brunswick and Hessian Officers During the American Revolution*, trans. William L. Stone (Albany, NY: Joel Munsell's Sons, 1891), 158; Charles S. Sydnor, *Gentlemen Freeholders: Political Practices in Washington's Virginia* (Chapel Hill: University of North Carolina Press, 1952), chapters 3, 4; Rhys Isaac, *The Transformation of Virginia, 1740–1790* (Chapel Hill: University of North Carolina Press for the Omohundro Institute of Early American History and Culture, 1999), 111–113; Wood, *Radicalism*, 41–42.

45. Baxter, *House*, 48–51; Richard C. Kugler, "The Whale Oil Trade, 1750–1775," *Seafaring in Colonial Massachusetts*, vol. 52 (Boston: The Colonial Society of Massachusetts, 1980), 153–154.

46. John Hancock to Barnard and Harrison, August 17, 1764, John Hancock Letterbook (business), 1762–1783, HFP, BLSC.

47. John Hancock to Harrison and Barnard, April 17, 1766, John Hancock Letterbook (business), 1762–1783, HFP, BLSC; Baxter, *House*, 227–229.

48. John Hancock to Harrison, Barnard, & Spragg, September 2 and September 18, 1767, John Hancock Letterbook (business), 1762–1783, HFP, BLSC.

49. "The Old State House Historic Structure Report," Boston Landmarks Commission, City of Boston online, 6–11.

50. Baxter, *House*, 223.

51. Thomas Hancock Probate Records, 13484, Suffolk County, MA: Probate File Papers online database, New England Historic Genealogical Society.

52. Baxter, *House*, 223–224; Fowler, *Baron*, 48–49.

53. "From John Adams to William Tudor, Sr., 1 June 1817," FO.

54. John Hancock to Barnard and Harrison, August 17, 1764 and January 21, 1765, John Hancock to Harrison, Barnard, & Spragg, September 2 and September 18, 1767, John Hancock Letterbook (business), 1762–1783, HFP, BLSC; Baxter, *House*, 48–51, 227–229; Thomas M. Doerflinger, *A Vigorous*

Spirit of Enterprise: Merchants and Economic Development in Revolutionary Philadelphia (Chapel Hill: University of North Carolina Press for the Omohundro Institute of Early American History and Culture, 1986), 135–146, 157–161.

2: BECOMING A MAN OF THE PEOPLE

1. JRD, November 5, 1764, in *Letters and Diary of John Rowe*, ed. Anne Rowe Cunningham (Boston: W. B. Clarke, 1903), 68.

2. Pierre Du Simitière, "Image of Boston Pope's Day, 1767," in *The Papers of Francis Bernard, volume 2: 1759–1763*, ed. John W. Tyler (Boston: The Colonial Society of Massachusetts, 2015), 425; Sherwood Collins, "Boston's Political Street Theatre: The Eighteenth-Century Pope Day Pageants," *Educational Theatre Journal* 25, no. 4 (December 1973): 407–408; *BG*, November 11, 1765, GB; Francis D. Cogliano, "Deliverance from Luxury: Pope's Day, Conflict, and Consensus in Colonial Boston, 1745–1765," *Studies in Popular Culture* 15, no. 2 (1993): 17, 20.

3. Francis Bernard to John Pownall, November 26, 1765, in Tyler, *Francis Bernard*, 2: 422; Alfred F. Young, "Ebenezer Mackintosh: Boston's Captain General of the Liberty Tree," in *Revolutionary Founders: Rebels, Radicals, and Reformers in the Making of the of the Nation*, ed. Alfred F. Young, Gary B. Nash, and Ray Raphael (New York: Alfred A. Knopf, 2011), 20; Cogliano, "Deliverance," 15–17, 20–22; Jack Tager, *Boston Riots: Three Centuries of Social Violence* (Boston: Northeastern University Press, 2001), 44–51.

4. Brendan McConville, "Pope's Day Revisited: 'Popular' Culture Reconsidered," *Explorations in Early American Culture* 4 (2000): 260, 265–266; Young, "Ebenezer Mackintosh," 17–19.

5. Collins, "Boston's Political Street Theatre," 403; Cogliano, "Deliverance," 19.

6. Francis Bernard to John Pownall, November 1, 1765 and November 26, 1765, in Tyler, *Francis Bernard*, 2: 397, 423; Young, "Ebenezer Mackintosh," 17–19.

7. Francis Bernard to John Pownall, November 26, 1765, in Tyler, *Francis Bernard*, 2: 422; JRD, November 5, 1764, in Cunningham, *Diary*, 67–68; McConville, "Pope's Day Revisited," 260, 266; Cogliano, "Deliverance," 21.

8. Francis Bernard to John Pownall, November 26, 1765, in Tyler, *Francis Bernard*, 2: 422; Young, "Ebenezer Mackintosh," 20–21; Justin du Rivage, *Revolution Against Empire: Taxes, Politics, and the Origins of American*

Independence (New Haven, CT: Yale University Press, 2017), 43–44, 52, 102–108, 120.

9. Edmund S. Morgan and Helen M. Morgan, *The Stamp Act Crisis: The Prologue to Revolution* (Chapel Hill: University of North Carolina Press, 1953, 1995), 23–31; Woody Holton, *Liberty is Sweet: The Hidden History of the American Revolution* (New York: Simon & Schuster, 2021), 26–31, 39–41.

10. William Burke, *An Account of the European Settlements in America in Six Parts*, vol. 2 (London: R. and J. Dodsley, 1760), 174; Wayne Curtis, *And a Bottle of Rum: A History of the New World in Ten Cocktails* (New York: Three Rivers Press, 2007), 97–98; Stephen Conway, "British Governments, Colonial Consumers, and Continental European Goods in the British Atlantic Empire, 1763–1775," *The Historical Journal* 58, no. 3 (2015): 721–722.

11. John Hancock to Barnard and Harrison, January 21, 1765, John Hancock Letterbook (business), HFP, BLSC; Morgan and Morgan, *Stamp Act*, 35–36: Margaret Ellen Newell, *From Dependency to Independence: Economic Revolution in Colonial New England* (Ithaca, NY: Cornell University Press, 1998), 267–269, 276–281; C. M. Andrews, "The Boston Merchants and the Non-Importation Movement," in *Transactions 1916–1917*, vol. 19 (Boston: The Colonial Society of Massachusetts, 1918), 163–165.

12. John Hancock to Thomas Pownall, July 6, 1765, reel 2, microfilm edition of HFP, MHS, P277; Edmund S. Morgan, ed., *Prologue to Revolution: Sources and Documents on the Stamp Act Crisis, 1764–1766* (Chapel Hill: University of North Carolina Press, 1959), 35–43; du Rivage, *Revolution*, 115–116.

13. Jane Kamensky, *Revolution in Color: The World of John Singleton Copley* (New York: W. W. Norton, 2016), 24.

14. "From John Adams to William Tudor, Sr., 1 June 1817," FO; Kamensky, *Revolution in Color*, 8, 69–73, 95; Paul Staiti, "Character and Class," in Carrie Rebora Barratt, et al., *John Singleton Copley in America* (New York: The Metropolitan Museum of Art, 1995), 71–74.

15. Gary B. Nash, *The Urban Crucible: The Northern Seaports and the Origins of the American Revolution* (Cambridge, MA: Harvard University Press, 1986), 148, 157–159, 185; Cornelia H. Dayton and Sharon V. Salinger, *Robert Love's Warnings: Searching for Strangers in Colonial Boston* (Philadelphia: University of Pennsylvania Press, 2014), 15, 138–139.

16. Instructions of the Town of Boston to Its Representatives in the General Court, September 18, 1765, in *The Writings of Samuel Adams*, ed. Harry Alonzo Cushing, vol. 1 (New York: G. P. Putnam's Sons, 1904), 9.

17. Pauline Maier, *From Resistance to Revolution: Colonial Radicals and the Development of American Opposition to Britain, 1765–1776* (New York: W. W. Norton, 1991), 3–14, 26–35; Tager, *Boston Riots*, 14–51; Dirk Hoerder, *Crowd Action in Revolutionary Massachusetts, 1765–1780* (New York: Academic Press, 1977), 40–84; William Pencak, *War, Politics, & Revolution in Provincial Massachusetts* (Boston: Northeastern University Press, 1981), 185–191.

18. Instructions of the Town of Boston to Its Representatives in the General Court, September 18, 1765, in Cushing, *Samuel Adams*, 1: 9; Maier, *Resistance*, 81–86; Nash, *Urban Crucible*, 185, 208–209, 220; Francis Bernard to John Pownall, November 1, 1765, in Tyler, *Francis Bernard*, 2: 397; Jesse Lemisch, *Jack Tar vs. John Bull: The Role of New York's Seamen in Precipitating the Revolution* (New York: Garland Publishing, 1997), 51–58, 88–92.

19. Gordon Wood, *The Radicalism of the American Revolution* (New York: Vintage Books, 1991), 77–85.

20. Thomas Hutchinson to Richard Jackson, August 16, 1765, in *The Correspondence of Thomas Hutchinson, volume 1: 1740–1766*, ed. John W. Tyler (Boston: The Colonial Society of Massachusetts, 2014), 279; Francis Bernard to Lord Halifax, August 15, 1765, in Tyler, *Francis Bernard*, 2: 302.

21. Thomas Hutchinson to Richard Jackson, August 16, 1765, in Tyler, *Thomas Hutchinson*, 1: 279; Morgan and Morgan, *Stamp Act*, 129–131.

22. John Hancock to Jonathan Barnard, August 22, 1765, John Hancock Letterbook (business), HFP, BLSC; Maier, *Resistance*, 62–64.

23. Morgan and Morgan, *Stamp Act*, 150–161; Maier, *Resistance*, 54–57.

24. Brad A. Jones, *Resisting Independence: Popular Loyalism in the Revolutionary British Atlantic* (Ithaca, NY: Columbia University Press, 2021), 42–43; Kathleen DuVal, *Independence Lost: Lives on the Edge of the American Revolution* (New York: Random House, 2015), xv–xxi, 3, 7–12, 31–33, 53–56, 224–226; Alan Taylor, *American Colonies* (New York: Viking, 2001), 422–443. Some historians tally twenty-six British colonies in the Americas but Holly Brewer counts forty administrative units in 1776. Holly Brewer, "How Many Colonies in the Americas?," *Slavery, Law, & Power in the British Empire and Early America* website.

25. Bernard Bailyn, *The Ordeal of Thomas Hutchinson* (Cambridge, MA: The Belknap Press of Harvard University Press, 1974), 9–12, 51–68; Morgan and Morgan, *Stamp Act*, 217–225.

26. Esther Forbes, *Paul Revere and the World He Lived In* (Boston: Mariner Books, 1999), 22–23.

27. "The Hutchinson House," *The American Magazine of Useful & Entertaining Knowledge* (February 1836): 237; William Burgis, "A southeast view of ye great town of Boston in New England in America," Digital Commonwealth, Massachusetts Collection Online; John W. Tyler, "'Such Ruins Were Never Seen in America': The Looting of Thomas Hutchinson's House at the Time of the Stamp Act Riots," *Boston Furniture, 1700–1900* (Boston: The Colonial Society of Massachusetts, 2016), 153, 161, 163.

28. Thomas Hutchinson, *The History of the Province of Massachusetts Bay: From 1749 to 1774* (London: John Murray, 1828), 124; Samuel Adams to John Smith, August 20, 1765, in Cushing, *Samuel Adams*, 1: 60; Morgan and Morgan, *Stamp Act*, 132–135; Bailyn, *Ordeal*, 35–37.

29. John Hancock to Jonathan Barnard, January 25, 1766, John Hancock Letterbook (business), HFP, BLSC.

30. John Hancock to Jonathan Barnard, January 25, 1766, John Hancock Letterbook (business), HFP, BLSC; Samuel Adams to John Smith, August 20, 1765, in Cushing, *Samuel Adams*, 1: 60; Maier, *Resistance*, 62–64.

31. Maier, *Resistance*, 56–58; Hoerder, *Crowd Action*, 108–110.

32. *BG*, April 14, 1766, HD; Maier, *Resistance*, chapter 4; Morgan and Morgan, *Stamp Act*, chapter 11.

33. *BG*, April 14, 1766, HD; Amanda Ripley, *High Conflict: Why We Get Trapped and How We Get Out* (New York: Simon & Schuster, 2021), 4–5, 49–50.

34. Maier, *Resistance*, 96–108; Jones, *Resisting*, 45–47.

35. John Hancock to Jonathan Barnard, October 14, 1765, John Hancock Letterbook (business), HFP, BLSC.

36. John Hancock to Jonathan Barnard, August 22, 1765 and October 22, 1765, John Hancock Letterbook (business), HFP, BLSC; Alan Taylor, *American Revolutions: A Continental History, 1750–1804* (New York: W. W. Norton, 2016), 25–26.

37. John Hancock to Jonathan Barnard, October 14, 1765 and October 22, 1765, John Hancock Letterbook (business), HFP, BLSC; T. H. Breen, *Tobacco Culture: The Mentality of the Great Tidewater Planters on the Eve of Revolution* (Princeton, NJ: Princeton University Press, 1985), 121–131; T. H. Breen, *The Marketplace of Revolution: How Consumer Politics Shaped American Independence* (Oxford: Oxford University Press, 2004), 224.

38. John Hancock to Jonathan Barnard, October 14, 1765, October 22, 1765, and January 25, 1766, John Hancock Letterbook (business), HFP, BLSC; Bernard Bailyn, *The Ideological Origins of the American Revolution* (Cambridge, MA: The Belknap Press of Harvard University Press, 1992), 67–78, 99.

39. John Hancock to Jonathan Barnard, September 30, 1765, John Hancock Letterbook (business), HFP, BLSC; Breen, *Marketplace*, 220–225; Morgan and Morgan, *Stamp Act*, 272–275; Benjamin L. Carp, *Rebels Rising: Cities and the American Revolution* (New York: Oxford University Press, 2007), 4–6.

40. John Hancock to Jonathan Barnard, October 22, 1765; John Hancock to Devonshur and Reeve, December 21, 1765, John Hancock Letterbook (business), HFP, BLSC.

41. Francis Bernard to John Pownall, November 1, 1765, in Tyler, *Francis Bernard*, 2: 395, quote on 397; Morgan and Morgan, *Stamp Act*, 165–185.

42. Robert McCluer Calhoon, *Political Moderation in America's First Two Centuries* (New York: Cambridge University Press, 2009), 5–6; Cathy Matson, *Merchants & Empire: Trading in Colonial New York* (Baltimore: John Hopkins University Press, 1998), 266–271; Jones, *Resisting*, 51–52, 61.

43. David Conroy, *In Public Houses: Drink and Revolution of Authority in Colonial Massachusetts* (Chapel Hill: University of North Carolina Press, 1995), 59, 89–95, 255–263; Wood, *Radicalism*, 41–42.

44. Nathaniel B. Shurtleff, *A Topographical and Historical Description of Boston* (Boston: Alfred Mudge and Son, 1871), 610–611.

45. Conroy, *In Public Houses*, 16; Sharon Salinger, *Taverns and Drinking in Early America* (Baltimore: Johns Hopkins University Press, 2002), 21; Allan Forbes and Ralph M. Eastman, *Taverns and Stagecoaches of New England*, vol. 2 (Boston: State Street Trust Company, 1954), 26; Samuel A. Forman, *Dr. Joseph Warren: The Boston Tea Party, Bunker Hill, and the Birth of American Liberty* (Gretna, LA: Pelican Publishing Company, 2012), 110–114.

46. "Reminiscences by Gen. Wm. H. Sumner," *NEHGR* 8 (1854): 191; *Columbian Centinel*, October 23, 1793, GB; Maier, *Resistance*, 69–71.

47. Francis Bernard to John Pownall, November 26, 1765, in Tyler, *Francis Bernard*, 2: 422.

48. Francis Bernard to John Pownall, November 5, 1765, in Tyler, *Francis Bernard*, 2: 397–398; *BG*, November 4, 1765, GB.

49. Francis Bernard to John Pownall, November 5 and November 26, 1765, in Tyler, *Francis Bernard*, 2: 397, 399, 423; *BG*, November 4 and November 11, 1765, GB; McConville, "Pope's Day Revisited," 271, 272, 275.

50. Francis Bernard to John Pownall, November 26, 1765, in Tyler, *Francis Bernard*, 2: 423.

51. Francis Bernard to John Pownall, April 13, 1766, in *The Papers of Francis Bernard, volume 3: 1766–1767*, ed. Colin Nicolson (Boston: The Colonial Society of Massachusetts, 2013), 142; Morgan and Morgan, *Stamp Act*, 275–291; du Rivage, *Revolution against Empire*, 132–143, 180.

52. Morgan and Morgan, *Stamp Act*, 295; Jones, *Resisting*, 63–69.
53. Maier, *Resistance*, 109–111; du Rivage, *Revolution*, 144.
54. JRD, May 16, 1766, in Cunningham, *Diary*, 95; BG, May 19, 1766, HD.
55. BG, May 19 and May 26, 1766, HD.
56. BG, May 26, 1766, HD.
57. BG, May 26, 1766, HD.
58. Wood, *Radicalism*, 89.
59. JRD, May 19, 1766, in Cunningham, *Diary*, 95; Benjamin Bussey Thatcher, *Traits of the Tea Party; Being a Memoir of George R. T. Hewes* (New York: Harper & Brothers, 1835), 73; Conroy, *In Public Houses*, 264.
60. BG, May 26, 1766, HD.
61. BG, May 26, 1766, HD.

3: THE BOLD AND BRASH IDOL OF THE MOB

1. Memorial to the Right Honble The Lords Commissioners of His Majesty's Treasury from the Commissioners of the Customs of America, May 12, 1768, NA, Treasury Bundle, T1/465, 64.
2. Yale Avalon online, "Great Britain: Parliament—The Townshend Act, November 20, 1767," accessed June 1, 2020; Justin du Rivage, *Revolution Against Empire: Taxes, Politics, and the Origins of American Independence* (New Haven, CT: Yale University Press, 2017), 181–182.
3. Joseph Harrison to Marquis of Rockingham, June 17, 1768, in D. H. Watson, "Joseph Harrison and the Liberty Incident," *The William and Mary Quarterly* 20, no. 4 (October 1963): 588–589.
4. Oliver Morton Dickerson, "Opinion of Attorney General Jonathan Sewall of Massachusetts in the Case of the Lydia," *The William and Mary Quarterly* 4, no. 4 (October 1947): 499–504; Neal Nusholtz, "How John Adams Won the Hancock Trial," *Journal of the American Revolution*, August 16, 2016, accessed online; Testimony of Owen Richards and Robert Jackson, April 11, 1768, NA, Treasury Bundle, T1/465, 66.
5. March 8, 1773, *A Report of the Record Commissioners of the City of Boston Containing the Boston Town Records, 1770 Through 1777* (Boston: Rockwell and Churchill, 1887), 116–117; *The Massachusetts Spy*, March 3, 1774, GB.
6. Opinion of Jonathan Sewell, April 23, 1768, NA, Treasury Bundle, T1/465, 70; Dickerson, "Opinion," 499–504; Testimony of Owen Richards and Robert Jackson, April 11, 1768, NA, Treasury Bundle, T1/465, 66.

7. Testimony of Owen Richards and Robert Jackson, April 11, 1768, NA, Treasury Bundle, T1/465, 66.

8. Testimony of Owen Richards and Robert Jackson, April 11, 1768, NA, Treasury Bundle, T1/465, 67; Dickerson, "Opinion," 499–504; Thomas Hutchinson to Nathaniel Rogers, April 17, 1768, in *The Correspondence of Thomas Hutchinson, volume 2: 1767–1769*, ed. John W. Tyler (Boston: The Colonial Society of Massachusetts, 2020), 158.

9. Thomas Hutchinson to Nathaniel Rogers, April 17, 1768, in Tyler, *Thomas Hutchinson*, 2: 158.

10. Memorial to the Right Honble The Lords Commissioners, May 12, 1768, NA, Treasury Bundle, T1/465, 64; Samuel Fitch, Solicitor's Opinion, April 15, 1768, NA, Treasury Bundle, T1/465, 68–69.

11. Benjamin H. Irvin, "Tar, Feathers, and the Enemies of American Liberties, 1768–1776," *The New England Quarterly* 76, no. 2 (June 2003): 203–205.

12. Dickerson, "Opinion," 499–504; Opinion of Jonathan Sewell, April 23, 1768, NA, Treasury Bundle, T1/465, 71; Nina Sankovitch, *American Rebels: How the Hancock, Adams, and Quincy Families Fanned the Flames of Revolution* (New York: St. Martin's Press, 2020), 49–50.

13. Memorial to the Right Honble The Lords Commissioners, May 12, 1768, NA, Treasury Bundle, T1/465, 65; Memorial of the American Board of Customs to the Lords Commissioners of the Treasury, February 12, 1768, in *The Papers of Francis Bernard: Governor of Colonial Massachusetts, volume 4: 1760–1769*, ed. Colin Nicolson (Boston: The Colonial Society of Massachusetts, 2015), 377–378.

14. Francis Bernard to Lord Barrington, March 4, 1768, in Nicolson, *Francis Bernard*, 4: 363–366; Dickerson, "Opinion," 500, 504; Lisa Ford, *The King's Peace: Law and Order in the British Empire* (Cambridge, MA: Harvard University Press, 2021), 28–29.

15. *A Report of the Record Commissioners of the City of Boston, Containing the Boston Town Records, 1758 to 1769* (Boston: Rockwell and Churchill, 1886), 250; Memorial to the Right Honble The Lords Commissioners, May 12, 1768, NA, Treasury Bundle, T1/465, 64.

16. Memorial to the Right Honble The Lords Commissioners, May 12, 1768, NA, Treasury Bundle, T1/465, 64.

17. John Cotton to John Hancock, May 18, 1768, FCCC, A 137, HGARC.

18. Francis Bernard to John Hancock, May 18, 1768, FCCC, A 138, John Hancock to Francis Bernard, May 19, 1768, FCCC, A 147, HGARC.

19. Francis Bernard to the Earl of Hillsborough, May 30, 1768, in Nicolson, *Francis Bernard*, 4: 166–169.

20. John Hancock to Hill, Lamar, & Bissett, January 20, 1767, in G. G. Wolkins, "The Seizure of John Hancock's Sloop 'Liberty,'" *MHS-P*, vol. 55 (Boston: Massachusetts Historical Society, 1923), 262; John Hancock to Hill, Lamar, & Bissett, July 23, 1765, John Hancock Letterbook (business), HFP, BLSC.

21. "Case of the *Liberty*" by William De Grey, July 25, 1768, in Wolkins, "The Seizure," 273; O. M. Dickerson, "John Hancock: Notorious Smuggler or Near Victim of British Revenue Racketeers?" *The Mississippi Valley Historical Review* 32, no. 4 (March 1946): 520–521.

22. Examination of Mr. Hallowell at the Treasury Board, July 21, 1768, Arthur Lee Papers, 1741–1882, HL.

23. Deposition of Thomas Kirk, June 10, 1768, NA, Treasury Bundle, T1/465, 129; Dickerson, "John Hancock," 521.

24. Deposition of Thomas Kirk, June 10, 1768, NA, Treasury Bundle, T1/465, 129.

25. Deposition of Thomas Kirk, June 10, 1768, NA, Treasury Bundle, T1/465, 129.

26. Joseph Harrison and Benjamin Hallowell to the Commissioners of the Customs at Boston, June 11, 1768, NA, Treasury Bundle, T1/465, 145; Dickerson, "John Hancock," 518–520.

27. *BEP*, June 20, 1768, HD; Douglass Adair and John A. Schutz, eds., *Peter Oliver's Origin & Progress of the American Revolution: A Tory View* (San Marino, CA: The Huntington Library, 1961), 69.

28. "Case of the Liberty" by William De Grey, July 25, 1768, in Wolkins, "The Seizure," 274; *BEP*, June 20, 1768, HD; Examination of Mr. Hallowell, July 21, 1768, Arthur Lee Papers, 1741–1882, HL; Joseph Harrison to Marquis of Rockingham, June 17, 1768, in Watson, "Joseph Harrison," 590.

29. Earl of Hillsborough to Francis Bernard, July 30, 1768, in Nicolson, *Francis Bernard*, 4: 271–276; Pauline Maier, *From Resistance to Revolution: Colonial Radicals and the Development of American Opposition to Britain, 1765–1776* (New York: W. W. Norton, 1972, 1991), 9–11; Neil R. Stout, "Manning the Royal Navy in North America, 1763–1775," *American Neptune* 23 (1963): 184.

30. Deposition of Benjamin Hallowell, June 11, 1768 and Deposition of Joseph Harrison, June 11, 1768, NA, Treasury Bundle, T1/465, 131, 133; Francis Bernard to the Earl of Hillsborough, June 11, 1768, in Nicolson, *Francis Bernard*, 4: 185–186.

31. Deposition of Benjamin Hallowell, June 11, 1768, and Deposition of Joseph Harrison, June 11, 1768, NA, Treasury Bundle, T1/465, 131, 134; Francis

Bernard to the Earl of Hillsborough, June 11, 1768, in Nicolson, *Francis Bernard*, 4: 185–186.

32. Deposition of Richard Harrison, June 11, 1768, NA, Treasury Bundle, T1/465, 135; Francis Bernard to the Earl of Hillsborough, June 11, 1768, in Nicolson, *Francis Bernard*, 4: 185–186.

33. *BEP*, June 20, 1768, HD; Francis Bernard to the Earl of Hillsborough, June 6, 1768, in Nicolson, *Francis Bernard*, 4: 174–175. Some historians argue that the riot was more about impressment: Jesse Lemisch, "Jack Tar in the Street: Merchant Seamen in the Politics of Revolutionary America," *The William and Mary Quarterly* 25, no. 3 (July 1968): 392n86; Maier, *Resistance*, 124–125; John Rowe, however, was unequivocal: "A considerable mob tonight occasioned by a seizure belonging to Mr John Hancock," JRD, June 10, 1768, in *Letters and Diary of John Rowe*, ed. Anne Rowe Cunningham (Boston: W. B. Clarke, 1903), 165.

34. Joseph Harrison to Marquis of Rockingham, June 17, 1768, in Watson, "Joseph Harrison," 590–591.

35. Alan Taylor, *American Revolutions: A Continental History, 1750–1804* (New York: W. W. Norton, 2016), 4, 211–219; Maya Jasanoff, *Liberty's Exiles: American Loyalists in the Revolutionary World* (New York: Alfred A. Knopf, 2011), 8–9, 23–25; Aaron Sullivan, *The Disaffected: Britain's Occupation of Philadelphia during the American Revolution* (Philadelphia: University of Pennsylvania Press, 2019), 5–7; Paul H. Smith, "The American Loyalists: Notes on their Organization and Numerical Strength," *The William and Mary Quarterly* 25, no. 2 (April 1968): 261–269; N. E. H. Hull, Peter C. Hoffer, and Steven L. Allen, "Choosing Sides: A Quantitative Study of the Personality Determinants of Loyalist and Revolutionary Political Affiliation in New York," *The Journal of American History* 65, no. 4 (September 1978): 344–366; Mary Beth Norton, *1774: The Long Year of Revolution* (Alfred A. Knopf, 2020), xv–xvi; Daniel Vickers, "Ashley Bowen of Marblehead: Revolutionary Neutral," in *The Human Tradition in the American Revolution*, ed. Nancy L. Rhoden and Ian K. Steele (Wilmington, DE: Scholarly Resources, 2000), 90, 113; Brendan McConville, *The Brethren: A Story of Faith and Conspiracy in Revolutionary America* (Cambridge, MA: Harvard University Press, 2021), 7, 191–202.

36. Francis Bernard to the Earl of Hillsborough, June 11, 1768, in Nicolson, *Francis Bernard*, 4: 185–186.

37. Francis Bernard to the Earl of Hillsborough, June 11, 1768, in Nicolson, *Francis Bernard*, 4: 185–186; Joseph Harrison to Marquis of Rockingham,

NOTES TO PAGES 61–64 253

June 17, 1768, in Watson, "Joseph Harrison," 591; *BEP*, June 20, 1768, HD; Examination of Mr. Hallowell, July 21, 1768, Arthur Lee Papers, HL; Thomas Hutchinson to Richard Jackson, June 16, 1768, in Wolkins, "The Seizure," 281; Burning press gangs boats was a tradition dating to the 1740s. Marcus Rediker, "A Motley Crew of Rebels: Sailors, Slaves, and the Coming of the American Revolution," in *The Transforming Hand of Revolution: Reconsidering the American Revolution as a Social Movement*, ed. Ronald Hoffman and Peter J. Albert (Charlottesville: University Press of Virginia, 1995), 160–162, 170.

38. Memorial of the American Board of Customs, June 16, 1768, in Nicolson, *Francis Bernard*, 4: 377–378; Wolkins, "The Seizure," 275; Francis Bernard to the Earl of Hillsborough, June 14, 1768, in Nicolson, *Francis Bernard*, 4: 201–202.

39. Joseph Harrison to Marquis of Rockingham, June 17, 1768, in Watson, "Joseph Harrison," 592.

40. Examination of Mr. Hallowell, July 21, 1768, Arthur Lee Papers, HL; Dickerson, "John Hancock," 531; Wolkins, "The Seizure," 275; Christian Di Spigna, *Founding Martyr: The Life and Death of Dr. Joseph Warren, the American Revolution's Lost Hero* (New York: Crown 2018), 96.

41. Examination of Mr. Hallowell, July 21, 1768, Arthur Lee Papers, HL; Joseph Harrison and Benjamin Hallowell to John Robinson, June 12, 1768, NA, Treasury Bundle, T1/465, 149–150.

42. Examination of Mr. Hallowell, July 21, 1768, Arthur Lee Papers, HL.

43. Examination of Mr. Hallowell, July 21, 1768, Arthur Lee Papers, HL; Joseph Harrison to Marquis of Rockingham, June 17, 1768, in Watson, "Joseph Harrison," 589, 592.

44. Brad A. Jones, *Resisting Independence: Popular Loyalism in the Revolutionary British Atlantic* (Ithaca, NY: Columbia University Press, 2021), 85.

45. JRD, June 14, 1768, in Cunningham, *Diary*, 165–166; *BG*, June 20, 1768, GB; Francis Bernard to the Earl of Hillsborough, June 16, 1768, in Nicholson, *Francis Bernard*, 4: 207; Richard Archer, *As If an Enemy's Country: The British Occupation of Boston and the Origins of Revolution* (New York: Oxford University Press, 2010), 89–90.

46. Francis Bernard to the Earl of Hillsborough, June 16, 1768, in Nicholson, *Francis Bernard*, 4: 208.

47. The House of Representatives of Massachusetts to Dennys de Berdt, January 12, 1768, in *The Writings of Samuel Adams*, ed. Harry Alonzo Cushing, vol. 1 (New York: G.P. Putnam's Sons, 1904), 136–138.

48. JRD, August 1, 1768, in Cunningham, *Diary*, 171.

49. John Hancock to George Hayley, October 4, 1768, John Hancock Letter-book (business), HFP, BLSC; Ford, *King's Peace*, 44–48.

50. David Lisle to Thomas Bradshaw, May 14, 1768, NA, Treasury Bundle, T1/465, 77; Earl of Hillsborough to Francis Bernard, July 30, 1768, in Nicolson, *Francis Bernard*, 4: 271–276.

51. *BEP*, November 3, 1768, in *Boston Under Military Rule, 1768–1769, As Revealed in a Journal of the Times*, ed. Oliver Morton Dickerson (New York: Da Capo Press, 1970), 18; William M. Fowler, Jr., *The Baron of Beacon Hill: A Biography of John Hancock* (Boston: Houghton Mifflin, 1980), 98–99.

52. L. Kinvin Wroth and Hiller B. Zobel, eds., *Legal Papers of John Adams*, vol. 2 (Cambridge, MA: The Belknap Press of Harvard University Press, 1965), 197; Nusholtz, "How John Adams"; W. T. Baxter, *The House of Hancock: Business in Boston, 1724–1775* (Cambridge, MA: Harvard University Press, 1945), 266–268; JAD, 1768, in Charles Francis Adams, ed., *The Works of John Adams*, vol. 2 (Boston: Charles C. Little and James Brown, 1850), 216.

53. *BG*, July 24, 1769, HD; "The Burnings of the *Liberty*," *Boston 1775* (blog), August 20, 2019, https://boston1775.blogspot.com/2019/08/the-burnings-of-liberty.html.

54. John Wilkes to William Palfrey, July 24, 1769, September 27, 1769, and July 24, 1770, *Transactions 1937–1942*, vol. 34 (Boston: The Colonial Society of Massachusetts, 1943), 414–418; Joseph Harrison to Marquis of Rockingham, June 17, 1768, in Watson, "Joseph Harrison," 589; Maier, *Resistance*, 163–165.

55. John Hancock Speech, March 5, 1774, in Paul D. Brandes, *John Hancock's Life and Speeches: A Personalized Vision of the American Revolution, 1763–1793* (Lanham, MD: The Scarecrow Press, 1996), 215; Serena Zabin, *The Boston Massacre: A Family History* (Boston: Houghton Mifflin Harcourt, 2020), chapter 5; Bernard Bailyn, *The Ideological Origins of the American Revolution* (Cambridge, MA: The Belknap Press of Harvard University Press, 1992, 1967), 61–63, 112–115.

56. *BEP*, October 31, 1768, in Dickerson, *Boston Under Military Rule*, 17; Zabin, *Boston Massacre*, 109–125.

57. John Hancock to George Hayley, Esq., October 4, 1768, John Hancock Letterbook, HFP, BLSC.

4: BAD PRESS

1. *BG*, August 21, 1769, HD; JAD, August 14, 1769, vol. 1, MHS online; William Palfrey, "An Alphabetical List of the Sons of Liberty who din'd at Liberty Tree, Dorchester," MHS online; JRD, August 14, 1769, in *Letters and Diary of John Rowe*, ed. Anne Rowe Cunningham (Boston: W. B. Clarke, 1903), 191.

2. JAD, August 14, 1769, vol. 1, MHS online; Joseph Harrison to Marquis of Rockingham, June 17, 1768, in D. H. Watson, "Joseph Harrison and the Liberty Incident," *The William and Mary Quarterly* 20, no. 4 (October 1963): 592.

3. *BEP*, October 6, October 19, October 26, November 27, November 30, 1768, January 8, 1769, and April 11, 1769, in *Boston Under Military Rule, 1768–1769, As Revealed in a Journal of the Times*, ed. Oliver Morton Dickerson (New York: Da Capo Press, 1970), 3, 8, 9, 28–29, 47, 89.

4. JAD, August 14, 1769, vol. 1, MHS online; *BG*, August 21, 1769, HD; JRD, August 14, 1769, in Cunningham, *Diary*, 191; Alfred F. Young, *The Shoemaker and the Tea Party: Memory and the American Revolution* (Boston: Beacon Press, 1999), 94–98; Philip Davidson, *Propaganda and the American Revolution, 1763–1783* (New York: W. W. Norton, 1973), 174–176.

5. Samuel Adams to Jonathan Augustine Washington, March 21, 1775, in *The Writings of Samuel Adams, 1773–1777*, ed. Harry Alonzo Cushing, vol. 3 (New York: G. P. Putnam's Sons, 1907), 211; Charles Tilly, *The Politics of Collective Violence* (Cambridge: University of Cambridge Press, 2003), 75–76; John K. Alexander, *Samuel Adams: America's Revolutionary Politician* (Lanham, MD: Rowman & Littlefield, 2002), 44–45.

6. Esther Forbes, *Paul Revere and the World He Lived In* (Boston: Mariner Books, 1999), 197, 397–398.

7. JAD, August 14, 1769, vol. 1, MHS online; *BG*, August 21, 1769, HD; "Memories of 'Mr. Balch's Mimickry,'" *Boston 1775* (blog), August 16, 2019, https://boston1775.blogspot.com/2019/08/memories-of-mr-balchs-mimickry.html.

8. Sharon Salinger, *Taverns and Drinking in Early America* (Baltimore: Johns Hopkins University Press, 2002), 70, 220; *BG*, August 21, 1769, HD.

9. All toasts printed in *BG*, August 21, 1769, HD.

10. JRD, August 1, 1769, in Cunningham, *Diary*, 190.

11. John Hancock to George Hayley, August 24, 1768, John Hancock Letterbook (business), HFP, BLSC; Arthur Meier Schlesinger, *The Colonial Merchants*

and the American Revolution, 1763–1776 (New York: Longmans, Green and Co., 1918), 110–113, 120; T. H. Breen, *The Marketplace of Revolution: How Consumer Politics Shaped American Independence* (New York: Oxford University Press, 2004), 244–247.

12. Thomas Gage to Lord Hillsborough, December 4, 1769, in *The Correspondence of General Thomas Gage with the Secretaries of State, 1763–1775*, ed. Clarence Edwin Carter, vol. 1 (Archon Books, 1969), 242.

13. Schlesinger, *Colonial Merchants*, 110–113, 131; C. M. Andrews, "The Boston Merchants and the Non-Importation Movement," *Transactions 1916–1917*, vol. 19 (Boston: The Colonial Society of Massachusetts, 1918), 204–221; John W. Tyler, *Smugglers and Patriots: Boston Merchants and the Advent of the American Revolution* (Boston: Northeastern University Press, 1986), 113–116; Breen, *Marketplace*, 245–247; Pauline Maier, *From Resistance to Revolution: Colonial Radicals and the Development of American Opposition to Britain, 1765–1776* (New York: W. W. Norton, 1972, 1991), 114–115, 145–146; Thomas M. Doerflinger, "Philadelphia Merchants and the Logic of Moderation, 1760–1775," *The William and Mary Quarterly* 40, no. 3 (April 1983): 218–221.

14. Breen, *Marketplace*, 38, 60–64.

15. John Hancock to George Hayley, October 4, 1768, John Hancock Letterbook (business), HFP, BLSC; Michael Zakim, *Ready-Made Democracy: A History of Men's Dress in the American Republic, 1760–1860* (Chicago: University of Chicago Press, 2003), 11–22.

16. Anna Green Winslow diary, February 21, 1772, in *Diary of Anna Green Winslow: A Boston School Girl of 1771*, ed. Alice Morse Earle (Boston: Houghton Mifflin, 1895), 32; Mary Beth Norton, *Liberty's Daughters: The Revolutionary Experience of American Women, 1750–1800* (Boston: Little, Brown, 1980), 157–170; Alfred F. Young, "'Persons of Consequence': The Women of Boston and the Making of the American Revolution, 1765–1776," in *Liberty Tree: Ordinary People and the American Revolution* (New York: New York University Press, 2006), 115–117; Patricia Cleary, *Elizabeth Murray: A Woman's Pursuit of Independence in Eighteenth-Century America* (Amherst: University of Massachusetts Press, 2000), 137–138; Jeremy A. Stern, "Jane Franklin Mecom: A Boston Woman in Revolutionary Times," *Early American Studies* 4, no. 1 (Spring 2006): 149–158, 169–171; Linda K. Kerber, *Women of the Republic: Intellect and Ideology in Revolutionary America* (New York: W. W. Norton, 1986), 37–44, 48.

17. *BG*, August 21, 1769, HD; Francis Bernard to the Earl of Hillsborough, May 19, 1768, in *The Papers of Francis Bernard: Governor of Colonial Mas-*

sachusetts, volume 4: 1760–1769, ed. Colin Nicolson (Boston: The Colonial Society of Massachusetts, 2015), 162.

18. Joseph M. Adelman, *Revolutionary Networks: The Business and Politics of Printing the News, 1763–1789* (Baltimore: Johns Hopkins University Press, 2019), 81–83, 91; Davidson, *Propaganda*, 225–233; Eric Hinderaker, *Boston's Massacre* (Cambridge, MA: The Belknap Press of Harvard University Press, 2017), 134–137.

19. JAD, August 14, 1769, vol. 1, MHS online; *BG*, August 21, 1769, HD.

20. William Palfrey to John Hancock, February 5, 1771, Palfrey Family Papers, HL; John E. Alden, "John Mein: Scourge of Patriots," *Transactions 1937–1942*, vol. 34 (Boston: The Colonial Society of Massachusetts, 1943), 579–584; Isaiah Thomas, *The History of Printing in America*, vol. 2 (Worcester, MA: Isaac Sturtevant, 1810), 247, 439–440; Samuel Adams Drake, *Old Landmarks and Historic Personages of Boston* (Boston: J. R. Osgood, 1873), 106–107; *BG*, January 25, 1768, HD; *BG*, February 1, 1768, GB.

21. *BC*, June 1, 1769, GB; *BEP*, June 5, 1769, *Massachusetts Gazette*, June 8, 1769, HD.

22. *BC*, July 31–August 3, 1769, HD; JRD, July 31, 1769, in Cunningham, *Diary*, 190.

23. *BG*, October 2, 1769, HD; *BC*, August 21, 1769, GB.

24. *BC*, August 21, 1769, *BEP*, August 28, 1769, GB; Jared Sparks, ed., *Lives of John Ribault, Sebastian Rale, and William Palfrey*, The Library of American Biography, second series, vol. 7 (Boston: Charles C. Little and James Brown, 1845), 364.

25. John Hancock to George Hayley, December 21, 1768, John Hancock Letterbook (business), HFP, BLSC; *BEP*, August 28, 1769, GB.

26. *BC*, August 28, 1769, GB; Schlesinger, *Colonial Merchants*, 169.

27. *Newport Mercury*, September 4, 1769, GB; William M. Fowler, Jr., *The Baron of Beacon Hill: A Biography of John Hancock* (Boston: Houghton Mifflin, 1980), 304n38.

28. *BG*, October 2, 1769, HD; Thomas, *History of Printing*, 2: 247; O. M. Dickerson, "British Control of American Newspapers on the Eve of Revolution," *The New England Quarterly* 24, no. 4 (December 1951): 461–463; Adelman, *Revolutionary Networks*, 92.

29. JRD, September 5, 1769, in Cunningham, *Diary*, 191–192; Schlesinger, *Colonial Merchants*, 168–169; John Hancock to Hayley and Hopkins, September 6, 1769, and January 1, 1770, John Hancock Letterbook (business), HFP, BLSC.

30. John Mein, "A State of the Importations from Great-Britain into the Port of Boston" (Boston: Mein and Fleeming, 1769); Andrews, "Boston Merchants," 228–229, 250–251; Tyler, *Smugglers*, 163.

31. William Palfrey to John Wilkes, October 21, 1769, *MHS-P*, vol. 47 (Boston: Massachusetts Historical Society, 1914), 212; *Boston News-Letter*, October 26, 1769, GB.

32. *New York Journal*, January 18, 1770, GB; Schlesinger, *Colonial Merchants*, 132.

33. *BC*, October 26, 1769, *BG*, September 4, 1769, GB.

34. Alden, "Scourge," 586–587; Hiller B. Zobel, *The Boston Massacre* (New York: W. W. Norton, 1996), 155–162.

35. Alden, "Scourge," 587; *BEP*, October 30, 1769, GB.

36. Alden, "Scourge," 588; JRD, October 28, 1769, in Cunningham, *Diary*, 194; "The Pleadings Book: 1771–1773," FO; *BEP*, October 30, 1769, HD; J. L. Bell, "An assault, on the Body of the said George Gailer," *Boston 1775* (blog), November 4, 2019, https://boston1775.blogspot.com/2019/11/an-assault-on -body-of-said-george-gailer.html.

37. *BEP*, October 30, 1769, HD.

38. JRD, October 28, 1769, in Cunningham, *Diary*, 194.

39. *BG*, October 2, 1769, HD; Thomas Longman to John Hancock, July 22, 1769, HFP, MHS; John Hancock to Thomas Longman, October 28, 1765, in Abram English Brown, *John Hancock: His Book* (Boston: Lee and Shepard, 1898), 92–94; Andrews, "Boston Merchants," 229.

40. L. Kinvin Wroth and Hiller B. Zobel, eds., *Legal Papers of John Adams*, vol. 1 (Cambridge, MA: The Belknap Press of Harvard University Press, 1965), 200; Thomas Longman to John Hancock, December 4, 1769, HFP, MHS.

41. John Hancock to Thomas Longman, May 18, 1770, in Brown, *His Book*, 94; Thomas Longman to John Hancock, January 3, 1770, HFP, MHS.

42. Wroth and Zobel, *Legal Papers of John Adams*, 1: 202–203; Drake, *Old Land-marks*, 107; William Palfrey to John Hancock, February 5, 1771, Palfrey Family Papers, HL.

43. John Hancock to Thomas Longman, December 3, 1770, in Brown, *His Book*, 96.

44. William Palfrey to John Hancock, February 15, 1771, Palfrey Family Papers, HL; Longman v. Mein, Wright & Gill v. Mein 1770–1771 Editorial Note, MHS online, 200.

45. George Hayley to John Hancock, February 17, 1770, HFP, MHS; Tyler, *Smugglers*, 139–143.

46. JRD, January 19, 1770, in Cunningham, *Diary*, 196; *BEP*, January 29, 1770, GB; Richard Archer, *As If an Enemy's Country: The British Occupation of Boston and the Origins of Revolution* (New York: Oxford University Press, 2010),168–171; Tyler, *Smugglers*, 144–148; Benjamin L. Carp, *Defiance of the Patriots: The Boston Tea Party and the Making of America* (New Haven, CT: Yale University Press, 2010), 40–41.

47. *BC*, January 15, 1770, GB; Schlesinger, *Colonial Merchants*, 171–172; Dirk Hoerder, *Crowd Action in Revolutionary Massachusetts, 1765–1780* (New York: Academic Press, 1977), 216–219.

48. *BC*, January 15, 1770, GB; Andrews, "Boston Merchants," 225–226, 232–233; Cleary, *Elizabeth Murray*, 133–135; Schlesinger, *Colonial Merchants*, 158–159; Justin du Rivage, *Revolution Against Empire: Taxes, Politics, and the Origins of American Independence* (New Haven, CT: Yale University Press, 2017), 180.

49. *BC*, January 15, 1770, GB.

50. *BG*, February 26, 1770, GB; J. L. Bell, "Ebenezer Richardson: Customs informer and killer," *Boston 1775* (blog), May 22, 2006, https://boston1775 .blogspot.com/2006/05/ebenezer-richardson-customs-informer.html.

51. *BG*, February 26, 1770, GB; Zobel, *Boston Massacre*, 174–176; Archer, *Enemy's Country*, 178–179. Christopher Seider is sometimes spelled Snider and some accounts claim he was twelve years old.

52. *BG*, February 26, 1770, HD; JRD, February 26, 1770, in Cunningham, *Diary*, 197; Thomas Hutchinson to Lord Hillsborough, February 28, 1770, in *The Correspondence of Thomas Hutchinson, volume 3: 1770 (January-October)*, ed. John W. Tyler (Boston: The Colonial Society of Massachusetts, 2021), 95.

53. Thomas Preston to Thomas Gage, March 14, 1770, "A Fair Account," in Neil L. York, *The Boston Massacre: A History with Documents* (New York: Routledge, Taylor & Francis, 2010), 110, 148–149.

54. Archer, *Enemy's Country*, 185–198; Wroth and Zobel, *Legal Papers of John Adams*, 3: 266.

55. Thomas Preston to Thomas Gage, March 14, 1770, in York, *Boston Massacre*, 111; *BG*, March 12, 1770, GB; Zobel, *Boston Massacre*, 184–205.

56. Hinderaker, *Boston's Massacre*, 227–234.

57. John Hancock Speech, March 5, 1774, in Paul D. Brandes, *John Hancock's Life and Speeches: A Personalized Vision of the American Revolution, 1763-1793* (Lanham, MD: The Scarecrow Press, 1996), 213; "Memoranda of the year 1789," *MHS-P*, vol. 3 (Boston: Massachusetts Historical Society, 1859), 308–309; Serena Zabin, *The Boston Massacre: A Family History* (Boston: Houghton Mifflin Harcourt, 2020), 161–170; *BG*, March 12, 1770, GB.

58. William Tudor, *Deacon Tudor's Diary* (Boston: Press of Wallace Spooner, 1896), 33.

59. *BG*, March 12, 1770, GB; Zabin, *Boston Massacre*, 191–221.

60. D. Brenton Simons, *Witches, Rakes, and Rogues: Trues Stories of Scam, Scandal, Murder, and Mayhem in Boston, 1630–1775* (Carlisle, MA: Commonwealth Editions, 2005), 225–227; Alexander, *Samuel Adams*, 92–105; David McCullough, *John Adams* (New York: Simon & Schuster, 2001), 69–70.

5: LIFE OUTSIDE OF POLITICS

1. Sharon Salinger, *Taverns and Drinking in Early America* (Baltimore: Johns Hopkins University Press, 2002), 54, 115, 152; Elaine Forman Crane, *Ebb Tide in New England: Women, Seaports, and Social Change, 1630–1800* (Boston: Northeastern University Press, 1998), 177–183; *Documents of the City of Boston for the Year 1893*, vol. 3 (Boston: Rockwell and Churchill, 1894), 225; Frank W. C. Hersey, "The Misfortunes of Dorcas Griffiths," *Transactions, 1937-1942*, vol. 34 (Boston: The Colonial Society of Massachusetts, 1934), 15–16.

2. David Conroy, *In Public Houses: Drink and Revolution of Authority in Colonial Massachusetts* (Chapel Hill: University of North Carolina Press, 1995), 127–129.

3. Hersey, "Misfortunes," 22; Salinger, *Taverns*, 161–170; Conroy, *In Public Houses*, 99–119.

4. Benjamin Franklin, "Old Mistresses Apologue, 25 June 1745," FO.

5. "From John Adams to William Tudor, Sr., 1 June 1817," FO; Daniel Scott Smith, "The Demographic History of Colonial New England," *The Journal of Economic History* 32, no.1 (March 1972): 176–177; Michael R. Haines, "Long Term Marriage Patterns in the United States From Colonial Times to the Present," NBER Working Paper Series on Historical Factors in Long Run Growth (Cambridge, MA: National Bureau of Economic Research, March 1996), 6–7; Ellen K. Rothman, *Hands and Hearts: A History of Courtship in America* (Cambridge, MA: Harvard University Press, 1987), 22–23, 57–59; Nicole Eustace, "'The Cornerstone of a Copious Work': Love and Power in Eighteenth-Century Courtship," *Journal of Social History* 34, no. 3 (Spring 2001): 520–521.

6. Russell Leigh Jackson, "John Jackson and Some of His Descendants," *NEHGR* 97 (1943): 5–6; John Boyle, *A Journal of Occurrences in Boston, 1759–1778*, February 22, 1770, HL.

7.   JRD, April 24, 1770, in *Letters and Diary of John Rowe*, ed. Anne Rowe Cunningham (Boston: W. B. Clarke, 1903), 201.

8.   JRD, May 8, 1770, in Cunningham, *Diary*, 202; William Palfrey to John Hancock, February 15, 1771, William Palfrey Papers, HL; W. T. Baxter, *The House of Hancock: Business in Boston, 1724–1775* (Cambridge, MA: Harvard University Press, 1945), 268–289; John W. Tyler, *Smugglers and Patriots: Boston Merchants and the Advent of the American Revolution* (Boston: Northeastern University Press, 1986), 159–169, 175–176; Arthur Meier Schlesinger, *The Colonial Merchants and the American Revolution, 1763–1776* (New York: Longmans, Green and Co., 1918), 212–218, 241–246; Benjamin L. Carp, *Defiance of the Patriots: The Boston Tea Party and the Making of America* (New Haven, CT: Yale University Press, 2010), 77–78.

9.   *BG*, April 15, 22, 1771, HD.

10. William Palfrey to John Hancock, February 5, 1771, William Palfrey Papers, HL; Horace Bleackley, *Life of John Wilkes* (London: John Lane, The Bodley Head, 1917), 394.

11. William Palfrey to John Hancock, February 15, 1771, William Palfrey Papers, HL; Mary Caroline Crawford, *Old Boston Days & Ways: From the Dawn of the Revolution Until the Town Became a City* (Boston: Little, Brown, 1909), 126–128.

12. Daniel Scott Smith, "Parental Power and Marriage Patterns: An Analysis of Historical Trends in Hingham, Massachusetts," *Journal of Marriage and Family* 35, no. 3 (August 1973): 426; Rothman, *Hands and Hearts*, 26–27, 31–33.

13. "From John Adams to William Tudor, Sr., 1 June 1817," FO; Charles L. Nichols, "Samuel Salisbury—A Boston Merchant in the Revolution," *American Antiquarian Society Proceedings* (April 1925): 51.

14. Nina Sankovitch, *American Rebels: How the Hancock, Adams, and Quincy Families Fanned the Flames of Revolution* (New York: St. Martin's Press, 2020), 41–42; Clifford K. Shipton, *Sibley's Harvard Graduates*, vol. 7 (Boston: Massachusetts Historical Society, 1945), 109–111.

15. Edmund Quincy to Dorothy Quincy, June 18, 1773, in *Transactions, 1899, 1900*, vol. 6 (Boston: The Colonial Society of Massachusetts, 1904), 320; Shipton, *Sibley's*, 7: 113–114.

16. Edmund Quincy to Dorothy Quincy, June 18, 1773, in *Transactions* 6: 319; Eustace, "'Cornerstone,'" 518, 525; Joel Perlmann and Dennis Shirley, "When Did New England Women Acquire Literacy?," *The William and Mary Quarterly* 48, no. 1 (January 1991): 50–67; Joel Perlmann, Silvana R. Siddali,

and Keith Whitescarver, "Literacy, Schooling, and Teaching among New England Women, 1730–1820," *History of Education Quarterly* 37, no. 2 (Summer 1997): 117–139; Jennifer E. Monaghan, *Learning to Read and Write in Colonial America* (Amherst: University of Massachusetts Press, 2005), chapter 10; Lucy Porter Higgins, "'Dorothy Q.,' Who Became Dorothy H.," *Americana, American Historical Magazine* 14 (1920): 412.

17. "Reminiscences by Gen. Wm. H. Sumner," *NEHGR* 8 (1854): 188.
18. Hersey, "Misfortunes," 17–21.
19. Hersey, "Misfortunes," 22.
20. Hersey, "Misfortunes," 22; Samuel Adams Drake, *Old Landmarks and Historic Personages of Boston* (Boston: J. R. Osgood & Company, 1873), 293–294; Robert J. Taylor, ed., *Papers of John Adams*, vol. 2, December 1773–April 1775 (Cambridge, MA: The Belknap Press of Harvard University Press, 1977), 129–130; Nancy Rubin Stuart, *Defiant Brides: The Untold Story of Two Revolutionary-Era Women and the Radical Men They Married* (Boston: Beacon Press, 2013), 19–20.
21. Hersey, "Misfortunes," 17–19.
22. Schlesinger, *Colonial Merchants*, 253–254; Richard D. Brown, *Revolutionary Politics in Massachusetts: The Boston Committee of Correspondence and the Towns, 1772–1774* (Cambridge, MA: Harvard University Press, 1970), 34–35.
23. Edward M. Cook, Jr., *The Fathers of the Towns: Leadership and Community Structure in Eighteenth-Century New England* (Baltimore: Johns Hopkins University Press, 1976), 44–45, 51, 80–89; Edmund S. Morgan, *Inventing the People: The Rise of Popular Sovereignty in England and America* (New York: W. W. Norton, 1989), 247–249; Richard L. Bushman, *The Refinement of America: Persons, Houses, Cities* (New York: Vintage Books, 1992), xiv–xv, 40–41, 61–99.
24. *Boston Town Records, 1770 Through 1777* (Boston: Rockwell and Churchill, 1887), 21; Robert E. Brown, "Democracy in Colonial Massachusetts," *The New England Quarterly* 25, no. 3 (September 1952): 301–302; Alan Taylor, *American Revolutions: A Continental History, 1750–1804* (New York: W. W. Norton, 2016), 36.
25. "From John Adams to James Sullivan, 26 May 1776," FO; Allan J. Lichtman, *The Embattled Vote in America: From the Founding to the Present* (Cambridge, MA: Harvard University Press, 2018), 13–14; Brown, "Democracy," 302; Rosemarie Zagarri, "What Did Democracy Look Like? Voting in Early America," Mapping Early American Elections online, Roy Rosenzweig Center for History and New Media.

26. Charles Francis Adams, ed., *The Works of John Adams*, vol. 2 (Boston: Little and Brown, 1850), 112; Conroy, *In Public Houses*, 196–200; Worthington Chauncey Ford, ed., *The Writings of George Washington, 1758–1775*, vol. 2 (New York: G. P. Putnam's Sons, 1889), 52n2.

27. Samuel Adams to John Hancock, May 11, 1770, in *The Writings of Samuel Adams, 1770–1773*, ed. Harry Alonzo Cushing, vol. 2 (New York: G. P. Putnam's Sons, 1906), 9.

28. Douglass Adair & John A. Schutz, eds., *Peter Oliver's Origin & Progress of the American Revolution: A Tory View* (San Marino: The Huntington Library, 1961), 39; Jane Kamensky, *Revolution in Color: The World of John Singleton Copley* (New York: W. W. Norton, 2016), 212n87; Carrie Rebora Barratt, et al., *John Singleton Copley in America* (New York: The Metropolitan Museum of Art, 1995), 277. Art historians believe the portraits were painted between 1770 and 1772. Hancock likely commissioned them in 1770, after Adams convinced him to serve in the House. It is less probable that they were painted in 1771 or 1772—Hancock had pulled away from Adams and politics at that time.

29. Barratt, et al., *John Singleton Copley*, 275; Richard Beeman, *Our Lives, Our Fortunes, Our Sacred Honor: The Forging of American Independence 1774–1776* (New York: Basic Books, 2013), 42–43.

30. Richard Thompson Ford, *Dress Codes: How the Laws of Fashion Made History* (New York: Simon & Schuster, 2021), 31.

31. Bushman, *Refinement in America*, 65–71; Ford, *Dress Codes*, 96.

32. Gary B. Nash, *The Urban Crucible: The Northern Seaports and the Origins of the American Revolution* (Cambridge, MA: Harvard University Press, 1986), 218–224; Gordon S. Wood, *The Creation of the American Republic, 1776–1787* (Chapel Hill: University of North Carolina Press, 1998), 79–80, 110–112.

33. John Hancock to George Hayley, October 6, 1771, John Hancock to Thomas Longman, November 14, 1771, John Hancock Letterbook (business), HFP, BLSC; Baxter, *House*, 280–281; William M. Fowler, Jr., *The Baron of Beacon Hill: A Biography of John Hancock* (Boston: Houghton Mifflin, 1980), 138.

34. John Hancock to George Hayley, February 21, 1769, John Hancock Letterbook (business), HFP, BLSC.

35. Thomas Hutchinson, *The History of the Province of Massachusetts Bay: From 1749 to 1774* (London: John Murray, 1828), 346; Samuel Adams to Arthur Lee, April 12, 1773, in *The Writings of Samuel Adams, 1773–1777*, ed. Harry Alonzo Cushing, vol. 3 (New York: G. P. Putnam's Sons, 1907), 23.

36. JAD, February 9, 1772 and March 4, 1773, in Adams, *Works of John Adams*, 2: 294, 315; Sankovitch, *American Rebels*, 158; John A. Nagy, *Dr. Benjamin Church, Spy: A Case of Espionage on the Eve of the American Revolution* (Yardley, PA: Westholme Publishing, 2013), 40; Bernard Bailyn, *The Ordeal of Thomas Hutchinson* (Cambridge, MA: The Belknap Press of Harvard University Press, 1974), 178.

37. Bailyn, *Ordeal*, 177–178, 183.

38. Hutchinson, *History*, 344, 347; Thomas Hutchinson to Thomas Gage, December 1, 1771, in *The Correspondence of Thomas Hutchinson, volume 4: November 1770–June 1772*, ed. John W. Tyler (Boston: The Colonial Society of Massachusetts, 2022), 284.

39. November 2, 1772, *Boston Town Records*, 1770–7, 93; John K. Alexander, *Samuel Adams: America's Revolutionary Politician* (Lanham, MD: Rowman & Littlefield Publishers, 2002), 93–112.

40. James S. Loring, "Thomas Cushing," *The Historical Magazine and Notes and Queries Concerning the Antiquities, History, and Biography of America*, vol. 6 (New York: Charles B. Richardson, 1862), 213; Brown, *Revolutionary Politics*, 59–61.

41. Samuel Adams to James Warren, March 25, 1771, December 9, 1772, in *Warren-Adams Papers*, 1743–1777, vol. 1 (Massachusetts Historical Society, 1917), 8, 15; JAD, December 24, 30, 1772, in Adams, *John Adams*, 2: 306, 308.

42. Brown, *Revolutionary Politics*, 66–79; Ray Raphael, *The First American Revolution: Before Lexington and Concord* (New York: The Free Press, 2002), 33–38.

43. JRD, August 6, 1772 and August 23, 1772, in Cunningham, *Diary*, 232, 233; Nash, *Urban Crucible*, 204–210.

44. John Andrews Correspondence, February 24, 1772, *MHS-P*, vol. 8 (Boston: Massachusetts Historical Society, 1866), 322; Charles W. Akers, *The Divine Politician: Samuel Cooper and the American Revolution in Boston* (Boston: Northeastern University Press, 1982), 128–129; Clifford K. Shipton, *New England Life in the Eighteenth Century: Representative Biographies from Sibley's Harvard Graduates* (Cambridge, MA: The Belknap Press of Harvard University Press, 1995), 367.

45. Henry Pelham to [Peggy McIlvaine], March 1, 1772, in *Letters & Papers of John Singleton Copley and Henry Pelham, 1739–1776* (Boston: Massachusetts Historical Society, 1914), 184; *BEP*, January 27, 1772, GB; John S. Ezell, "When Massachusetts Played the Lottery," *The New England Quarterly* 22, no. 3 (September 1949): 325.

46. Samuel Adams to Arthur Lee, April 12, April 22, 1773, in Cushing, *Samuel Adams*, 3: 23, 36; Fowler, *Baron*, 136.

47. *BG*, May 11, 1772, HD; John Andrews to William Barrell, June 4, 1773, *MHS-P* 8: 323; David Hansen, "The First Corps of Cadets of Boston," *Proceedings of the Bostonian Society*, vol. 12 (1944), 27, 56.

48. John Andrews to William Barrell, June 4, 1773, *MHS-P* 8: 323–324; H. Telfer Mook, "Training Day in New England," *The New England Quarterly* 11, no. 4 (December 1938): 682–683; May 25, 1791 bill to John Hancock, FCCC, A292, HGARC.

49. First Corps of Cadets to John Hancock, August 18, 1774, FCCC, A155, HGARC; JRD, July 7, 1772, in Cunningham, *Diary*, 230.

50. Nick Bunker, *An Empire on the Edge: How Britain Came to Fight America* (New York: Alfred A. Knopf, 2014), 133–138, 149; Carp, *Defiance*, 73.

51. JAD, February 14, 1771, MHS online; William Palfrey to John Hancock, February 15, 1771, William Palfrey Papers, HL; Baxter, *House*, 281; Schlesinger, *Colonial Merchants*, 246.

52. Carp, *Defiance*, 78–84.

6: A CORONATION

1.   Benjamin L. Carp, *Defiance of the Patriots: The Boston Tea Party and the Making of America* (New Haven, CT: Yale University Press, 2010), 84–87.

2.   *BG*, November 8, 1773, HD.

3.   Thomas Hutchinson to John Hancock, November 11, 1773, FCCC, A150, HGARC; L. F. S. Upton, "Proceedings of Ye Body Respecting the Tea," *The William and Mary Quarterly* 22, no. 2 (April 1965): 291.

4.   *BG*, November 8, 1773, HD; Carp, *Defiance*, 89–90.

5.   JRD, November 17, 1773, in *Letters and Diary of John Rowe*, ed. Anne Rowe Cunningham (Boston: W. B. Clarke, 1903), 254; Carp, *Defiance*, 96–97.

6.   JRD, November 18, 1773, in Cunningham, *Diary*, 254; Carp, *Defiance of the Patriots*, 91–92.

7.   Abigail Adams to Mercy Otis Warren, December 5, 1773, in *Warren-Adams Papers, 1743-1777*, vol. 1 (Massachusetts Historical Society, 1917), 18; John Hancock to Haley, December 21, 1773, John Hancock Letterbook (business), HFP, BLSC; Carp, *Defiance*, 100–102, 109; Mary Beth Norton, *1774: The Long Year of Revolution* (New York: Alfred A. Knopf, 2020), 25.

8.   *BG*, December 13, 1773, HD.

9. Samuel Adams to Arthur Lee, December 31, 1775, in *The Writings of Samuel Adams, 1773–1777*, ed. Harry Alonzo Cushing, vol. 3 (New York: G. P. Putnam's Sons, 1907), 74; Harlow Giles Unger, *American Tempest: How the Boston Tea Party Sparked a Revolution* (Boston: Da Capo Press, 2011), 161.

10. *BG*, December 27, 1773, HD; Bernard Bailyn, *The Ordeal of Thomas Hutchinson* (Cambridge, MA: The Belknap Press of Harvard University Press, 1974), 238–243; June 2, 1773, *Journals of the House of Representatives, 1773–1774*, vol. 50 (Boston: Massachusetts Historical Society, 1981), 26; Thomas Hutchinson, *The History of the Province of Massachusetts Bay: From 1749 to 1774* (London: John Murray, 1828), 395.

11. *BG*, December 20, 1773, HD; Benjamin Bussey Thatcher, *Traits of the Tea Party; Being a Memoir of George R. T. Hewes* (New York: Harper & Brothers, 1835), 177–178; The Committee of Correspondence of Boston to Other Committees of Correspondence, December 17, 1773, in Cushing, *Samuel Adams*, 3: 72.

12. Upton, "Proceedings," 298. George Robert Twelve Hewes claimed to see Hancock at the destruction, recognizing his "ruffles." Historians have dismissed this claim. Thatcher, *Traits*, 193; Alfred F. Young, *The Shoemaker and the Tea Party: Memory and the American Revolution* (Boston: Beacon Press, 1999), 57; Carp, *Defiance*, 122–124, 237, chapter 6; Jeremiah Colburn, "The Command at the Battle of Bunker Hill, As Shown in the Statement of Major Thompson Maxwell," *NEHGR* 22 (January 1868): 57–58; William Willder Wheildon, "A Remarkable Military Life," *NEHGR* 45 (October 1891): 274; Robert J. Allison, *The American Revolution: A Concise History* (New York: Oxford University Press, 2011), 17.

13. John Hancock to Haley, December 21, 1773, John Hancock Letterbook (business), HFP, BLSC.

14. JRD, December 16 and December 17, 1773, in Cunningham, *Diary*, 258; "From Benjamin Franklin to the Massachusetts House Committee of Correspondence, 2 February 1774," FO; Arthur Meier Schlesinger, *The Colonial Merchants and the American Revolution, 1763–1776* (New York: Longmans, Green and Co., 1918), 298–300; John W. Tyler, *Smugglers and Patriots: Boston Merchants and the Advent of the American Revolution* (Boston: Northeastern University Press, 1986), 211–212; Norton, *1774*, 48–55, 84.

15. *BG*, March 7, 1774, HD.

16. JRD, March 5, 1774, in Cunningham, *Diary*, 264.

17. Noah Webster to E. S. Thomas, July 29, 1840, in Ebenezer Smith Thomas, *Reminiscences of the Last Sixty-five Years*, vol. 2 (Hartford: Case, Tiffany, and Burnham, 1840), 169; Young, *Shoemaker*, 96–97.

18. John Hancock speech, March 5, 1774, in Paul D. Brandes, *John Hancock's Life and Speeches: A Personalized Vision of the American Revolution, 1763–1793* (Lanham, MD: The Scarecrow Press, 1996), 211–212.

19. John Hancock speech, March 5, 1774, in Brandes, *John Hancock's Life*, 213, 214.

20. *BEP*, March 7, 1774, GB; *A Report of the Record Commissioners of the City of Boston, Containing the Selectmen's Minutes from 1769 Through April, 1775* (Boston: Rockwell and Churchill, 1893), 205–212; *A Report of the Record Commissioners of the City of Boston, Containing the Boston Town Records, 1770 Through 1777* (Boston: Rockwell and Churchill, 1887), 162; William Palfrey to Hayley, January 10, 1774, John Hancock Letterbook (business), HFP, BLSC.

21. John Hancock speech, March 5, 1774, in Brandes, *John Hancock's Life*, 214; *BG*, March 12, 1770, HD; Adams's Minutes of Crown Evidence, November 28, 1770, Legal Papers of John Adams, vol. 3, 112, MHS online.

22. John Hancock speech, March 5, 1774, in Brandes, *John Hancock's Life*, 214, 215.

23. John Hancock speech, March 5, 1774, in Brandes, *John Hancock's Life*, 216–218.

24. John Hancock speech, March 5, 1774, in Brandes, *John Hancock's Life*, 219; *BEP*, March 7, 1774, GB.

25. *BG*, March 7, 1774, HD; JAD, March 5, 1774, MHS online.

26. Thomas, *Reminiscences*, 169; William M. Fowler, Jr., *The Baron of Beacon Hill: A Biography of John Hancock* (Boston: Houghton Mifflin, 1980), 165, 314n6; Brandes, *John Hancock's Life*, 208–209.

27. John Hancock, An Oration Delivered March Fifth, 1774 (Boston: Edes and Gill, 1774), HD, 4; Thomas Randolph Adams, "American Independence, The Growth of an Idea," *Transactions, 1956-1963*, vol. 43 (Boston: The Colonial Society of Massachusetts, 1966), 5, 104.

28. George P. Anderson, "A Note on Ebenezer Mackintosh," *Transactions, 1924-1926*, vol. 26 (Boston: The Colonial Society of Massachusetts, 1927), 350.

29. Anderson, "Ebenezer Mackintosh," quote on 350; *BG*, March 14, 1774, HD; David Hansen, "The First Corps of Cadets of Boston," *Proceedings of the Bostonian Society* 12 (1944), 31; JRD, March 8, 1774, in Cunningham, *Diary*, 265.

30. Henry Pelham to John Singleton Copley, July 17, 1774, *MHS-C* 71, series 7 (Boston: Massachusetts Historical Society, 1914), 232; *BG*, May 23, 1774, HD; JRD, May 17, 1774, in Cunningham, *Diary*, 270–271.

31. J. L. Bell, *The Road to Concord: How Four Stolen Cannon Ignited the Revolutionary War* (Yardley, PA: Westholme Publishing, 2016), 4–5; Justin du Rivage, *Revolution Against Empire: Taxes, Politics, and the Origins of American Independence* (New Haven, CT: Yale University Press, 2017), 171.

32. Richard D. Brown, *Revolutionary Politics in Massachusetts: The Boston Committee of Correspondence and the Towns, 1772–1774* (Cambridge, MA: Harvard University Press, 1970), 140–141.

33. "By the Governor. A Proclamation for Dissolving the General Court," June 17, 1774, *Journals of the House of Representatives, 1773–1774* 50: 291.

34. General Gage, Transcript of verbal reply to the Cadets, August 18, 1774, FCCC, A143, Corps of Cadets Committee to Thomas Gage, August 15, 1774, FCCC, A134, First Corps of Cadets to Thomas Gage, August 15, 1774, FCCC, A159, HGARC; John Andrews Letters, August 16, 1774, *MHS-P*, vol. 8 (Boston: Massachusetts Historical Society, 1866), 342.

35. John Andrews Letters, September 27, 1774, *MHS-P* 8: 369; Henry Pelham to John Singleton Copley, July 17, 1774, *MHS-C* 71: 232; Boston Committee of Correspondence, Circular Letter, September 27, 1774. Accessed online through State Library of Massachusetts.

36. John Andrews Letters, September 26 and September 27, 1774, *MHS-P* 8: 368, 369; Norton, 1774, 209–210.

37. Thomas Gage to Lord Dartmouth, October 30, 1774, in *The Correspondence of General Thomas Gage with the Secretaries of State, 1763–1775*, ed. Clarence Edwin Carter, vol. 1 (Archon Books, 1969), 380; Rakove, *Revolutionaries*, 31, 46–47; Ray Raphael, *The First American Revolution: Before Lexington and Concord* (New York: The Free Press, 2002), 51–52.

38. John Adams to Benjamin Rush, May 21, 1807, in *The Works of John Adams*, ed. Charles Francis Adams, vol. 9 (Boston: Little, Brown, 1854), 597; Brad A. Jones, *Resisting Independence: Popular Loyalism in the Revolutionary British Atlantic* (Ithaca, NY: Columbia University Press, 2021), 108–116; Brendan McConville, *The Brethren: A Story of Faith and Conspiracy in Revolutionary America* (Cambridge, MA: Harvard University Press, 2021), 46–53.

39. The Committee of Correspondence of Boston to the Committee of Correspondence in Philadelphia, Boston, May 13, 1774, in Cushing, *Samuel Adams*, 3: 110; Norton, 1774, 94–101, 132–140.

40. Brown, *Revolutionary Politics*, 210–211; Raphael, *First American Revolution*, 68–132, 151–156.

41. Richard Alan Ryerson, *The Revolution is Now Begun: The Radical Committees of Philadelphia, 1765–1776* (Philadelphia: University of Pennsylvania Press, 1978), 40–60.

42. Christian Di Spigna, *Founding Martyr: The Life and Death of Dr. Joseph Warren, the American Revolution's Lost Hero* (New York: Crown, 2018), 149–151.

43. Alan Taylor, *American Revolutions: A Continental History, 1750–1804* (New York: W. W. Norton, 2016), 123; Richard Beeman, *Our Lives, Our Fortunes, Our Sacred Honor: The Forging of American Independence 1774–1776* (New York: Basic Books, 2013), 166, 173.

44. Bell, *Road to Concord*, 101–102.

45. Norton, *1774*, 270–279; October 26, 1774, *The Journals of Each Provincial Congress of Massachusetts in 1774 and 1775* (Boston: Dutton and Wentworth, 1838), 34.

46. John Andrews Letters, October 29, 1774, *MHS-P* 8: 380–381; Henry Pelham to John Singleton Copley, July 17, 1774, *MHS-C* 71: 233.

47. Henry Pelham to John Singleton Copley, July 17, 1774, *MHS-C* 71: 232; Thomas Gage to Earl of Dartmouth, September 2, 1774, *The Parliamentary History of England from the Earliest Period to the Year 1803*, vol. 18 (London, T. C. Hansard, 1813), 95–97.

48. John Andrews Letters, September 26, 1774, *MHS-P* 8: 368.

49. Journal of Thomas Hutchinson, July 1, 1774, *MHS-P*, vol. 15 (Boston: Massachusetts Historical Society, 1878), 329–330; *Newport Mercury*, October 17, 1774, GB.

50. John F. Watson to A. Holmes, February 13, 1832, *MHS-P*, vol. 5 (Boston: Massachusetts Historical Society, 1862), 211; J. A. Leo Lamay, "The American Origins of 'Yankee Doodle,'" *The William and Mary Quarterly* 33, no. 3 (July 1976): 441–451.

51. *Boston City Records, 1770–1776*, 216; Di Spigna, *Founding Martyr*, 158–160.

52. John Burke Diary, March 6, 1775, in *The British in Boston: Being the Diary of Lieutenant John Barker of the King's Own Regiment*, ed. Elizabeth Ellery Dana (Cambridge, MA: Harvard University Press, 1924), 25–26.

53. John Burke Diary, March 6, 1775, in Dana, *British in Boston*, 26.

54. John Burke Diary, March 6, 1775, in Dana, *British in Boston*, 26.

55. March 19, 1775, in Frank Moore, *The Diary of the Revolution* (Hartford, CT: The J. B. Burr Publishing Company, 1876), 53, 54.

56. John Andrews Letters, March 20, 1775, *MHS-P* 8: 401.

7: WAR AND ATTEMPTS AT PEACE

1. Richard P. Kollen, *The Patriot Parson of Lexington, Massachusetts: Reverend Jonas Clarke and the American Revolution* (Charleston, SC: The History Press, 2016), 28–31.

2. Richard Godbeer, *Sexual Revolution in Early America* (Baltimore: Johns Hopkins University Press, 2002), 228–238, 246–250.

3. Richard Kollen, "Lexington's Reverend John Hancock," Lexington Historical Society upload, www.lexingtonhistory.org, 7; Elias Phinney, *History of the Battle of Lexington, On the Morning of the 19th April, 1775* (Boston: Phelps and Farnam, 1825), 33; Jonas Clarke, *Opening of the War of the Revolution* (Lexington, MA: Lexington Historical Society, 1901).

4. Nick Bunker, *An Empire on the Edge: How Britain Came to Fight America* (New York: Alfred A. Knopf, 2014), 349–363; David Hackett Fischer, *Paul Revere's Ride* (New York: Oxford University Press, 1994), 76–77.

5. Fischer, *Paul Revere's Ride*, 43–48, 58–64; J. L. Bell, *The Road to Concord: How Four Stolen Cannon Ignited the Revolutionary War* (Yardley, PA: Westholme Publishing, 2016).

6. Letter to Jeremy Belknap, in *Paul Revere's Three Accounts of His Famous Ride*, ed. Edmund S. Morgan (Boston: A Revolutionary War Bicentennial Commission and Massachusetts Historical Society Publication, 1967); Arthur Tourtellot, *Lexington and Concord: The Beginning of the War of the American Revolution* (New York: W. W. Norton, 2000), 92–101; Fischer, *Paul Revere's Ride*, 97–112, 129–137.

7. Abner Cheney Goodell, Jr., *The Trial and Execution, for Petit Treason, of Mark and Phillis: Slaves of Capt. John Codman* (Cambridge, MA: John Wilson and Son, 1883), 1–30.

8. Gordon Wood, *The Radicalism of the American Revolution* (New York: Vintage Books, 1991), 59; Phinney, *Battle of Lexington*, 16.

9. Phinney, *Battle of Lexington*, 16, 17.

10. Patricia A. Cunningham, "Eighteenth Century Nightgowns: The Gentleman's Robe in Art and Fashion," *Dress* 10, no. 1 (1984): 2–5; Linda Baumgarten, *What Clothes Reveal: The Language of Clothing in Colonial and Federal America* (Williamsburg, VA: The Colonial Williamsburg Foun-

dation, 2002), 108–112; William Sullivan, Letter IV, January 27, 1833, *Familiar Letters on Public Characters* (Boston: Russell, Odiorne, and Metcalf, 1834), 12.

11. "Reminiscences by Gen. Wm. H. Sumner," *NEHGR* 8 (1854): 187; Phinney, *Battle of Lexington*, 34; Wood, *Radicalism*, 24–42.

12. "Reminiscences," 187; Samuel Sewall, *The History of Woburn* (Boston: Wiggin and Lunt, 1868), 365.

13. "Reminiscences," 188.

14. Phinney, *Battle of Lexington*, 34.

15. The Deposition: Corrected Copy, and Letter to Jeremy Belknap, in Morgan, *Three Accounts*.

16. Letter to Jeremy Belknap, in Morgan, *Three Accounts*; Phinney, *Battle of Lexington*, 34; Tourtellot, *Lexington and Concord*, 123–143.

17. "Reminiscences," 188.

18. Bell, *Road to Concord*, 160–161.

19. Thomas Gage to Lord Dartmouth, April 22, 1975, in *The Correspondence of General Thomas Gage with the Secretaries of State, 1763–1775*, ed. Clarence Edwin Carter, vol. 1 (Hamden, CT: Archon Books, 1969), 396; Tourtellot, *Lexington and Concord*, 151–167; Robert Gross, *The Minutemen and Their World* (New York: Hill and Wang, 1976, 2001), 125–130.

20. Lieutenant Mackenzie of the Royal Welsh Fusiliers Description of the Battle of Lexington, April 19, 1775, *MHS-P*, vol. 5 (Boston: Massachusetts Historical Society, 1890), 394.

21. "Reminiscences," 188; Sewall, *Woburn*, 365–366; Geo. J. Varney, *The Story of Patriots' Day* (Boston: Lee and Shepard Publishers, 1895), 99.

22. "Reminiscences," 188.

23. Jacqueline Barbara Carr, *After the Siege: A Social History of Boston 1775–1800* (Boston: Northeastern University, 2005), 22–30.

24. Sewall, *Woburn*, 366; Varney, *Patriots' Day*, 100.

25. John Hancock to the gentlemen committee of safety, April 24, 1775, in William Lincoln, ed., *The Journals of the Provincial Congress of Massachusetts in 1774 and 1775, and of the Committee of Safety* (Boston: Dutton and Wentworth, 1838), 170; Richard Beeman, *Our Lives, Our Fortunes, Our Sacred Honor: The Forging of American Independence 1774–1776* (New York: Basic Books, 2013), 112–115, 155–156.

26. Fischer, *Paul Revere's Ride*, 106.

27. Herbert S. Allan, *John Hancock: Patriot in Purple* (New York: The Macmillan Company, 1948), 34–35, quote on 34.

28. Silas Deane to Elizabeth Deane, August 31–September 4, 1774, May 12, 1775, in *Letters of Delegates to Congress, 1774–1789*, ed. Paul H. Smith, et al., vol. 1 (Washington, DC: Library of Congress, 1976–2000), 29–30, 345–348; Allan Forbes and Ralph M. Eastman, *Taverns and Stagecoaches of New England*, vol. 2 (Boston: State Street Trust Company, 1954), 3; Stacy Schiff, *A Great Improvisation: Franklin, France, and the Birth of America* (New York: Henry Holt and Company, 2005), 205–206.

29. John Hancock to Dorothy Quincy, May 7, 1775, HFP, MHS.

30. John Hancock to Dorothy Quincy, May 7, 1775, HFP, MHS.

31. Caesar Rodney to Thomas Rodney, May 11, 1775, in Smith, et al., *Letters*, 1: 343–344; Silas Deane to Elizabeth Deane, May 12, 1775, in Smith, et al., *Letters*, 1: 345–347.

32. Richard Caswell to William Caswell, May 11, 1775, in Smith, et al., *Letters*, 1: 340; Hewes to Samuel Johnston, May 11, 1775, in Smith, et al., *Letters*, 1: 342–343.

33. Clare A. Lyons, *Sex among the Rabble: An Intimate History of Gender & Power in the Age of Revolution, Philadelphia, 1730–1830* (Chapel Hill: University of North Carolina Press for the Omohundro Institute of Early American History and Culture, 2006), chapter 2.

34. "Independence Hall Complex, Independence Hall, 500 Chestnut Street, Philadelphia, Philadelphia County, PA" (sheet 9 of 45), Library of Congress.

35. Beeman, *Our Lives, Our Fortunes*, 218.

36. Worthington C. Ford, et al., *Journals of the Continental Congress, 1774–1789*, vol. 2 (Washington, DC, 1904–1937), 58–59; Beeman, *Our Lives, Our Fortunes*, 218–219.

37. Thomas Gage, "By his excellency the Hon. Thomas Gage, Governor, and commander in chief in and over his Majesty's Province of Massachusetts-Bay vice admiral of the same. A proclamation" (New York, 1775), Library of Congress online.

38. Samuel Adams to Mrs. [Betsy] Adams, July 28, 1775, in *The Writings of Samuel Adams, 1773–1777*, ed. Harry Alonzo Cushing, vol. 3 (New York: G. P. Putnam's Sons, 1907), 221; Pauline Maier, *The Old Revolutionaries: Political Lives in the Age of Samuel Adams* (New York: Alfred A. Knopf, 1980), 17.

39. Lynn Montross, *The Reluctant Rebels: The Story of the Continental Congress, 1774–1789* (New York: Harper & Brothers Publishers, 1950), 85–86; Beeman, *Our Lives, Our Fortunes*, 250–253.

40. Beeman, *Our Lives, Our Fortunes*, 276–277.
41. John Hancock to Certain Colonies, April 30, 1776, in *Letters of Delegates to Congress, January to May 1776*, ed. Paul H. Smith, et al., vol. 3 (Washington, DC: Library of Congress, 1978), 605.
42. JAD, June and July 1775, AFP, MHS online.
43. John Adams to Abigail Adams, May 29, 1775, AFP, MHS online; Maurizio Valsania, *First Among Men: George Washington and the Myth of American Masculinity* (Baltimore: Johns Hopkins University Press, 2022), 226–244.
44. JAD, June and July 1775, AFP, MHS online.
45. JAD, June and July 1775, AFP, MHS online.
46. Ford, et al., *Journals*, 2: 91; Beeman, *Our Lives, Our Fortunes*, 230–231.
47. JAD, June and July 1775, AFP, MHS online.
48. Eliphalet Dyer to Joseph Trumball, June 17, 1775, in *Letters of Delegates to Congress, September to December 1775*, ed. Paul H. Smith, et al., vol. 2 (Washington, DC: Library of Congress, 1977), 499–500.
49. "From George Washington to Martha Washington, 18 June 1775," FO; Ron Chernow, *Washington: A Life* (New York: Penguin Books, 2010), quote on 185; Joanne B. Freeman, *Affairs of Honor: National Politics in the New Republic* (New Haven, CT: Yale Nota Bene, 2002), 167–168; Barry Schwartz, *George Washington: The Making of an American Symbol* (New York: The Free Press, 1987), 119–131, 149–155.
50. James L. Nelson, *With Fire and Sword: The Battle of Bunker Hill and the Beginning of the American Revolution* (New York: Thomas Dunne Books, 2011), 294–304.
51. John Hancock to Dorothy Quincy, May 18, 1775, HFP, MHS; Samuel Adams to James Warren, June 28, 1775, in *Warren-Adams Papers*, vol. 1, 1743–1777 (Massachusetts Historical Society, 1917), 70.
52. "To George Washington from John Hancock, 10 July 1775," FO; John Hancock to Certain Colonies, June 4, 1776, in *Letters of Delegates to Congress, May 16. 1776 to August 15, 1776*, ed. Paul H. Smith, et al., vol. 4 (Washington, DC: Library of Congress, 1979), 136–137; Ray Raphael, *The First American Revolution: Before Lexington and Concord* (New York: The Free Press, 2002), 59–66.
53. John Hancock to Dorothy Quincy, June 10, 1775, in Smith, et al., *Letters*, 1: 472; Ellen C. D. Q. Woodbury, *Dorothy Quincy: Wife of John Hancock with Events of Her Time* (Washington, DC: The Neale Publishing Company, 1901), 84.
54. Woodbury, *Dorothy Quincy*, 84.

55. Matthew L. Davis, *Memoirs of Aaron Burr with Miscellaneous Selections from His Correspondence*, vol. I (New York: Harper & Brothers, 1836), 182.

56. Davis, *Memoirs*, 182; Woodbury, *Dorothy Quincy*, 90–91; Nancy Isenberg, *Fallen Founder: The Life of Aaron Burr* (New York: Viking, 2007), 60–61.

57. John Hancock to Dorothy Quincy, August 14, 1775, HFP, MHS.

58. John Adams to James Warren, September 17, 1775, in Smith, et al., *Letters*, 2: 24.

8: DECLARING INDEPENDENCE

1. John Adams to Abigail Adams, December 3, 1775, in *Letters of Delegates to Congress, September to December 1775*, ed. Paul H. Smith, et al., vol. 2 (Washington, DC: Library of Congress, 1977), 430.

2. John Adams to Abigail Adams, November 4, 1775, in Smith, et al., *Letters*, 2: 296.

3. "Reminiscences by Gen. Wm. H. Sumner," *NEHGR* 8 (1854): 189.

4. "Reminiscences," 189; Diary of Christopher Marshall, November 21–27, 1775, in *Extracts from the Diary of Christopher Marshall*, ed. William Duane (Albany, NY: Joel Munsell, 1877), 51–53, quote on 52; Edmund Quincy to Kate Quincy, May 27, 1776, in *Dorothy Quincy: Wife of John Hancock with Events of Her Time*, ed. Ellen C. D. Q. Woodbury (Washington, DC: The Neale Publishing Company, 1901), 111; Nancy F. Cott, *The Bonds of Womanhood: "Woman's Sphere" in New England, 1780–1835* (New Haven, CT: Yale University Press, 1977), 187–193.

5. "Reminiscences," 189.

6. John Adams to James Warren, October 13, 1775, in Smith, et al., *Letters*, 2: 24; John Hancock to Thomas Cushing, February 1, 1776 and March 7, 1776, in *Letters of Delegates to Congress, January to May 1776*, ed. Paul H. Smith, et al., vol. 3 (Washington, DC: Library of Congress, 1978), 183, 348; William M. Fowler, Jr., *The Baron of Beacon Hill: A Biography of John Hancock* (Boston: Houghton Mifflin, 1980), 203–204.

7. Pamela Ehrlich, "A Hancock Family Story: Restoring Connections," *Antiques & Fine Art Magazine* 17, no. 1 (Spring 2018): 151–152. The RISD Museum houses the Hancock miniatures in storage.

8. John Hancock to Samuel Cooper, July 20, 1776, in *Letters of Delegates to Congress, May 16. 1776 to August 15, 1776*, ed. Paul H. Smith, et al., vol. 4 (Washington, DC: Library of Congress, 1979), 501; Josiah Bartlett to John Langdon, October 7, 1776, in *Letters of Delegates to Congress, August to De-*

cember 1776, ed. Paul H. Smith, et al., vol. 5 (Washington, DC: Library of Congress, 1979), 312.

9. George Nuki and Peter A. Simkin, "A concise history of gout and hyperuricemia and their treatment," *Arthritis Research & Therapy* 8, no. 1 (2006): 1; Benjamin Franklin, *Poor Richard's Almanac and Other Papers* (Boston: Houghton Mifflin, 1886), 44–48.

10. "From John Adams to William Tudor, Sr., 1 June 1817," FO; John Hancock to Thomas Cushing, January 17, 1776 and February 1, 1776, in Smith, et al., *Letters*, 3: 105, 182; Josiah Bartlett to John Langdon, October 7, 1776, in Smith, et al., *Letters*, 5: 312.

11. John Hancock to Thomas Cushing, February 16, 1776. Smith, et al., *Letters*, 3: 264.

12. JAD, "[Wednesday Feb. 28. 1776.]," FO; Lynn Montross, *The Reluctant Rebels: The Story of the Continental Congress, 1774–1789* (New York: Harper & Brothers Publishers, 1950), 130–132; Richard Beeman, *Our Lives, Our Fortunes, Our Sacred Honor: The Forging of American Independence 1774–1776* (New York: Basic Books, 2013), 329–330, 357–359.

13. John Hancock to Thomas Cushing, January 17, February 13, 1776, in Smith, et al., *Letters*, 3: 105, 243.

14. Thomas Cushing to John Hancock, January 30, 1776, Gratz Mss, Case 1, Box 4, Historical Society of Pennsylvania.

15. Samuel Adams to James Warren, April 16, 1776, *Warren-Adams Papers, 1743-1777*, vol. 1 (Massachusetts Historical Society, 1917), 224; JAD, "[Fryday March 15. 1776.]," FO.

16. JAD, "[Wednesday Feb. 28. 1776.]," FO; Jack Rakove, *Revolutionaries: A New History of the Invention of America* (Boston: Houghton Mifflin Harcourt, 2009), 73–75; Nancy L. Rhoden, "William Smith: Philadelphia Minister and Moderate," in *The Human Tradition in the American Revolution*, ed. Rhoden and Ian K. Steele (Wilmington, DE: Scholarly Resources, 2000), 74–75; Thomas M. Doerflinger, "Philadelphia Merchants and the Logic of Moderation, 1760–1775," *The William and Mary Quarterly* 40, no. 3 (April 1983): 224–225; Eugene R. Slaski, "Thomas Willing: A Study in Moderation, 1774–1778," *The Pennsylvania Magazine of History and Biography* 100, no. 4 (October 1976): 499–501.

17. JAD, "[Fryday March 15. 1776.]" and "[Wednesday Feb. 28. 1776.]," FO.

18. "To John Adams from Benjamin Rush, 20 July 1811," FO.

19. Pauline Maier, *American Scripture: Making the Declaration of Independence* (New York: Vintage Books, 1998), 28–30.

20. John Hancock to Thomas Cushing, January 17, 1776, in Smith, et al., *Letters*, 3: 105–106; Alan Taylor, *American Revolutions: A Continental History, 1750–1804* (New York: W. W. Norton, 2016), 155–159.

21. John Adams to Horatio Gates, March 23, 1776, in Smith, et al., *Letters*, 3: 431; John Hancock to Thomas Cushing, February 13, 1776, in Smith, et al., *Letters*, 3: 244; Edmund Cody Burnett, *The Continental Congress: A definitive history of the Continental Congress from its inception in 1774 to March 1789* (New York: W. W. Norton, 1941), 138.

22. "His Majesty's most gracious speech to both Houses of Parliament," October 26, 1775, Eighteenth Century Collections Online; Joseph Ellis, *Revolutionary Summer: The Birth of American Independence* (New York: Vintage Books, 2014), 12–14; Beeman, *Our Lives, Our Fortunes*, 330–341.

23. Isaac Cazneau to John Hancock, April 4, 1776, Personal Letters, 1776–1793, HFP, BLSC; Jacqueline Barbara Carr, *After the Siege: A Social History of Boston 1775–1800* (Boston: Northeastern University Press, 2005), 20–30.

24. Isaac Cazneau to John Hancock, April 4, 1776, Personal Letters, 1776–1793, HFP, BLSC; Account of damage done to the estate of John Hancock by the British army during Siege of Boston, December 1776, American Revolutionary War Manuscripts Collection, BPL; Carr, *After the Siege*, 31–32.

25. Isaac Cazneau to John Hancock, April 4, 1776, Personal Letters, 1776–1793, HFP, BLSC.

26. Isaac Cazneau to John Hancock, April 4, 1776, Personal Letters, 1776–1793, HFP, BLSC; Account of damage done to the estate of John Hancock by the British army during Siege of Boston, December 1776, American Revolutionary War Manuscripts Collection, BPL.

27. John Hancock to George Washington, December 22, 1775, in Smith, et al., *Letters*, 2: 509; Richard Smith Diary, December 21 and December 22, 1775, in Smith, et al., *Letters*, 2: 513; Worthington C. Ford, et al., *Journals of the Continental Congress, 1774–1789*, vol. 3 (Washington, DC, 1904–1937), 442–445.

28. John Hancock to George Washington, December 22, 1775, in Smith, et al., *Letters*, 2: 509; Mrs. Lincoln Phelps, ed., "Reminiscences of the Hancocks," *Our Country in its Relations to the Past, Present and Future* (Baltimore: John D. Toy, 1864), 298.

29. Arthur Gilman, "The Hancock House and Its Founder," *The Atlantic Monthly* 11, no. 68 (June 1863): 707.

30. William Bant to John Hancock, March 25, 1776, Account of damage done to the estate of John Hancock by the British army, December 1776, Amer-

ican Revolutionary War Manuscripts Collections, BPL; "George Washington to John Hancock, 19 March 1776," FO; Isaac Cazneau to John Hancock, April 4, 1776, Personal Letters, 1776–1793, HFP, BLSC.

31. John Hancock to George Weedon, August 28, 1776, in Smith, et al., *Letters*, 5: 78; Elizabeth A. Fenn, *Pox Americana: The Great Smallpox Epidemic of 1775–82* (New York: Hill and Wang, 2001), 20–21.

32. Fenn, *Pox*, 31–36, 82–85.

33. Fenn, *Pox*, 36–42.

34. "To George Washington from John Hancock, 16 May 1776," FO; Fenn, *Pox*, 15–20.

35. "From George Washington to John Hancock, 20 May 1776," FO.

36. "To George Washington from John Hancock, 21 May 1776," FO.

37. "To George Washington from John Hancock, 21 May 1776," FO, n3.

38. John Hancock to Thomas Cushing, May 17, 1776, in Smith, et al., *Letters*, 4: 26; "Enclosure: John Hancock to John Adams, 16 July 1776," FO; Abigail Adams to John Adams, July 13, 1776, FO.

39. John Hancock to William Cooper, July 6, 1776, in Smith, et al., *Letters*, 4: 26; Bill to John Hancock, October 31, 1783, HFP, MHS; John B. Blake, "Smallpox Inoculation in Colonial Boston," *Journal of the History of Medicine and Allied Sciences* 8, no. 3 (July 1953): 290–292.

40. Charles Coleman Sellers, "Portraits and Miniatures by Charles Willson Peale," *Transactions of the American Philosophical Society* 42, no. 1 (1952): 220.

41. John Hancock to Thomas Cushing, May 17, 1776, in Smith, et al., *Letters*, 4: 26.

42. Lydia Hancock Probate Records, 16409, *Suffolk County, MA: Probate File Papers*, online database, New England Historic Genealogical Society, digitized by FamilySearch.org; Jared Hardesty, *Unfreedom: Slavery and Dependence in Eighteenth-Century Boston* (New York: New York University Press, 2016), 16.

43. Hardesty, *Unfreedom*, 55–61, 77.

44. Lydia Hancock Probate Records, 16409, *Suffolk County, MA: Probate File Papers*; Hardesty, *Unfreedom*, 54.

45. Hardesty, *Unfreedom*, 16.

46. *Journals of the House of Representatives*, 1773–1774, vol. 50 (Boston: Massachusetts Historical Society, 1981), 85, 104, 221, 224; Thomas J. Davis, "Emancipation Rhetoric, Natural Rights, and Revolutionary New England: A Note on Four Black Petitions in Massachusetts, 1773–1777," *The New*

NOTES TO PAGES 162–166

England Quarterly 62, no. 2 (June 1989): 248–263, quote on 255; Jared Ross Hardesty, *Black Lives, Native Lands, White Worlds: A History of Slavery in New England* (Amherst: Bright Leaf, an imprint of University of Massachusetts Press, 2019), 119–123; Joanne Pope Melish, *Disowning Slavery: Gradual Emancipation and "Race" in New England, 1780–1860* (Ithaca, NY: Cornell University Press, 1998), 56–57, 64–65; Chernoh M. Sesay, Jr., "The Revolutionary Black Roots of Slavery's Abolition in Massachusetts," *The New England Quarterly* 87, no.1 (March 2014): 111–125.

47. Daniel R. Coquillette, "Sectionalism, Slavery, and the Threat of War in Josiah Quincy Jr.'s 1773 Southern Journal," *The New England Quarterly* 79, no. 2 (June 2006): 200–201; "Abigail Adams to John Adams, 22 September 1774," FO; Taylor, *American Revolutions*, quote on 116.

48. Hardesty, *Black Lives*, 50–52; Wendy Warren, *New England Bound: Slavery and Colonization in Early America* (New York: Liveright, 2016), 129.

49. Vincent Carretta, *Phillis Wheatley: Biography of a Genius in Bondage* (Athens: University of Georgia Press, 2011), 1–11, 37–44, 68–72, 101–104, quote on 72.

50. Carretta, *Phillis Wheatley*, 37–44, 68–72, 101–104.

51. Samuel Adams to James Warren, June 6, 1776, in *Warren-Adams Letters*, 1: 255–256.

52. Larrie D. Ferreiro, *Brothers at Arms: American Independence and the Men of France & Spain Who Saved It* (New York: Alfred A. Knopf, 2016), xiv.

53. Ferreiro, *Brothers at Arms*, xvi–xxiv.

54. Beeman, *Our Lives, Our Fortunes*, 370–375, 407–413; Brad A. Jones, *Resisting Independence: Popular Loyalism in the Revolutionary British Atlantic* (Ithaca, NY: Cornell University Press, 2021), 148–153.

55. John Hancock to Certain States, July 6, 1776, in Smith, et al., *Letters*, 4: 396; Rakove, *Revolutionaries*, 73–75.

56. John Hancock to William Cooper, July 6, 1776, in Smith, et al., *Letters*, 4: 394.

9: THE ART OF POPULARITY

1. John Hancock to Robert Treat Paine, January 13, 1777, in *Letters of Delegates to Congress, January to April 1777*, ed. Paul H. Smith, et al., vol. 6 (Washington, DC: Library of Congress, 1980), 91.

2. Benjamin Harrison to Robert Morris, December 25, 1776, in *Letters of Delegates to Congress, August 16–December 31, 1776*, ed. Paul H. Smith, et al.,

vol. 5 (Washington, DC: Library of Congress, 1979), 665; Oliver Wolcott to Laura Wolcott, January 1, 1777, in Smith, et al., *Letters*, 6: 14; Benjamin Harrison to Robert Morris, January 8, 1777, in Smith, et al., *Letters*, 6: 58; Matthew A. Crenson, *Baltimore: A Political History* (Baltimore: Johns Hopkins University Press, 2017), 14–15, 45–47.

3. Benjamin Rush to Julia Rush, January 31, 1777, in Smith, et al., *Letters*, 6: 184; John Adams to Abigail Adams, February 7, 1777, in Smith, et al., *Letters*, 6: 228.

4. John Adams to Abigail Adams, February 7, 1777, in Smith, et al., *Letters*, 6: 228; John Hancock to Robert Morris, January 14, 1777, in Smith, et al., *Letters*, 6: 99; John Hancock to Robert Treat Paine, January 13, 1777, in Smith, et al., *Letters*, 6: 91.

5. April 10, 1775, Harvard University Corporation Records: minutes, corporation records vol. 3, digital, Harvard University; Josiah Quincy, *The History of Harvard University*, vol. 3 (Cambridge: John Owen, 1840), 183–187, 195–209; Donald J. Proctor, "John Hancock: New Soundings on an Old Barrel," *The Journal of American History* 64, no. 3 (December 1977): 661–669.

6. Richard Beeman, *Our Lives, Our Fortunes, Our Sacred Honor: The Forging of American Independence 1774–1776* (New York: Basic Books, 2013), 198, 378–379; Alan Taylor, *American Revolutions: A Continental History, 1750–1804* (New York: W. W. Norton, 2016), 316, 362–363.

7. John Hancock to Robert Morris, January 2, January 14, February 18, 1777, in Smith, et al., *Letters*, 6: 21, 99, 313.

8. John Hancock to Robert Morris, February 18, 1777, in Smith, et al., *Letters*, 6: 313; Robert Morris to John Hancock, February 21, 1777, in Smith, et al., *Letters*, 6: 339; Richard Godbeer, *The Overflowing of Friendship: Love Between Men and the Creation of the American Republic* (Baltimore: John Hopkins University Press, 2009), 5–9, 55–61, 71–76.

9. John Hancock to Robert Morris, February 27, 1777, in Smith, et al., *Letters*, 6: 383; John Hancock to Dorothy Quincy, March 3 and March 5, 1777, in Smith, et al., *Letters*, 6: 396, 397; Sharon Salinger, *Taverns and Drinking in Early America* (Baltimore: Johns Hopkins University Press, 2002), 211.

10. Walther Rathjen, "Dental Technology, Oral Health and Aesthetic Appearance: A Historical View," *ICON* 13 (2007): 107–108; Jennifer Van Horn, "George Washington's Dentures: Disability, Deception, and the Republican Body," *Early American Studies* 14, no. 1 (Winter 2016): 4–9.

11. John Hancock to Dorothy Quincy, March 3 and March 10, 1777, in Smith, et al., *Letters*, 6: 397, 422; Salinger, *Taverns*, 214.

12. John Hancock to Dorothy Quincy, March 5 and March 10, 1777, in Smith, et al., *Letters*, 6: 398, 422, 423; John Hancock to Dorothy Quincy, March 11, 1777, in Abram English Brown, *John Hancock: His Book* (Boston: Lee and Shepard Publishers, 1898), 219.

13. John Hancock to Dorothy Quincy, March 11, 1777, in Brown, *John Hancock*, 219, 220; John Hancock to Dorothy Quincy, March 5, 1777, in Smith, et al., *Letters*, 6: 397–398.

14. John Hancock to Dorothy Quincy, March 11, 1777, in Brown, *John Hancock*, quote on 220.

15. John Adams to Abigail Adams, August 13 and August 14, 1777, AFP, MHS online, 1.

16. John Hancock to Dorothy Quincy, March 11, 1777, in Brown, *John Hancock*, quote on 220; John Hancock to Dorothy Hancock, June 29, 1778, *MHS-P*, vol. 97 (Boston: Massachusetts Historical Society, 1986), 147; Enoch Edwards to John Hancock, August 10, 1786, Personal Letters 1776–1793, HFP, BLSC.

17. "Excerpts from the Day-Books of David Evans, Cabinet-Maker, Philadelphia, 1774–1811," *The Pennsylvania Magazine of History and Biography* 27, no. 1 (1903): 49; August 11, 1777, Personal Bills, 1773–1777, Mss: 766, HFP, BLSC; Pamela Ehrlich, "A Hancock Family Story: Restoring Connections," *Antiques & Fine Art Magazine* 17, no. 1 (Spring 2018): 151–152.

18. John Hancock to Dorothy Hancock, September 17, 1777, in *Letters of Delegates to Congress, May to September 1777*, ed. Paul H. Smith, et al., vol. 7 (Washington, DC: Library of Congress, 1981), 685; John Hancock to Dorothy Hancock, October 1, 1777, in *Letters of Delegates to Congress, September 1777 to January 1778*, ed. Paul H. Smith, et al., vol. 8 (Washington, DC: Library of Congress, 1981), 38.

19. John Hancock to Dorothy Hancock, October 1, 1777, in Smith, et al., *Letters*, 8: 38.

20. John Hancock to Dorothy Hancock, October 1, 1777, in Smith, et al., *Letters*, 8: 38, 39; John Adams to Abigail Adams, September 30, 1777, AFP, MHS online; Aaron Sullivan, *The Disaffected: Britain's Occupation of Philadelphia During the American Revolution* (Philadelphia: University of Pennsylvania Press, 2019), 63–64.

21. John Hancock to Dorothy Hancock, October 8, 1777, in Smith, et al., *Letters*, 8: 77; Lynn Montross, *The Reluctant Rebels: The Story of the Continental Congress, 1774–1789* (New York: Harper, 1950), 210–211.

22. John Hancock to Dorothy Hancock, October 1, 1777, in Smith, et al., *Letters*, 8: 39.

23. John Hancock to Dorothy Hancock, October 8 and October 18, 1777, in Smith, et al., *Letters*, 8: 78–79, 137.

24. John Hancock to Dorothy Hancock, October 1 and October 8, 1777, in Smith, et al., *Letters*, 8: 39, 77; John Hancock to Dorothy Hancock, June 29, 1778, *MHS-P* 97: 148.

25. John Hancock to Robert Morris, October 5, 1777, in Smith, et al., *Letters*, 8: 55.

26. John Hancock to Thomas Jefferson, October 25, 1777, in Smith, et al., *Letters*, 8: 180; John Hancock to William Palfrey, October 19, 1777, in Smith, et al., *Letters*, 8: 144; John Hancock to George Washington, October 17, 1777, in Smith, et al., *Letters*, 8: 131.

27. John Hancock to Dorothy Hancock, June 29, 1778, *MHS-P* 97: 147; Edmund Cody Burnett, *The Continental Congress: A Definitive History of the Continental Congress from Its Inception in 1774 to March 1789* (New York: W. W. Norton, 1941), 259–260, 267; Larrie D. Ferreiro, *Brothers at Arms: American Independence and the Men of France & Spain Who Saved It* (New York: Alfred A. Knopf, 2016), 73, 95–99.

28. John Hancock to Dorothy Hancock, July 1, 1778, in *Letters of Delegates to Congress, June to September 1778*, ed. Paul H. Smith, et al., vol. 10 (Washington, DC: Library of Congress, 1983), 217; Montross, *Reluctant Rebels*, 173–174, 181–187.

29. Samuel Adams to James Warren, October 30, 1777, in Smith, et al., *Letters*, 8: 212; October 31, 1777, *Journals of the American Congress: From 1774 to 1788*, vol. 2 (Washington: Way and Gideon, 1823), 308.

30. Samuel Adams to James Warren, October 30 and November 4, 1777, in Smith, et al., *Letters*, 8: 212, 226; October 8, 1777, November 4, 1777, July 7, 1778, *Journals of the American Congress*, 2: 282, 312, 616.

31. John Hancock to George Washington, October 17, 1777, in Smith, et al., *Letters*, 8: 132; "From George Washington to John Hancock, 22 October 1777," FO; "From George Washington to John Hancock, 2 November 1777," FO.

32. Samuel Adams to John Adams, December 8, 1777, in *The Writings of Samuel Adams, 1773–1777*, ed. Harry Alonzo Cushing, vol. 3 (New York: G. P. Putnam's Sons, 1907), 417; William Ellery and Henrietta C. Ellery, "Diary of the Hon. William Ellery, of Rhode Island: October 20 to November 15,

1777," *The Pennsylvania Magazine of History and Biography* 11, no. 3 (October 1887): 323.

33. JAD, November 17, 1777, AFP, MHS online, 22.

34. A Private Letter from New England, December 30, 1777, in *Letters of Brunswick and Hessian Officers During the American Revolution*, trans. William L. Stone (Albany, NY: Joel Munsell's Sons, 1891), 158; Malcolm Barnard, *Fashion as Communication*, 2nd ed., (London: Routledge, 2006), 2–5, 20–22; Kate Haulman, *The Politics of Fashion in Eighteenth-Century America* (Chapel Hill: University of North Carolina Press, 2011), 175, 184–185.

35. John Boyle, A Journal of Occurrences in Boston, November 19, 1777, HL; James Warren to John Adams, June 7, 1778, in *Warren-Adams Papers*, vol. 2, 1778–1814 (Massachusetts Historical Society, 1925), 20; A Private Letter from New England, December 30, 1777, in Stone, *Letters of Brunswick*, 158; Mary Caroline Crawford, *Old Boston Days & Ways: From the Dawn of the Revolution Until the Town Became a City* (Boston: Little, Brown, 1909), 250.

36. October 31, 1777, *Journals of the American Congress*, 2: 308.

37. Burnett, *Continental Congress*, 233–240, 318–321.

38. John Hancock to Dorothy Hancock, June 20, 23, 1778, in Smith, et al., *Letters*, 10: 145, 179; John Hancock to Dorothy Hancock, June 29, 1778, *MHS-P* 97: 147, 148.

39. John Hancock to Dorothy Hancock, June 20, 23, 1778, in Smith, et al., *Letters*, 10: 145, 179.

40. John Hancock to Dorothy Hancock, June 23, 1778, in Smith, et al., *Letters*, 10: 178; John Hancock to Dorothy Hancock, June 29, 1778, *MHS-P* 97: 147–148; Sullivan, *Disaffected*, 143; Burnett, *Continental Congress*, 343.

41. John Hancock to Dorothy Hancock, June 29, 1778, *MHS-P* 97: 147; June 24, 1778, Worthington C. Ford, et al., *Journals of the Continental Congress, 1774–1789*, vol. 2 (Washington, DC, 1904–1937), 602; JAD, August 29, 1774, FO; Salinger, *Taverns*, 54.

42. Ellery and Ellery, "Diary of the Hon. William Ellery," 477; Walter Staib, *A Sweet Taste of History* (Guilford, CT: Lyons Press, 2013), xv; Burnett, *Continental Congress*, 343–344.

43. John Hancock to Dorothy Hancock, June 29, 1778, *MHS-P* 97: 147; Samuel Adams to Samuel Phillips Savage, August 11, 1778, in *The Writings of Samuel Adams, 1778–1802*, ed. Harry Alonzo Cushing, vol. 4 (New York: G. P. Putnam's Sons, 1908), 49.

44. July 26 and August 8, 1778, "Diary of Ezekiel Price," *NEHGR* 19 (Boston: David Clapp & Son, 1865): 334; January 30, 1776, *Journals of the House of*

Representatives of Massachusetts, vol. 51, part 2, 1775–1776 (Boston: Massachusetts Historical Society, 1983), 225.

45. William B. Wilcox, "British Strategy in America, 1778," *The Journal of Modern History* 19, no. 2 (June 1947): 111; Ezra Stiles diary, July 11, 1778, in *The Literary Diary of Ezra Stiles*, ed. Franklin Bowditch Dexter, vol. 2 (New York: Charles Scribner's Sons, 1901), 294; Paul Revere to Rachel Revere, August 1778, in Esther Forbes, *Paul Revere and the World He Lived In* (Boston: Mariner Books, 1999), quote on 343.

46. John Hancock to Dorothy Quincy, August 19, 1778, HFP, MHS.

47. John Hancock to Jeremiah Powell, August 14, 1778, Massachusetts State Archives, vol. 199, 418; Louis Gottschalk, *Lafayette Joins the American Army* (Chicago: University of Chicago Press, 1937, 1965), 250–257; Charles P. Whittemore, *A General of the Revolution: John Sullivan of New Hampshire* (New York: Columbia University Press, 1961), 90–98, 102–103.

48. Ferreiro, *Brothers at Arms*, 143; Fred Anderson, *Crucible of War: The Seven Years' War and the Fate of Empire in British North America, 1754–1766* (New York: Vintage Books, 2000), 11; Brendan McConville, *The Brethren: A Story of Faith and Conspiracy in Revolutionary America* (Cambridge, MA: Harvard University Press, 2021), 73–77.

49. Paul Revere to John Rivoire, July 1, 1782, in Elbridge Henry Goss, *The Life of Colonel Paul Revere*, vol. 2 (Boston: Joseph George Cupples, 1891), 511; "From Benjamin Franklin to [Samuel Cooper], 27 February 1778," FO; Forbes, *Paul Revere*, 4–5, 12.

50. Abigail Adams to John Adams, September 29, 1778, AFP, MHS online, 2–3; Salinger, *Taverns*, 1–2; Christian McBurney, "Why did a Boston Mob Kill a French Officer?," *Journal of the American Revolution*, October 23, 2014, accessed online, https://allthingsliberty.com/2014/10/why-did-a-boston-mob-kill-a-french-officer/.

51. Fitz-Henry Smith, Jr., *The French at Boston During the Revolution* (Boston: Privately Printed, 1913), 35–38; McBurney, "Boston Mob."

52. "From George Washington to Major General William Heath, 22 September 1778," FO.

53. H. E. Scudder, ed., *Recollections of Samuel Breck with Passages from His Notebooks* (Philadelphia: Porter & Coates, 1877), 48; Lafayette to d'Estaing, August 22, 1778, *Revue d'Histoire Diplomatique* 6 (January 1892): 423; "To George Washington from Major General Lafayette, 1 September 1778," FO; Smith, Jr., *French at Boston*, 35; John Hancock Probate Records, 20215,

Suffolk County, MA: Probate File Papers, online database; Haulman, *Politics of Fashion*, 178–181. Merci to Mathilde Piton for her translation.

54. "To George Washington from Major General Nathanael Greene, 16 September 1778," FO; "To George Washington from Major General Lafayette, 1 September 1778," FO.

55. "Reminiscences by Gen. Wm. H. Sumner," *NEHGR* 8 (1854): 189; Walter Kendall Watkins, "The Hancock House and Its Builder," *Old-Time New England* 17, no. 1 (July 1926): 19.

56. "Reminiscences," 189, 190.

57. Ellen C. D. Q. Woodbury, *Dorothy Quincy: Wife of John Hancock with Events of Her Time* (Washington: The Neale Publishing Company, 1901), 237–238; Josiah Quincy, *A Municipal History of the Town and City of Boston* (Boston: Charles C. Little and James Brown, 1852), 151–152; Sarah Vowell, *Lafayette in the Somewhat United States* (New York: Riverhead Books, 2015), 3–8.

58. "Reminiscences," 190; Abigail Adams to John Adams, October 21 and October 25, 1778, AFP, MHS online, 1, 2.

59. "To George Washington from Major General Nathanael Greene, 16 September 1778," FO; "Reminiscences," 189.

60. "Reminiscences," 189.

61. M. Le Comte D'Estaing, *Extrait Du Journal D'Un Officier de la Marine* (1782), 51; James Warren to Samuel Adams, September 25, 1778, in *Warren-Adams Letters* 2: 48; Smith, Jr., *French at Boston*, 43.

62. JRD, October 29, 1778, in *Letters and Diary of John Rowe*, ed. Anne Rowe Cunningham (Boston: W. B. Clarke, 1903), 323; Benjamin Guild Diary, October 29, 1778, Diaries of Benjamin Guild, 1776, 1778, Harvard University.

63. John Hancock to Jeremiah Powell, September 28, 1778, HFP, MHS; Abigail Adams to John Adams, October 25, 1778, AFP, MHS online, 1; James Warren to Samuel Adams, September 25, 1778, *Warren-Adams Letters* 2: 48.

64. Comte d'Estaing to Unknown. September 5, 1778, in Henri Doniol, *Histoire de la Participation de la France a l'establissement des États-Unis d'Amérique*, vol. 3 (Paris: Imprimerie Nationale, 1888), 363; Joseph S. Nye, Jr., "Soft Power," *Foreign Policy* 80 (Autumn 1990): 153-171.

65. JRD, November 5, December 25, December 26, 1778, in Cunningham, *Diary*, 323, 325.

10: TRAITOR TO HIS CLASS

1. John Hancock to Thomas Hancock, January 14, 1761, *MHS-P*, vol. 43
    (Boston: Massachusetts Historical Society, 1910), 196–197; William Pychon
    Diary, October 25, 1780, in *The Diary of William Pynchon of Salem*, ed.
    Fitch Edward Oliver (Boston: Houghton Mifflin, 1890), 77.

2. Jill Lepore, *These Truths: A History of the United States* (New York: W. W.
    Norton, 2018), 111–114; Jack Rakove, *Revolutionaries: A New History of the
    Invention of America* (Boston: Houghton Mifflin Harcourt, 2009), 181–195;
    Stephen E. Patterson, *Political Parties in Revolutionary Massachusetts* (Madison:
    University of Wisconsin Press, 1973), 161–196, 214–220, 234–239.

3. Richard D. Brown and Jack Tager, *Massachusetts: A Concise History* (Amherst:
    University of Massachusetts Press, 2000), 96; Patterson, *Political Parties*,
    221–226; Leonard L. Richards, *Shays's Rebellion: The American Revolution's
    Final Battle* (Philadelphia: University of Pennsylvania, 2002), 70–74.

4. William Gordon to John Adams, July 22, 1780, *MHS-P*, vol. 63 (Boston:
    Massachusetts Historical Society, 1931), 436; Samuel Adams to John Adams,
    July 10, 1780, in Robert J. Taylor, ed., *Massachusetts, Colony to Common-
    wealth: Documents on the Formation of Its Constitution, 1775–1780* (New
    York: W. W. Norton, 1961), 166; Samuel Adams to Betsy Adams, February 1,
    1781, in *The Writings of Samuel Adams, 1778–1802*, ed. Harry Alonzo Cushing,
    vol. 4 (New York: G. P. Putnam's Sons, 1908), 247; Van Beck Hall, *Politics
    Without Parties: Massachusetts, 1780–1791* (Pittsburgh, PA: University of
    Pittsburg Press, 1972), 132–133.

5. Clifford K. Shipton, *Sibley's Harvard Graduates, 1741–1745*, vol. 11 (Boston:
    Massachusetts Historical Society, 1960), 515–519, 535–537.

6. Samuel Adams to Betsy Adams, October 10, 1780, in Cushing, *Samuel
    Adams*, 4: 210; September 4, 1780, *A Report of the Record Commissioners of
    the City of Boston Containing the Boston Town Records, 1778 to 1783* (Boston:
    Rockwell and Churchill, 1895), 150; Brown, *Massachusetts*, 92–98.

7. William Pynchon Diary, October 25, 1780, in Oliver, *Diary*, 77; William
    Gordon, *The History of the Rise, Progress, and Establishment of the Inde-
    pendence of the United States of America*, vol. 3 (New York: John Woods,
    1801), 139.

8. Kimberly S. Alexander, *Treasures Afoot: Shoe Stories from the Georgian Era*
    (Baltimore: Johns Hopkins University Press, 2018), 157.

9. William Pynchon Diary, October 26, 1780, in Oliver, *Diary*, 77; Gordon,
    History, 3: 139.

10. Gordon, *History*, 3: 139–140; Charles W. Akers, *The Divine Politician: Samuel Cooper and the American Revolution in Boston* (Boston: Northeastern University Press, 1982), 312–314.

11. Samuel Adams to Samuel Cooper, December 25, 1778, in Cushing, *Samuel Adams*, 4: 108; William M. Fowler, Jr., *Samuel Adams: Radical Puritan* (New York: Addison-Wesley Educational Publishers, Inc., 1997), 155–156; Gordon S. Wood, *The Creation of the American Republic, 1776–1787* (Chapel Hill: University of North Carolina Press, 1998), 47–55, 108–110, 417–421; Hall, *Politics*, 83–84.

12. James Warren to Arthur Lee, December 18, 1780, in Richard Henry Lee, *Life of Arthur Lee*, vol. 2 (Boston: Wells and Lilly, 1829), 273.

13. Mercy Otis Warren to John Adams, November 15, 1780, in *Warren-Adams Papers, 1778–1814*, vol. 2 (Boston: Massachusetts Historical Society, 1925), 147; Edith B. Gelles, "Bonds of Friendship: The Correspondence of Abigail Adams and Mercy Otis Warren," *MHS-P*, vol. 108 (Boston: Massachusetts Historical Society, 1998), 61; Woody Holton, *Abigail Adams* (New York: Free Press, 2009), 158, 244; Rosemarie Zagarri, *A Woman's Dilemma: Mercy Otis Warren and the American Revolution* (Wheeling, IL: Harlan Davidson, 1995), xv–xvi, 86–90, 98–102.

14. Wood, *Creation*, 395–397.

15. John Adams to Benjamin Rush, June 19, 1789, FO; James Warren to Arthur Lee, December 18, 1780, in Lee, *Arthur Lee*, 2: 272; Hall, *Politics*, 133–136, especially notes 2, 4, 5; Patterson, *Political Parties*, 198–199.

16. Woody Holton, *Unruly Americans and the Origins of the Constitution* (New York: Hill and Wang, 2007), 27–28.

17. Sean Condon, *Shays's Rebellion: Authority and Distress in Post-Revolutionary America* (Baltimore: Johns Hopkins University Press, 2015), 10, 16.

18. Holton, *Unruly*, 31–36, 131, 267; Woody Holton, "'From the Labour of Others': The War Bonds Controversy and the Origins of the Constitution in New England," *The William and Mary Quarterly* 61, no. 2 (April 2004): 272–277; Holton, *Abigail Adams*, 272–277.

19. Hall, *Politics*, 23–43, 118–119, 184–196; Condon, *Shays's*, 20–26, 38–40; Brown, *Massachusetts*, 100; Richards, *Shays's*, 4, 85; Allan Kulikoff, "The Progress of Inequality in Revolutionary Boston," *The William and Mary Quarterly* 28, no. 3 (July 1971): 376–384, 409.

20. John Hancock to James Scott, November 14, 1783, John Hancock Letterbook (business), HFP, BLSC; Chris Starbuck to William Hoskins, May 6, 1783, Jonathan Payson to William Hoskins, August 11, 1783, Letters received

by William Hoskins, 1783 January-May and 1783–September 1786, HFP, BLSC.

21. William Pynchon Diary, June 25, 1778, in Oliver, ed., *Diary*, 54; *Independent Chronicle*, February 5, 1778, GB.

22. William Hoskins to Joseph Otis, April 16, 1783, William Hoskins to James Warren, February 1, 1783, John Hancock Letterbook (business), HFP, BLSC.

23. John Hancock to James Scott, November 14, 1783, John Hancock Letterbook (business), HFP, BLSC; John Wendall to John Hancock, September 12, 1782, Real Estate, 1781–2, HFP, BLSC; W. T. Baxter, *The House of Hancock: Business in Boston, 1724–1775* (Cambridge, MA: Harvard University Press, 1945), 280–287.

24. Lynn Montross, *The Reluctant Rebels: The Story of the Continental Congress, 1774–1789* (New York: Harper & Brothers Publishers, 1950), 318–319, 377; February 3, 1781, in *Journals of the Continental Congress*, ed. Worthington C. Ford, et al., vol. 19 (Washington, DC: 1912), 112.

25. Edwin M. Bacon, ed., *Supplement to the Acts and Resolves of Massachusetts*, vol. 1 (Boston: Geo. H. Ellis, 1896), 96–97, 120, 138, 139; Samuel Adams to John Lovell, May 15, 1782, in Cushing, *Samuel Adams*, 4: 273.

26. Bacon, *Supplement to the Acts* 1: 96, 120, 138, 146, 147; James Sullivan to Benjamin Lincoln, November 18, 1782, in *Life of James Sullivan: With Selections from his Writings*, ed. Thomas C. Amory, vol. 2 (Boston: Phillips, Sampson, and Company, 1859), 387; Hall, *Politics*, 96–118, 133–134, 150–152.

27. John Hancock to John Wendell, May 22, 1782, in Barrett Wendell, "A Gentlewoman of Boston: 1742–1805," *American Antiquarian Proceedings* 29 (October 1919): quote on 266–267.

28. James Sullivan to Benjamin Lincoln, November 18, 1782, in Amory, *James Sullivan*, 2: 388; Mrs. Lincoln Phelps, ed., "Reminiscences of the Hancocks," *Our Country in its Relations to the Past, Present and Future* (Baltimore: John D. Toy, 1864), 302–303; January 27, 1833, William Sullivan, *Familiar Letters on Public Characters* (Boston: Russell, Odiorne, and Metcalf, 1834), 12.

29. William Heath to John Hancock, April 18, 1783, *MHS-C* 5, series 7 (Boston: Massachusetts Historical Society, 1905), 389; William Gordon to Elbridge Gerry, December 24, 1783, *MHS-P* 63: 500; John Hancock to James Scott, November 14, 1783, John Hancock Letterbook (business), HFP, BLSC; William M. Fowler, Jr., *The Baron of Beacon Hill: A Biography of John Hancock* (Boston: Houghton Mifflin, 1980), 258–259, 337n51.

30. John Hancock to Rufus King, November 30, 1785, Rufus King to John Adams, December 10, 1785, in *Life and Correspondence of Rufus King*,

1775–1794, ed. Charles R. King, vol. 1 (New York: G. P. Putnam's Sons, 1894), 114, 117; November 23, 1785, Worthington C. Ford, et. al., ed., *Journals of the Continental Congress*, vol. 29 (Washington, DC, 1933), 879; June 5, 1786, *Journals of the Continental Congress*, Worthington C. Ford, et al., ed., vol. 30 (Washington, DC, 1934), 328.

31. "From John Adams to William Tudor, Sr., 1 June 1817," FO.
32. John Hancock to James Scott, November 14, 1783, John Hancock Letterbook (business), HFP, BLSC.
33. John Hancock to James Scott, November 14, 1783, John Hancock Letterbook (business), HFP, BLSC; Phelps, *Our Country*, 301; "Inventory of all the Estate of his late Excellency John Hancock, Esq.," Suffolk County Probate Case 20215, New England Historic Genealogical Society Online.
34. "Reminiscences by Gen. Wm. H. Sumner," *NEHGR* 8 (1854): 189.
35. "Reminiscences," 189.
36. Ellen C. D. Q. Woodbury, *Dorothy Quincy: Wife of John Hancock with Events of Her Time* (Washington: The Neale Publishing Company, 1901), 195.
37. *American Herald*, January 29, 1787, *Massachusetts Centinel*, January 31, 1787, GB; Pamela Ehrlich, "A Hancock Family Story: Restoring Connections," *Antiques & Fine Art Magazine* 17, no. 1 (Spring 2018): 152, 153n19.
38. *Independent Chronicle*, February 1, 1787, BG, February 5, 1787, *Massachusetts Centinel*, February 3, 1787, GB.
39. John Hancock to Henry Knox, March 14, 1787, HFP, MHS.
40. John Hancock to Henry Knox, March 14, 1787, HFP, MHS.
41. John Hancock to Henry Knox, March 14, 1787, HFP, MHS; "The Worcester Magazine from the Fourth Week in March to the First Week in April 1787," 3, no. 1 (Worcester: Isaiah Thomas, 1787): 76; May 6, 1787, Domestic Bills, 1787 February-November, HFP, BLSC.
42. Speech by James Bowdoin, May 31, 1785, *Acts and Resolves of the Commonwealth of Massachusetts, 1784–1785* (Boston: Adams & Nourse, 1784), 708–709; Gordon E. Kershaw, *James Bowdoin: Patriot and Man of the Enlightenment* (Brunswick, ME: Bowdoin College, 1976), 82; Holton, *Unruly*, 75, 129, 133.
43. Reverend Bezaleel Howard Reflection, 1787, in Richard D. Brown, "Shays's Rebellion and Its Aftermath: A View from Springfield, Massachusetts, 1787," *The William and Mary Quarterly* 40, no. 4 (October 1983): 602–603.
44. Reverend Bezaleel Howard Reflection, 1787, in Brown, "Shays's," 598, quote on 602; Condon, *Shays's*, 17–18, 46–57, 67–68, 73–74; Richards, *Shays's*, 6, 8–12, 26–27, 111; Hall, *Politics*, 166–184, 208, 212.

45. James Warren to John Adams, May 18, 1787, in *Warren-Adams Letters* 2: 292; Richards, *Shays's*, 16–19; Hall, *Politics*, 214–216.

46. September 28, 1786, *Acts and Resolves of the Commonwealth of Massachusetts, 1786–1787* (Wright & Potter Printing Company, 1893), 928; William Pencak, "Samuel Adams and Shays's Rebellion," *The New England Quarterly* 62, no. 1 (March 1989): 64.

47. Samuel Adams to Noah Webster, April 30, 1784, in Cushing, *Samuel Adams*, 4: 305, 306; Pencak, "Samuel Adams," 67.

48. Massachusetts Archives, vol. 189, List of Subscribers, 217–218, accessed digitally. Samuel Gore and Moses Grant were subscribers and Boston Tea Party participants. Benjamin L. Carp, *Defiance of the Patriots: The Boston Tea Party and the Making of America* (New Haven, CT: Yale University Press, 2010), 236; Richards, *Shays's*, 11, 13–14, 23–25; Condon, *Shays's*, 82–88.

49. Brown, *Massachusetts*, 104–105; Condon, *Shays's*, 91–95, 106–112.

50. Kershaw, *James Bowdoin*, 86; Condon, *Shays's*, 107.

51. Jonathan Smith, "The Depression of 1785 and Daniel Shays' Rebellion," *The William and Mary Quarterly* 5, no. 1 (January 1948): 89, 94; *Massachusetts Centinel*, April 4, 1787, GB; Hall, *Politics*, 90, 227, 235–237, 242, 270–271; "John Quincy Adams to John Adams, 30 June 1787," FO.

52. Hall, *Politics*, 236–242.

53. *Massachusetts Centinel*, April 4, 1787, GB.

54. *Massachusetts Centinel*, April 7, 1787, GB.

55. John Hancock Speech, October 18, 1787, in Paul D. Brandes, *John Hancock's Life and Speeches: A Personalized Vision of the American Revolution, 1763–1793* (Lanham, MD: The Scarecrow Press, 1996), 301; Condon, *Shays's*, 111–115, 117; Richards, *Shays's*, 39–41; Hall, *Politics*, 249–253.

56. John Hancock Speech, October 18, 1787, in Brandes, *John Hancock's Life*, 301; Holton, *Unruly*, 76; Richards, *Shays's*, 119.

57. James Warren to John Adams, May 18, 1787, in *Warren-Adams Letters* 2: 292–293; Christopher Gore to Rufus King, June 7, 1789, in King, *Rufus King*, 1: 361.

11: DEFENDING MASSACHUSETTS FROM THE UNITED STATES

1. Jeremy Belknap Minutes, January 15–17, 1788, *MHS-P*, vol. 3 (Boston: Massachusetts Historical Society, 1859), 296; Henry Jackson to Henry Knox, January 20, 1788, in *The Documentary History of the Ratification of the Constitution Digital Edition*, ed. John P. Kaminski, Gaspare J. Saladino,

Richard Leffler, Charles H. Schoenleber, and Margaret A. Hogan, vol. 7 (Charlottesville: University of Virginia Press, 2009), 1536–1537.

2. George Benson to Nicholas Brown, January 30, 1788, in Kaminski, et al., *Documentary History*, 7: 1548; James T. Austin, *The Life of Elbridge Gerry*, vol. 2 (Boston: Wells and Lilly, 1829), 75; William Vincent Wells, *The Life and Public Services of Samuel Adams*, vol. 3 (Boston: Little, Brown, 1865), 259; Ebenezer Smith Thomas, *Reminiscences of the Last Sixty-Five Years*, vol. 1 (Hartford: Case, Tiffany, and Burnham, 1840), 243.

3. Wells, *Samuel Adams*, 3: 259.

4. Woody Holton, *Unruly Americans and the Origins of the Constitution* (New York: Hill and Wang, 2007), 4–9, 16–18, 158–159, 180–198, 272–274; George William Van Cleve, *We Have Not a Government: The Articles of Confederation and the Road to the Constitution* (Chicago: University of Chicago Press, 2017), 8–9, 229–242, 270–276.

5. Van Cleve, *We Have Not*, 258–259; Van Beck Hall, *Politics Without Parties: Massachusetts, 1780–1791* (Pittsburgh, PA: University of Pittsburgh Press, 1972), 263–264; *The Records of the Federal Convention of 1787*, ed. Max Farrand, vol. 2 (New Haven, CT: Yale University Press, 1911), 646.

6. Jill Lepore, *These Truths: A History of the United States* (New York: W. W. Norton, 2018), 128; Alan Taylor, *American Revolutions: A Continental History, 1750–1804* (New York: W. W. Norton, 2016), 386–387.

7. Pauline Maier, *Ratification: The People Debate the Constitution, 1787–1788* (New York: Simon & Schuster, 2010), 166; George H. Haynes, "The Conciliatory Proposition in the Massachusetts Convention of 1788," *Proceedings of the American Antiquarian Society* 29 (October 1919): 299; "From George Washington to James Madison, 5 February 1788," FO; "From George Washington to Benjamin Lincoln, 31 January 1788," FO.

8. Neal J. Roese and Kathleen D. Vohs, "Hindsight Bias," *Perspectives on Psychological Science* 7, no. 5 (September 2012): 411–416; Baruch Fischhoff, "Hindsight ≠ Foresight: The Effect of Outcome Knowledge on Judgment Under Uncertainty," *Journal of Experimental Psychology: Human Perception and Performance* 1, no. 3 (1975): 288–299.

9. From Tristram Dalton, February 3, 1788, in Kaminski, et al., *Documentary History*, 7: 1569; Eben F. Stone, "Parsons and the Constitutional Convention of 1788," *Historical Collections of the Essex Institute*, vol. 35 (Salem, MA: Essex Institute, 1899), 88; Richard D. Brown and Jack Tager, *Massachusetts: A Concise History* (Amherst: University of Massachusetts Press, 2000), 107–108; Hall, *Politics*, 286–293.

10. Holton, *Unruly*, 187–191, 200–206; Lepore, *These Truths*, 129–130.
11. Tristram Dalton to Michael Hodge, January 30, 1788, Thomas Russell to John Langdon, January 30, 1788, From Tristram Dalton, February 3, 1788, Rufus King to Henry Knox, February 3, 1788, in Kaminski, et al., *Documentary History*, 7: 1560, 1562, 1569, 1571; Stone, *Historical Collections*, 34: 88.
12. Jeremy Belknap Minutes, January 31, 1788, *MHS-P* 3:302; *BG*, February 4, 1788, GB.
13. John Hancock Speech, January 31, 1788, in Paul D. Brandes, *John Hancock's Life and Speeches: A Personalized Vision of the American Revolution, 1763–1793* (Lanham, MD: The Scarecrow Press, 1996), 321.
14. *BG*, February 22, 1788, GB; Tristram Dalton to Michael Hodge, January 30, 1788, in Kaminski, et al., *Documentary History*, 7: 1560; Samuel Bannister Harding, *The Contest Over the Ratification of the Federal Constitution in the State of Massachusetts* (New York: Longmans, Green, and Co., 1896), 85; Maier, *Ratification*, 192–196.
15. Rufus King to James Madison, January 30, 1788, in Kaminski, et al., *Documentary History*, 7: 1561.
16. *BG*, February 22, 1788, GB; John Hancock Speech, January 31, 1788, in Brandes, *John Hancock's Life*, 323, 325; Maier, *Ratification*, 200, 519n44.
17. Henry Van Schaack to Peter Van Schaack, February 4, 1788, in Kaminski, et al., *Documentary History*, 7: 1575.
18. Henry Jackson to Henry Knox, February 6, 1788, in Kaminski, et al., *Documentary History*, 7: 1580.
19. John Hancock Speech, February 6, 1788, in Brandes, *John Hancock's Life*, 328; Edmund Quincy, *Life of Josiah Quincy* (Boston: Ticknor and Fields, 1867), 38–39.
20. Austin, *Elbridge Gerry*, 2: 76; John Hancock Speech, February 6, 1788, in Brandes, *John Hancock's Life*, 328.
21. William Widgery to George Thatcher, February 9, 1788, in Kaminski, et al., *Documentary History*, 7: 1690; Jeremy Belknap Minutes, February 6, 1788, *MHS-P* 3: 303; Maier, *Ratification*, 207–208.
22. Henry Van Schaack to Peter Van Schaack, February 4, 1788, in Kaminski, et al., *Documentary History*, 7: 1575; "The Convention of Massachusetts," *Magazine of American History* 14, no.6 (December 1885): 540; William Widgery to George Thatcher, February 9, 1788, in Kaminski, et al., *Documentary History*, 7: 1690.
23. Maier, *Ratification*, 209; Brandes, *John Hancock's Life*, 329n1.

24. Henry Jackson to Henry Knox, February 6, 1788, in Kaminski, et al., *Documentary History*, 7: 1580.

25. *Massachusetts Gazette*, February 8, 1788, *Vermont Gazette*, February 18, 1788, in Kaminski, et al., *Documentary History*, 7: 1495–1496; 1497n9; Henry Jackson to Henry Knox, February 10, 1788, in Kaminski, et al., *Documentary History*, 7: 1585.

26. *Debates and Proceedings in the Convention of the Commonwealth of Massachusetts Held in the Year 1788* (Boston: William White, 1856), 332.

27. Holton, *Unruly*, x–xi, 2, 277; Maier, *Ratification*, 202, 431–432, 468; Kenneth R. Bowling, "'A Tub to the Whale': The Founding Fathers and Adoption of the Federal Bill of Rights," *Journal of the Early Republic* 8, no. 3 (Autumn 1988): 223–224; Haynes, "Conciliatory Proposition," 309.

28. Elbridge Gerry to William Cushing, undated, in Austin, *Elbridge Gerry*, 2: 75; Rufus King to Henry Knox, February 3, 1788, Henry Jackson to Henry Knox, February 10, 1788, in Kaminski, et al., *Documentary History*, 7: 1572, 1585; Leonard L. Richards, *Shays's Rebellion: The American Revolution's Final Battle* (Philadelphia: University of Pennsylvania, 2002), 150; Harding, *Contest*, 85–86.

29. "To George Washington from Benjamin Lincoln, 24 September 1788," FO; Rufus King to Henry Knox, February 3, 1788, in Kaminski, et al., *Documentary History*, 7: 1572; *Massachusetts Centinel*, January 9, 1788, GB; "To George Washington from William Gordon, 3 April 1788," FO; Christopher Gore to Rufus King, August 30, 1788, in King, *Rufus King*, 1: 343.

30. *New-Hampshire Gazette*, August 21, 1788, *Independent Chronicle*, August 21, 1788, *Providence Gazette and Country Journal*, September 6, 1788, *United States Chronicle*, September 4, 1788, GB; August 16 and August 18, 1788, John Quincy Adams Diary, *The Diary of John Quincy Adams: A Digital Collection*, vol. 12, 214, 215, vol. 13, 33, MHS online.

31. Alexander Keyssar, *Why Do We Still Have the Electoral College?* (Cambridge, MA: Harvard University Press, 2020), 26–28.

32. Henry Jackson to Henry Knox, January 11, 1789, in Herbert S. Allan, *John Hancock: Patriot in Purple* (New York: The Macmillan Company, 1948), 339; "To George Washington from Benjamin Lincoln, 24 September 1788," FO; Benjamin Rush to Jeremy Belknap, October 7, 1788, *MHS-C* 4, series 6 (Boston: Massachusetts Historical Society, 1891), 419.

33. "To George Washington from Benjamin Lincoln, 24 September 1788," FO; "From John Adams to Mercy Otis Warren, 20 July 1807," FO; Hall, *Politics*, 305–308.

34. *The Western Star*, December 4, 1792, GB; Hall, *Politics*, 294–295, 319; Stephen Higginson, *The Chapters in the Life of John Hancock* (New York: 1857), 8, 39, 49, 66.

35. From M. CLAVIERE to M. BRISSOT de WARVILLE, July 30, 1788, in Jacques Pierre Brissot de Warville, *New Travels in the United States of America*, Performed in 1788, Evans Early America Imprint Collection, 66.

36. From M. CLAVIERE to M. BRISSOT de WARVILLE, July 30, 1788, in De Warville, *New Travels*, 66; Charles S. Sydnor, *Gentlemen Freeholders: Political Practices in Washington's Virginia* (Chapel Hill: University of North Carolina Press, 1952), chapters 3 and 4; Allan Kulikoff, "The Progress of Inequality in Revolutionary Boston," *The William and Mary Quarterly* 28, no. 3 (July 1971): 387–388.

37. "Memories of Mr. Balch's Mimicry," *Boston 1775* (blog), August 16, 2019, https://boston1775.blogspot.com/2019/08/memories-of-mr-balchs-mimicry.html; Scudder, ed., *Samuel Breck*, 108–109; James T. Austin, ed., *The Life of Elbridge Gerry*, vol. 1 (Boston: Wells and Lilly, 1828), 363–364; *Independent Chronicle*, August 7 and August 14, 1788, GB; John Hancock to Dorothy Quincy, ca. 1784, HFP, MHS; Hall, *Politics*, 317n135; Gordon Wood, *The Radicalism of the American Revolution* (New York: Vintage Books, 1991), 77–89.

38. Galusha Burchard Balch, *Genealogy of the Balch Families in America* (Salem, MA: Eben Putnam, 1897), 67; "Legends of Nathaniel Balch," *Boston 1775* (blog), December 30, 2019, https://boston1775.blogspot.com/2019/12/legends-of-nathaniel-balch.html.

39. Genevieve Cummins, *How the Watch was Worn: A Fashion for 500 Years* (Woodbridge, UK: Antique Collectors' Club, 2010), 19–41. The portrait is owned by the Katzen Arts Center, but not on display. Tom Dietzel and Elizabeth Loranth kindly shared their knowledge about watch chains.

40. Hall, *Politics*, 285n80, 321, 325; John K. Alexander, *Samuel Adams: America's Revolutionary Politician* (Lanham, MD: Rowman & Littlefield, 2002), 209–214.

41. John Hancock to General Court, June 1, 1790, in Brandes, *John Hancock's Life*, 369; Alan Taylor, *American Republics: A Continental History of the United States, 1783–1850* (New York: W. W. Norton, 2021), 5–6, 20–21, 39.

42. John Hancock to the General Court, June 1, 1790 and November 12, 1792, in Brandes, *John Hancock's Life*, 369–370, 412.

43. Emily Blanck, *Tyrannicide: Forging an American Law of Slavery in Revolutionary South Carolina and Massachusetts* (Athens: University of Georgia Press, 2014), 99, 103–104, 128–133; Emily Blanck, "Seventeen Eighty-Three:

The Turning Point in the Law of Slavery and Freedom in Massachusetts," *The New England Quarterly* 75, no. 1 (March 2002): 35–39.

44. Gloria McCahon Whiting, "Emancipation without the Courts or Constitution: The Case of Revolutionary Massachusetts," *Slavery & Abolition* 41, no. 3 (2020): 462–468, 469; Joanne Pope Melish, *Disowning Slavery: Gradual Emancipation and "Race" in New England, 1780–1860* (Ithaca, NY: Cornell University Press, 1998), 96.

45. "Queries Respecting the Slavery and Emancipation of Negroes in Massachusetts, Proposed by the Judge Tucker of Virginia, and Answered by Rev. Dr. Jeremy Belknap," *MHS-C* 4, series 1 (John H. Eastburn, 1835), 204–205; Peter P. Hinks, "Free Blacks and Kidnapping in Antebellum Boston," *Historical Journal of Massachusetts* 20, no. 1 (Winter 1992): 18–19.

46. Granville Sharp, "An essay on slavery: proving from Scripture its inconsistency with humanity and religion" (Burlington, NJ: Isaac Collins, 1773); "Inventory of all the Estate of his late Excellency John Hancock, Esq.," Suffolk County Probate Case 20215, New England Historic Genealogical Society Online; Presidential Committee on Harvard & the Legacy of Slavery, "Harvard & the Legacy of Slavery," April 25, 2022, 65.

47. *American Mercury*, December 31, 1792, GB.

48. *The Connecticut Courant*, February 11, 1793, GB; Melish, *Disowning Slavery*, 168–169.

49. *Federal Spy*, January 15, 1793, *Massachusetts Mercury*, January 17, 1793, GB.

50. John Hancock to the General Court, June 6, 1792, in Brandes, *John Hancock's Life*, 397; Holton, *Unruly*, 267–268; Richards, *Shays's*, 153–158.

51. John Hancock Speech, June 6, 1792 and January 30, 1793, in Brandes, *John Hancock's Life*, 398, 416–417.

52. John Hancock Speech, November 7, 1792, in Brandes, *John Hancock's Life*, 407; *BG*, December 10, 1792, *Independent Chronicle*, January 13, 1792, GB; Carr, *After the Siege*, 209–221.

53. Jeremy Belknap to Ebenezer Hazard, January 30, 1790, *MHS-C* 3, series 5 (Boston: Massachusetts Historical Society, 1877), 212.

54. "To George Washington from John Hancock, 21 October 1789," FO; "From George Washington to John Hancock, 22 October 1789," FO; "From George Washington to John Hancock, 23 October 1789," FO.

55. February 1, 1833, William Sullivan, *Familiar Letters on Public Characters* (Boston: Russell, Odiorne, and Metcalf, 1834), 17; George Washington Diary, "[Diary entry: 24 October 1789]," FO; *BG*, October 26, 1789, GB; "Historic Processions in Boston," *The Bostonian Society Publications*, vol. 5 (1908), 81.

56. February 1, 1833, Sullivan, *Familiar Letters*, 17–18; George Washington Diary, "[Diary entry: 24 October 1789]," FO; "Historic Processions in Boston," 78–82; *BG*, October 26, 1789, *Independent Chronicle*, October 29, 1789, GB.

57. George Washington Diary, "[Diary entry: 24 October 1789]," FO.

58. Joseph Willard to John Hancock, February 19, 1785, *Transactions, 1904-1906*, vol. 10 (Boston: The Colonial Society of Massachusetts, 1907), 321–322.

59. George Washington Diary, "[Diary entry: 25 October 1789]," FO; *Massachusetts Centinel*, January 30, 1790, GB.

60. George Washington Diary, "[Diary entry: 25 October 1789]," FO; "To George Washington from John Hancock, 25 October 1789," FO.

61. February 1, 1833, Sullivan, *Familiar Letters*, 18; "Reminiscences by Gen. Wm. H. Sumner," *NEHGR* 8 (1854): 190.

62. George Washington Diary, "[Diary entry: 25 October 1789]," FO.

63. *BG*, October 26, 1789, GB; George Washington Diary, "[Diary entry: 26 October 1789]," FO; February 1, 1833, Sullivan, *Familiar Letters*, 17.

64. Quincy, *Josiah Quincy*, 38, 39.

65. *Encyclopedia Britannica Online*, s.v. "epergne," accessed October 27, 2020. https://www.britannica.com/art/epergne. A man named James Dehorty was paid wages by John Hancock in 1787, signing his mark on the receipt. November 26, 1787, Receipts, HFP, BLSC; Quincy, *Josiah Quincy*, 39.

66. Quincy, *Josiah Quincy*, 39.

67. Quincy, *Josiah Quincy*, 39.

68. John Hancock to Samuel Adams, August 31, 1793, Thomas Hancock to John Hancock, July 3, 1793, Domestic Letters, 1793, HFP, BLSC; *Columbian Centinel*, December 21, 1792, GB.

69. *BG*, September 23, 1793, *Independent Chronicle*, October 10, 1793, GB; John Hancock to Samuel Adams, August 31, 1793, Domestic Letters, 1793, HFP, BLSC.

70. *BG*, September 23, 1793, GB.

71. Thomas, *Reminiscences*, 244.

72. *Independent Chronicle*, October 10, 1793, GB.

73. *BG*, November 29, 1790, GB.

EPILOGUE

1. *BG*, October 21, 1793, GB.

2. *BG*, October 21, 1793, GB; Henry Howell Williams Journal, October 14, 1793, in William H. Sumner, *A History of East Boston* (Boston: T. E. Tilton

and Company, 1858), 332; Boston Town Records, October 11, 1793, *A Volume of Records relating to the Early History of Boston Containing Boston Town Records, 1784 to 1796* (Boston: Municipal Printing Office, 1903), 344.

3.   Henry Howell Williams Journal, October 14, 1793, in Sumner, *East Boston*, 332.

4.   BG, October 21, 1793, GB; *Columbian Centinel*, October 30, 1793, GB.

5.   BG, October 21, 1793, GB.

6.   *Columbian Centinel*, October 16, 1793, GB; *BG*, October 21, 1793, GB; Samuel Adams Drake, *Old Boston Taverns and Tavern Clubs* (Boston: W. A. Butterfield, 1917), 94–95.

7.   *Massachusetts Mercury*, October 15, 1793, GB; *Columbian Gazetteer*, October 21, 1793, GB; Henry Howell Williams Journal, October 14, 1793, in Sumner, *East Boston*, 332; Mary Caroline Crawford, *Old Boston Days & Ways: From the Dawn of the Revolution Until the Town Became a City* (Boston: Little, Brown, 1909), 295; "Funeral Processions in Boston," *The Bostonian Society Publications*, vol. 4 (1907), 131–136.

8.   "From John Adams to Joseph Ward, 6 June 1809," FO; Alfred F. Young, *The Shoemaker and the Tea Party: Memory and the American Revolution* (Boston: Beacon Press, 1999), 94–98, 117, 125; David Waldstreicher, *In the Midst of Perpetual Fetes: The Making of American Nationalism, 1776–1820* (Chapel Hill: University of North Carolina Press, 1997), 117–126.

9.   Pauline Maier, *American Scripture: Making the Declaration of Independence* (New York: Alfred A. Knopf, 1997), 159–160, 197; Verner Clapp, "The Declaration of Independence: A Case Study in Preservation," *Special Libraries* 62 (December 1971): 503–504.

10. Thomas Jefferson to William P. Gardner, February 19, 1813, in *The Works of Thomas Jefferson*, ed. Paul Leicester Ford, vol. 11 (Correspondence and Papers 1806–1816), accessed September 15, 2021, via Online Library of Liberty.

11. John Sanderson, *Biography of the Signers to the Declaration of Independence*, 2nd ed., vol. 1 (Philadelphia: William Brown and Charles Peters, 1828), 17; James Truslow Adams, "Portrait of an Empty Barrel," *Harper's Monthly Magazine* 61 (September 1930): 425; *Merriam-Webster*, s.v. "John Hancock," accessed June 3, 2021, https://www.merriam-webster.com/dictionary/JohnHancock.

12. Suffolk County (MA) Probate Records, 1636–1899, 20215, FamilySearch .org, image 215, 309; W. T. Baxter, *The House of Hancock: Business in Boston, 1724–1775* (Cambridge, MA: Harvard University Press, 1945), 292;

William M. Fowler, Jr., *The Baron of Beacon Hill: A Biography of John Hancock* (Boston: Houghton Mifflin, 1980), 281; Mabel M. Swan, "The Furniture of His Excellency, John Hancock," *The Magazine Antiques* 31, no. 3 (March 1937): 119–120; Rebecca J. Bertrand, "Myth and Memory: The Legacy of the John Hancock House" (master's thesis, University of Delaware, 2010), 66–69; May 13, 1795, *A Volume of Records Relating to the Early History of Boston Containing Boston Town Records, 1784 to 1796* (Boston: Municipal Printing Office, 1903), 396–397; Lorna Condon and Richard C. Nylander, "A Classic in the Annals of Vandalism," *Historic New England* 6, no. 1 (Summer 2005): 4–5; Ellen C. D. Q. Woodbury, *Dorothy Quincy: Wife of John Hancock with Events of Her Time* (Washington: The Neale Publishing Company, 1901), 230–232; *Independent Chronicle*, August 1, 1796, GB. Some items listed for auction in 1817 included "Original Portraits, by Copely [sic]" of Joseph Warren and Samuel Adams. *Columbian Centinel*, August 9, 1817, GB.

13. "Report of Committee on the Preservation of the Hancock House 1863," City Document No. 56, June 3, 1863. *Documents of the City of Boston for the Year 1863*, vol. 2 (Boston: J. E. Farwell, 1863), 9; Michael Holleran, *Boston's "Changeful Times": Origins of Preservation & Planning in America* (Baltimore: Johns Hopkins University Press, 1998), 92.

14. "Preservation of the Hancock House 1863." *Documents of the City of Boston for the Year 1863*, 2: 6, 9; Charles B. Hosmer, Jr., *Presence of the Past: A History of the Preservation Movement in the United States before Williamsburg* (New York: G. P. Putnam's Sons, 1965), 39.

15. Hosmer, *Presence*, 21–22, 277; "Bostonians! Save the old John Hancock Mansion," Historic New England Online, Prints and Engravings Collection; Quincy, *Josiah Quincy*, 38; Marc Callis, "The Beginning of the Past: Boston and the Early Historic Preservation Movement," *Historical Journal of Massachusetts* 32, no. 2 (Summer 2004): 120.

16. Holleran, *Boston's "Changeful Times,"* 94–109, quote on 94; Hosmer, *Presence*, 40, 102–107, 198–199, 229–238.

17. *Boston Daily Advertiser*, September 11, 1896, GB.

18. The Chicago building has a new name (360 Chicago), but residents still know it as the John Hancock. The Boston building has likewise been renamed (200 Clarendon) but is commonly referred to as the John Hancock building by locals and visitors alike.

19. From John Adams to William Tudor, Sr., 1 June 1817," FO.

ACKNOWLEDGMENTS

In the spirit of 1760s Boston, I raise a glass of rum punch and huzzah the people and places that made this book possible.

First, to the keepers of history—the libraries, archives, and historical institutions that have preserved sources relevant to Hancock's life. Fortunately, I live in Boston, home to one of the finest libraries in the country. The Boston Public Library's staff was helpful, even during—especially during—a pandemic. The Baker Library at Harvard University digitized Hancock's business records, which made it easy to continue researching despite archives having to remain closed. Libraries that provided free images and documents include the Library of Congress, New York Public Library, and the Library Company of Philadelphia, and I am grateful for their open access policies. I am also obliged to the Massachusetts Historical Society for housing some of Hancock's family records and the National Archives in London for their collection of colonial bureaucratic documents. The Colonial Society of Massachusetts recently compiled, digitized, and published much of the correspondence of Governors Bernard and Hutchinson, an enormous job from which I benefited. Founders Online from the National Archives is an invaluable digital archive whose collection seems to grow daily. The Rhode Island School of

Design Museum has a miniature portrait of Hancock in storage that I was able to see because Conor Moynihan kindly arranged it. Maureen O'Brien shared her knowledge during the viewing.

While it has been many years since anyone closely examined Hancock's life, I am not the first to write about him, and I acknowledge those who wrote biographies decades ago. They include William M. Fowler, W. T. Baxter, and Herbert S. Allan. Their works enhanced my understanding of the way Hancock has been presented over the years and pointed to some sources I might not have otherwise found. Someone who has led me to other obscure references is J. L. Bell. He is an unrivaled expert on Boston's colonial past and has a knack for tracing sources to their origins. His *Boston 1775* blog posts about the nickname "King Hancock" were very helpful.

I was fortunate to have been Alan Taylor's student many years ago as an undergraduate, and in the time since, he has been supportive and encouraging of my work. I am particularly grateful for our conversation about this book. He helped me to see where I could enhance some of my arguments, which boosted me long past our meeting.

I am indebted to the team at Harvard University Press. Kathleen McDermott believed Hancock's life was a story that needed to be told. Aaron Wistar assisted with getting the manuscript ready for publication and Katrina Vassallo's reading ensured the book was ready to go out in the world. Henry Sene Yee designed a stunning cover. The anonymous peer reviewers pushed me to make my arguments sharper and I appreciate their close reads.

One of my biggest thanks goes to Lynne Griffin, who taught me so much about how to write for a wider audience. She pushed me to trust my own voice and to always consider my readers. My agent, Amy Bishop, sharpened the book's focus and has been a terrific advocate.

In 2013, I founded a tour company that introduces guests to the revolutionary (and drunken) history of Boston. I am fortunate to work with an incredible group of people at Ye Olde Tavern Tours. They are smart, enthusiastic, and loyal, and their work has enabled me to research and write more freely. Kelly Monday, Brian Mahoney, Rachel Young, Kristen Carey, and Elizabeth Loranth are amazing people and I'm lucky to know them. I also thank all the guests who have joined our tours over the years. Their questions about John Hancock and the American Revolution helped me understand what people were curious about and refined the way I approached this book.

I also appreciate those who remind me of life outside of eighteenth-century Boston. This is especially true of my lively and hilarious family in San Diego. I am grateful, too, for sharing laughter, cheese boards, beer, and book club talks with friends near and far. Writing is inherently a solo activity, but I was lucky to have the company of Divya Babin in the early days of this project. We silently typed alongside each other and then commiserated about problems that were coming up with our individual works. One of my dearest friends, Colleen Lumbard, read drafts of several chapters, and her sharp eye honed my argument and perspective. She was also there to acknowledge the many milestones that happen as a book gets written and made. Markus Donegan is as supportive a friend as one could ask for. He listened and cheered during every stage of the process—always ready with a bottle of champagne to celebrate even the smallest of victories.

Lastly, I thank Adam. His interest in history is minimal, but I rarely feel that. He talked through so much of Hancock's life with me and listened as I retold stories over and over, trying to get the tone right. He also consistently makes me laugh, even offering occasional jokes about the American Revolution. I have it good.

INDEX